RHETORIC, CULTURAL STUDIES, AND LITERACY

Selected Papers from the 1994 Conference
of the Rhetoric Society of America

RHETORIC, CULTURAL STUDIES, AND LITERACY
Selected Papers from the 1994 Conference of the Rhetoric Society of America

Edited by

John Frederick Reynolds
City College of CUNY

LAWRENCE ERLBAUM ASSOCIATES, PUBLISHERS

1995   Hillsdale, New Jersey   Hove, UK

Lawrence Erlbaum Associates, Inc., Publishers
365 Broadway
Hillsdale, New Jersey 07642

Cover design by Mairav Salomon-Dekel
Text design by Elaine B. Dawson

Library of Congress Cataloging-in-Publication Data

Rhetoric Society of America. Conference (1994 : Norfolk, VA.)
   Rhetoric, cultural studies, and literacy : selected papers from the 1994
Conference of the Rhetoric Society of America / edited by John Frederick
Reynolds
      p.   cm.
   Selected papers from the sixth biennial conference convened by the
Rhetoric Society of America, May 19–21, 1994, at the Waterside Marriott
Hotel and Convention Center in Norfolk, VA.
   Includes bibliographical references and index.
   ISBN 0-8058-1608-9 (alk. paper).—ISBN 0-8058-1609-7
   1. Rhetoric—Congresses.   2. Literacy—Congresses.   3. Language
and culture—Congresses.   I. Reynolds, John Frederick, 1952– .   II.
Title.
P301.R4714   1994
808—dc20
                                             95-12224
                                               CIP

Books published by Lawrence Erlbaum Associates are printed on
acid-free paper, and their bindings are chosen for strength and durability.

Printed in the United States of America
10 9 8 7 6 5 4 3 2 1

Contents

Preface

The Rhetoric Society of America, organized in 1968 for the advancement of the study of rhetoric, convened its sixth biennial conference May 19–21, 1994, at the Waterside Marriott Hotel and Convention Center in Norfolk, Virginia. The conference was co-hosted by Old Dominion University and the City of Norfolk, and organized around the theme "Rhetoric, Cultural Studies, and Literacy." Approximately 260 national and international teacher-scholars from the disciplines of English, speech communication, philosophy, film and media studies, composition studies, rhetoric, comparative literature, and humanities attended.

The conference was chaired by RSA President Kathleen E. Welch, Professor of English at the University of Oklahoma, who organized a diverse and stimulating 3-day program of 71 panels featuring 220 speakers, with the assistance of the 1994 RSA Program Committee: S. Michael Halloran of the Department of Language, Literature, and Communication at Rensselaer Polytechnic Institute; Kay Halasek of the Department of English at The Ohio State University; Jody Enders of the Departments of French and Italian at the University of California at Berkeley; conference assistants J. Blake Scott and Melody Bowdon, then of the Department of English at the University of Oklahoma; and local arrangements coordinator Fred Reynolds, then of Old Dominion University, who was assisted throughout the conference by Susan T. Desilets, Clayann Gilliam Panetta, and Michael Dunn.

The 1994 conference keynote addresses were delivered by Donovan J. Ochs and Sharon Crowley, both of the Department of Rhetoric at the University of Iowa. The Charles Kneupper Memorial Address for 1994 was delivered by

Edward Schiappa of Purdue University. All three of these addresses are reprinted here in their entirety. Of the more than 100 manuscripts submitted for consideration for inclusion in this volume designed to represent the conference, 17 were ultimately selected after a careful review by a committee co-chaired by Robert L. McDonald of the Virginia Military Institute and Christina G. Russell of James Madison University, who grouped the final selections and introduce them here.

ACKNOWLEDGMENTS

I want to publicly thank Rob and Christina for managing the difficult reviewing process so thoughtfully, promptly, and professionally. Also my then-assistant Clayann Gilliam Panetta for coordinating the many filings, mailings, and correspondences associated with the refereeing process. A small grant from the College of Arts and Letters at Old Dominion University supported final page-preparation work, which was done with remarkably good humor by the college's research services support person, Elaine B. Dawson, whom I can never thank enough for all her help during my Old Dominion years. Finally, many thanks are due to senior editor Hollis Heimbouch and all of the good people at Lawrence Erlbaum Associates, who continue to support me, my colleagues, my field, and the Rhetoric Society itself in many tangible ways.

John Frederick Reynolds

1

Epideictic, Ethos, and Educators

Donovan J. Ochs
University of Iowa

Stryker, Robert F. Rank and organization: Specialist 4, United States Army, Company C, 1st Battalion, 26th Infantry, 1st Infantry Division. Place and date: Near Loc Ninh, Republic of Vietnam, 7 November 1967. Entered service at: Syracuse, N.Y. Date and place of birth: November 9, 1944, Auburn, N.Y. Citation: For conspicuous gallantry and intrepidity at the risk of his life above and beyond the call of duty. Specialist Robert Stryker, United States Army, distinguished himself by conspicuous gallantry and intrepidity on 7 November 1967 while serving with Company C, 1st Battalion, 26th Infantry, 1st Infantry Division in the Republic of Vietnam. On this date Specialist Stryker was serving as a grenadier in a multi-company reconnaissance in force near Loc Ninh. As his unit moved through the dense underbrush, it was suddenly met with a hail of rocket, automatic weapons and small arms fire from enemy forces concealed in fortified bunkers and in the surrounding trees. Reacting quickly, Specialist Stryker fired into the enemy positions with his grenade launcher. During the devastating exchange of fire, Specialist Stryker detected enemy elements attempting to encircle his company and isolate it from the main body of the friendly force. Undaunted by the enemy machine gun and small arms fire, Specialist Stryker repeatedly fired grenades into the trees, killing enemy snipers and enabling his comrades to sever the attempted encirclement. As the battle continued, Specialist Stryker observed several wounded members of his squad in the killing zone of an enemy claymore mine. With complete disregard for his own safety, he threw himself upon the mine as it was detonated. He was mortally wounded as his body absorbed the blast and shielded his comrades from the explosion. His unselfish actions were responsible for saving the lives of at least six of his fellow soldiers. Specialist Stryker's great personal bravery was in keeping with the highest traditions of the military service and reflects great credit upon himself, his unit, and the United States Army.

—*Medal of Honor Recipients*, 951

1

The epideictic citation I just read is that of a person awarded the Medal of Honor, the highest military award in our country. As rhetoricians you have already correctly classified the language of this citation as epideictic, the discourse of praise. As rhetoricians you already know that the term, *epideictic*, covers a broad spectrum of language uses—panegyrics, encomia, eulogies, dedications, award ceremonies, product advertisements, to name only a few. Although we are indebted to Aristotle for identifying the genre—epideictic, discourse of praise and blame—we come away from a reading of the *Rhetorica* with more questions than answers, more puzzles than solutions, more complications than resolutions. I invite you to work through with me some of these questions, puzzles, and complications because I am convinced that all of us teachers of discourse, as educators, need to be more aware of the raw power, the energy to constrain and change, held by epideictic. Along the way I hope to call your attention to some of the ethical problems that are part and parcel of epideictic praise.

When I began my research for this presentation I started with Aristotle and reviewed his observations on virtue and vice, the noble and base. "Praise," he observed, "is the expression in words of the eminence of a person's good qualities, and therefore we must display one's actions as a product of such qualities" (I. 9.28–30). No problem here. Easy to understand. A person has certain *good* qualities of character, virtues if you will, and acts, *does* something, that reveals these qualities, and someone puts this connection into *words* for an audience. Simple. Safe. Clear. Child's play. But, Aristotle makes another observation: "To praise a person is in one respect akin to urging a course of action" (I. 9.36). Big problems here. Not safe. Not simple. We've just entered moral territory. Community values, ideologies, networks of interpretation,[1] criteria for admission and exclusion, unquestioned ethical yardsticks against which one's behavior is measured—all these are now in play when epideictic is deployed. Epideictic can wear a mask of virtuoso display, parading with garlands of rhetorical figures and tropes, but beneath the verbal tinsel lurks a moral force. Epideictic can also be clothed in simple and plain language, but a moral force is still present.

I am indebted to many of our scholarly colleagues for their insights about epideictic. A partial roll call will provide a quick review of what we now know.

Casey's study of Reagan's use of epideictic found that it functioned to seek increased assent to commonly accepted cultural values.

Madden found that Reagan's military eulogies served to "legitimate political authority" and "to subvert the public's capacity for effective dissent against war" (4).

Reber concluded that epideictic is used to communicate "fundamental American values" (3). Perelman also holds that view, by the way.

Cleland and, more recently, Park discovered that epideictic is not only a conservative form, but can "shape a community by opening up a vision of the possible" (Park 31).[2] Epideictic can serve politically radical ends.

Studies done by the Poulakos brothers (see, for example, John Poulakos 300–307; Takis Poulakos 317–328), and by Rosenfield (131–155) tell us that epideictic not only functions in the arena of the possible but also in that of ethics.

Condit's research helped us understand epideictic "as a public communication that serves a threefold set of paired functions—definition/understanding, display/ entertainment, and shaping/sharing of community."

Clearly, any language form capable of this many practical functions with such power to capture and enslave or release and free our minds deserves careful study and close scrutiny.

As I continued my research I next asked a big question: What must one do in our culture to be praised? Phrased another way: What are the criteria different communities to which we belong use in determining whom to praise? We know Aristotle's community, the polis of Athens, was aristocratic, warlike, hegemonic, paternal, racist, and sexist. We know the qualities of character, the criteria, the Athenians used to award praise. I wanted to learn what our criteria are.

To win the highest award in our military community, the Congressional Medal of Honor, "The deed . . . must have been one of personal bravery or self-sacrifice so conspicuous as to clearly distinguish the individual for gallantry and intrepidity above his comrades" and must have been "above and beyond the call of duty, in an action involving actual conflict with an opposing armed force" (*Medal of Honor* 10).

What qualities of character are specified? Courage, bravery, fearlessness, altruistic self-sacrifice. Excluded, at this time, were women. Armed combat is unquestioned. One must be more heroic than one's colleagues. Clearly, the epideictic citation I read at the outset is a direct descendant of the Athenian funeral speech and the Aristocratic Roman *laudatio funebris*. In fact, Minerva, the goddess who guided men in the dangers of war, "Where victory is gained by cunning, prudence, courage and perseverance" ("Minerva" 1045) appears on the medal itself. As an ex-combat infantry soldier, I view the criteria one way; as a rhetorician another; as a teacher yet another.

But we are all citizens. Most of us are members of the community we call the United States. The highest award? The Presidential Medal of Freedom. The criteria? "Meritorious contributions to security or the national interest of the United States, world peace, cultural, or other significant public or private endeavors" (Borthick and Britton 45).

Who wins such awards and for what reasons? Let me answer that question by reading an excerpt from President Bush's epideictic speech awarding the Medal of Freedom:

> America's greatness lies not in its Government but in its people. And it's not enough to be free; we must serve each other.
>
> Each of us, each of today's award winners certainly understands this, and each is a great American. Their names read like a roll call of American heroes:

Harry Schlaudeman, a tireless crusader for democracy, who after a life of public service came out of retirement 2 years ago to ensure Nicaragua's peaceful transition to democracy.

David Brinkley, the elder statesman of broadcast journalism. His record speaks for itself.

Richard Petty, who rose from humble beginnings in Level Cross, North Carolina, to become the king of stock car racing.

General Vessey, who was the ultimate never-say-die soldier, the last four-star combat veteran of World War II to retire. And General Vessey came out of retirement to counsel my predecessor and me and to help us reach full accounting of all our Vietnam veterans. And he's still engaged in this pursuit.

Elie Wiesel is another type of veteran of World War II, who survived the Holocaust and still today keeps watch against the forces of hatred.

Isaac Stern, one of the great violinists of our time, who has brought music to countless others.

I. M. Pei, the modernist architect whose work graces skylines worldwide.

To much of America, Johnny Carson was late-night TV. And with decency and style, he's made America laugh and think. (*Weekly Compilation* 2333–2345)

Epideictic seems to function in this category quite differently from that of the military community. Here the actions of the awardees depends on repetition as well as exceeding the norm. The actions must be altruistic, to be sure, but the virtues of character are persistence, determination, effort, and perseverance that lead to some type of recognizable success. These are noble virtues in the moral arena. Urging community members to persist successfully in activities that benefit our country cannot be faulted. Nor should they be. Nor am I. But, note, again, what is backgrounded, distanced, obscured. Cooperative teamwork is excluded. Only the star, the individual, is praised, not the supporting cast, not those who helped the person with their loyalty, assistance, and encouragement.

But we belong to other communities. Most people spend a good share of their lives working for a business or company. Because this is so I asked what criteria are used by businesses to single out and praise members of their business communities. I sent my question to the top 20 companies on the Fortune 500 list. All of us would correctly predict that business communities reward longevity. At 5, 10, 15, and so on, years of employment, these anniversary markers are recognized, publicized, and gifts are given. We might be surprised, however, and instructed at some of the qualitative criteria some of these large communities use. Let me share some with you.

Exxon singles out for praise "an employee whose ingenuity resulted in significant impact on earnings or business results or who for a particular achievement received national or international recognition."[3] The quality of ingenuity is clearly central. Increasing the community's financial strength is the key virtue.

The Chairman's Award at United Technologies Corporation is given for "extraordinary employee performance that exceeds position responsibility."[4] Here, distance from the norm is central. Increasing the community's financial strength is implied.

The Chairman's Club Award at Proctor and Gamble is based on meeting and quantifiably far exceeding sales quotas.[5] Here, measurable results are central. Increasing the community's financial strength is the key virtue.

Texaco has an elaborate recognition system. To be selected as a Star Quality Ambassador, their top award, employees or *teams* must "demonstrate exemplary customer service; make exceptionally valuable improvements in a process; or make valuable contributions to improving results."[6] Two elements deserve notice. First, team efforts, not just a single person, receive Texaco's highest praise. Second, the printed criteria stress the operative term, *value*, which clearly relates to the communities' prosperity. Voltaire once said, "By appreciation we make excellence in others our own property." Texaco's top-ranked epideictic is reserved for those who, by their actions, enhance and intensify the financial excellence of the community.

Were you to skim the *Manager's Guide to IBM United States Marketing and Services Recognition Manual* you would be overwhelmed. The number, types, and categories of awards rivals that of the military. Echoes of Aristotle's statement about praise and recommending a course of action is embedded in IBM's philosophy of recognition:

> Recognition in its simplest form is an acknowledgment for a past accomplishment— for something already completed. Viewed in broader terms, recognition is an investment in IBM's future, an incentive for employees to strive toward excellence.[7]

The IBM language is clear enough. Praising publicly a past virtuous action sets the standard against which future actions will be measured. I see a problem here. A serious problem. Possibly an inherent contradiction. Person A is praised. Fine. The norm is exceeded. Fine. The raised standard also raises the norm. Person B, then, must meet and exceed the raised norm. Across time a community either sets standards and criteria for legitimate praise so high that attainment is impossible— or—this ratcheting upward, ever upward, renders the criteria mere rhetoric. Excellence as an ideal incentive becomes unattainable or a disincentive.

IBM partially addressed this difficulty in language curiously reminiscent of Thucydides's injunction, "People can endure to hear others praised only so long as they can severally persuade themselves of their own ability to equal the actions recounted: when this point is passed, envy comes in and with it incredulity" (103). Sensitive to Thucydides' caution IBM insists that its managers, before making an individual award, "be sure the accomplishment being rewarded is an isolated event and that its magnitude, in and of itself, is sufficient to gain the general acknowledgment of those who are working with the employee receiving the award."[8] Something seems amiss here. Something confusing. Does a community, as a community, actually set the standards for praise? Or, is something else at work? Why do we ourselves often feel envy, incredulity, skepticism, and distrust when one of our colleagues is singled out for special recognition and public praise? If, indeed, a community sets the standards for praise, and someone meets these, then what accounts for community members experiencing, and often expressing, ill will toward the recipient? Try this for a possible answer. We have been intellectually handcuffed to Aristotle and Cicero, to the concepts of the polis and Roman Republic, a bit too long in our understanding of epideictic. Rhetorical systems of epideictic derived from Aristocracy and oligarchy do not translate well into communities characterized by egalitarianism. True, some of the many communities to which we may belong—the military, for example—fit the classical paradigm of epideictic. Why? Because the leaders, those in control, those with reward power and *not* the members of the community set the standards for recognition and praise.

But, we all belong to many communities—religious, recreational, social, familial. We all belong to what I will call the educational community . . . we teach. As teachers we are epideictic rhetors on a daily basis. Let me repeat that claim. As teachers we are epideictic rhetors on a daily basis.

How so, you rightly ask.

We are epideictic rhetors when we grade student work. We are epideictic rhetors when we write letters of recommendation. We are epideictic rhetors when we write tenure and promotion documents, when we review journal articles for publication, when we write book reviews, when we recommend that a publisher accept a prospectus, when we single out a colleague and *build a case* for a special award.

Time out. Did you notice how ordinary and comfortable that legal metaphor sounded? We *build a case*. We argue. We become attorneys in court. We seek justice not with evidence and enthymeme but with our narrative and someone else's virtuous action and accomplishment. Is this a problem? I think so in at least two ways. As a dramatic form, narrative can influence and persuade, but narrative cannot argue from premise to evidence to inferential conclusion. Second, the ethos, reputation, and linguistic virtuosity of the person crafting the praise becomes more important than the awardee's virtuous action and accomplishment. To see how these problems play out let's return to that list where we are epideictic rhetors.

We award grades. When challenged, we defend by pointing out where the student's virtuous action and accomplishment—a fancy way of describing a student paper or speech—where the student's virtuous actions failed to meet certain criteria. But these criteria are not those of the students' community at all. Where do they come from? From the traditional, received wisdom of the discipline? Maybe. From the individual teacher, the epideictic rhetor? Most assuredly.

We write letters of recommendation. We craft our discourse of praise narrating someone's qualities and accomplishments. But our goal is not that of publicly recognizing a community member and recommending a moral course of action for those in the community. Not at all. I maintain it is the reputation of the letter writer that counts in urging that someone be hired or admitted or given clearance or trusted.

Many of you serve on tenure committees, and many of you review manuscripts for various journals. In these roles you, me, all of us use epideictic rhetoric. Here again the criteria are not those of the untenured faculty community, nor those of the unpublished faculty community. Not at all. Someone or some group with more power sets the standards. As writers of epideictic praise in these contexts we are forced and constrained to argue, to build a case. And that, I submit, is a type and kind of epideictic, far, far different from a medal of honor citation, or a Medal of Freedom speech, or IBM's Presidential Club recognition.

By this point I hope you can see a few of the problems attached to the language of praise. All of our language use excludes. Words are incapable of capturing all of reality. Epideictic magnifies this inherent flaw.

By foregrounding and featuring, epideictic automatically backgrounds and eliminates. By holding up for admiration, epideictic automatically uncouples an individual from his or her community. By plotting a course on a moral compass, epideictic automatically and powerfully excludes alternate ethical directions.

Epideictic can energize and exalt; it can also demoralize and incapacitate. In a pluralistic society epideictic can impose one community's standards for praise on another community.

And yet. And yet as humans we all need to be recognized, to be praised, to be awarded and rewarded, to be made to feel special. There is our collective challenge. As practicing rhetoricians can we discover ways to use the necessary and positive features of epideictic and disengage the negative aspects?

I want to offer you a partial solution, a solution that might work in some epideictic situations, and it is contained in a story.

A few weeks ago I attended a United States Federal Court Swearing-In Ceremony. One of my former doctoral students was being sworn in as the first female U.S. Federal Marshal in the State of Iowa and the first female U.S. Marshal with a Ph.D. in our nation's history. A U.S. Federal Prosecutor and a U.S. Public Defender were also sworn in. The Federal Courtroom was packed with judges, senators, lawyers, coworkers, family and friends, and dozens of reporters. An Iowa Supreme Court Judge gave a modest encomium for each of the three. Then, each presented a type and quality of speech I'd never heard before. Maybe they could be called speeches of acknowledgment, but that label does not capture their substance. If the encomia of the judge were Act I in the epideictic drama, these speeches were Act II. I've yet to receive manuscripts, but let me work from paraphrase to give you a sense of these Act II speeches.

While he was being sworn in as the first Black Federal Prosecutor in Iowa, the man's two-year-old child threw a fit, and the mother carried the child out of the room. The man stood at the podium, ready to begin his speech and said, "Where's my wife? I can't start without my wife." Two highway patrol officers took the youngster somewhere, and three others whisked the wife and mother back into the courtroom. His speech began:

"Many of you know my wife and I were divorced. But when I was in the hospital with brain cancer, she came and held my hand and prayed with me. Since then, we've remarried and have two children. Without her help and support I would not be able to receive this honor."

He went on to specify and recognize and acknowledge and give details about the individual excellences various members of his community had given him. The secretarial staff, his law partners, his church members all were singled out and held up for praise. Community was restored. Those who were backgrounded, uncoupled, and excluded by epideictic discourse were foregrounded, reunited, and included by the awardee's skillful and magnanimous use of directed and developed praise. These were far more than simple "Thank You speeches." Far, far more than the empty Academy Awards' speeches. They were antistrophes to epideictic.[9]

I hope, as a discipline, as rhetoricians, as educators, we can find more.

Thank you.

ACKNOWLEDGMENTS

Special recognition must be given to John Karayannides, Research Assistant and MBA Candidate at the University of Iowa. Without his help, this study would not have been possible.

ENDNOTES

1. I am indebted to my colleague, Sharon Crowley, for this description of an ideology.

2. Park provides the most thorough analytical review of scholarship on epideictic of those I consulted. I am indebted to her careful work.

3. Letter received from R.W. Gentry, Senior Advisor, Human Resources Department, Exxon Corporation, dated November 29, 1993.

4. Letter and brochure received from Ellen McGroary, Human Resources Manager, Corporate Headquarters, United Technologies, dated November 9, 1993.

5. Letter and bulletin received from Susan Grote, Supervisor of Sales Recruiting, Proctor and Gamble, dated November 12, 1993.

6. Letter and *Texaco Gas Recognition Guide* received from William C. McLead, Manager, Quality Resources Center, Texaco, Inc., dated November 19, 1993.

7. Letter and *Recognition Guide* received from Richard L. Brescia, Program Manager, IBM, dated December 10, 1993. Cf. *Guide*, p. 1–1.

8. *IBM Guide*, p. 3.1.

9. I am indebted to my colleague, Fred Antczak, for this most apt phrase.

WORKS CITED

Aristotle, *Rhetorica*, trans. W. Rhys Roberts, in *The Basic Works of Aristotle*, ed. Richard McKeon (New York: Random House, 1941).

Borthick, David, and Jack Britton. *Medals, Military, and Civilian of the United States*. Tulsa, OK: M.C.N. Press, 1984.

Casey, Michael John. "Ronald Reagan's Epideictic Rhetoric within the Context of the State of the Union Address during the Cold War, 1945–1985," Ph.D. Diss., Washington State U, 1986.

Cleland, Maryland M. "Sophistic Epideictic Rhetoric: A Classical Theory and a Contemporary Interpretation," Ph.D. Diss., Northern Illinois U, 1989.

The Complete Writings of Thucydides: The Peloponnesian War. Trans. R. Crawley. New York: The Modern Library.

Condit, Celeste Michelle. "The Functions of Epideictic: The Boston Massacre Orations as Exemplar." *Communication Quarterly* 33 (1985): 284–299.

Maden, Michael Patrick. "A 'Covenant with Death': The President's Epideictic Message of Legitimation and National Sacrifice," Ph.D. Diss., U of Iowa, 1989.

Medal of Honor Recipients: 1863–1973. Washington: GPO, 1973.

"Minerva." *Harper's Dictionary of Classical Literature and Antiquities*. Ed. H.T. Peck. New York: American Book Co., 1923.

Park, Lynn. "A Practical Exploration of Epideictic," M.A. Thesis, Arizona State U, 1993.

Poulakos, John. "Gorgias' and Isocrates' Use of the Encomium." *Southern Speech Communication Journal* 51 (1986): 300–307.

Poulakos, Takis. "Isocrates' Use of Narrative in the *Evagoras*: Epideictic Rhetoric and Moral Action." *Quarterly Journal of Speech* 73 (1987): 317–328.

Reber, Thomas Clark. "Modern Epideictic Discourse: The Commemorative Speech in Twentieth Century America," Ph.D. Diss., U of Texas at Austin, 1989.

Rosenfield, Lawrence. "The Practical Celebration of Epideictic." *Rhetoric in Transition: Studies in the Nature and Uses of Rhetoric*. Ed. Eugene E. White. University Park: Pennsylvania State UP, 1980. 131–155.

Weekly Compilation of Presidential Documents 28, no. 50: 2333–2345.

2 Biting the Hand That Feeds Us: Nineteenth-Century Uses of a Pedagogy of Taste

Sharon Crowley
University of Iowa

I recently returned to the Midwest after living out West for over 20 years. Rediscovering the habits and tastes associated with the great middle region of the country has been a bit more of a jolt than I expected. Driving east to Iowa last summer, for example, my traveling companion and I stopped for lunch at a little roadside restaurant in Nebraska, just past the Colorado border at Julesburg. The luncheon buffet featured meat loaf with potatoes and gravy, boiled peas, orange jello salad with carrots inside and mayonnaise on top, and apple pie with vanilla ice cream for dessert. My traveling companion, who grew up in California and now lives in Arizona, could not resist the quip: "I think we're not in L.A. any more, Dorothy." Next morning, in a restaurant somewhere along Interstate 80, a friendly waitress graciously supplied us with this caution about Midwestern eating habits: "Honey," she said, "people don't eat fruit for breakfast." And during the last year, my colleague Don Ochs has reintroduced me to that quintessentially Midwestern lunchroom treat—the Velveeta cheese sandwich.

I hope you see that in these anecdotes about tastes the joke is on me, rather than on Midwesterners. Until I returned to the Midwest, I did not realize what a snob I had lately become about such things as espresso coffee and olive oil, things to which I had no access as a child growing up in the sandhills of Nebraska. My latter-day taste for these things, which I mistakenly assumed was shared by all right-thinking people, is of course just as localized as anyone's.

Pierre Bourdieu's study of taste, called *Distinction* (1984), establishes that the acquisition of taste is a local matter. We learn to like and dislike the things we do from the people we grow up with. Hence, our native tastes are pretty much decided for us. According to Bourdieu, we alter our tastes when we change our

11

class affiliation. (It is equally accurate to say that when we change our class affiliation we change our tastes.) However, Bourdieu's finding seems counter-intuitive to many people. His informants resolutely rejected his findings about the connection of class affiliation to taste; over and over again they protested that their tastes, and those of others, were "innate."

Bourdieu's contemporary French informants repeated an assumption that was held by American rhetoric teachers in the first half of the 19th century. These teachers also taught their students that taste was innate. Paradoxically enough, they nevertheless offered instruction in its development.[1]

I have long been puzzled about why the pedagogy of taste played such a large role in 19th-century American school rhetoric; in addition to its paradoxical nature, the development of taste seems, on the face of it, an odd project for rhetoric teachers to take on, given its provenance in modern philosophical aesthetics and its pedagogical impulse toward self-improvement rather than civic intervention. Indeed, I argue today that the pedagogy of taste adumbrated in early 19th-century school rhetoric texts operated according to the principles of discrimination and exclusion. Its object was to create a community whose members could easily discern, and hence exclude, nonmembers.

TRADITIONS OF TASTE

Historians have delineated several modern European traditions of taste. British interest in literary taste dates at least from the early 18th century. An unautho-rized edition of Pope's "Epistle to Burlington," also called "Miscellany on Taste, or Of False Taste," was published in London in 1731. Pope's editors credit this version of the epistle with stirring up interest in taste among learned circles in London, although other scholars argue that its ideas were commonplaces already in general circulation. By the 1750s, in any case, the notion of taste was prominently featured in philosophical discussions of aesthetics: David Hume published "Of a Standard of Taste" in 1757, and Alexander Gerard published his *Essay on Taste* in 1759.

Terry Eagleton traced a rich German tradition of thought about taste in his *Ideology of the Aesthetic* (1990). This tradition reached a kind of apogee with the publication of Immanuel Kant's *Critique of Judgement* in 1790. It was Kant who posited the existence of a "pure" taste, a taste that appreciated works of art and natural beauty as things in themselves. By positing this notion, Kant rationalized the familiar distinction now made between "high" and "low" tastes.

A Scottish tradition of thinking about taste seems to have influenced American rhetoricians more than either English or German thought. Its theorists defined taste as that capacity, or faculty, that permits persons to discriminate the good from the bad in works of art as well as the virtuous from the vicious in the realm of morality. In this tradition, which probably stems from the work of Frances

Hutcheson, the exercise of taste was directly connected to the exercise of public responsibility.[2] The most influential expositor of this tradition of taste in rhetorical theory was Hugh Blair, who devoted the first two chapters of his *Lectures on Rhetoric and Belles Lettres* (1783) to taste. In *Rhetoric in North America* (1991) Nan Johnson established a firm connection between Blair's philosophy of taste and the cultivation of civic and moral virtue. According to Johnson:

> defining rhetoric as a discipline that directs the cultivation of taste, Blair views the study of rhetoric and belles lettres as a process of edification, a means by which the individual can prepare for the discharge of "the higher and more important duties of life." (36; 1965 ed., p. 12)

Thanks no doubt to Blair's influential example, 19th-century American school rhetoric texts composed in the belles-lettres tradition developed a full-fledged pedagogy of taste.[3]

By the mid-19th century, however, Blair's firm connection of taste to civic virtue had all but disappeared from mainstream school rhetoric texts. In what follows, I examine the accounts of taste given in four rhetoric textbooks that were very popular before and during the Civil War: Samuel Newman's *System of Rhetoric* (1827), James Boyd's *Elements of English Composition* (1860); Henry Coppee's *Elements of Rhetoric* (1860); and G.P. Quackenbos's *Advanced Course in Composition and Rhetoric* (1864). I think you will see quickly enough that these teachers are discussing something very different from Blair's ideology of taste as the cultivation of civil commitment.

TASTE AS A FACULTY

Boyd, Coppee, Newman, and Quackenbos agree that taste is a faculty, which, in the faculty psychology that undergirds the rhetorical theory of the time, elevates it to the same status as the faculties of reason, emotion, or imagination. They uniformly treat taste as the capacity to grasp and evaluate emotional experiences. Coppee defined *taste* as "the faculty by which we discern and enjoy the beauties of Nature and Art" (61); Boyd named it "that faculty by which we are enable to perceive and relish the beauties of composition" (43); Quackenbos wrote that *taste* is "that faculty of the mind which enables it to perceive, with the aid of reason to judge of, and with the help of imagination to enjoy, whatever is beautiful or sublime in the works of nature and art" (170); Newman argued that "the decisions of taste are judgments passed on whatever is designed to excite emotions of beauty, of grandeur, or of sublimity" (42).

Boyd posited that anyone who would exercise taste must possess five faculties: first, a lively imagination; second, a "*clear* and *distinct apprehension of things*" (this ability is called *method* by other theorists of the period); third, "quick perception" of "those objects that gratify the secondary senses, particularly sublimity, beauty, harmony, and imitation"; fourth, *sympathy*, the ability to share moral pain and pleasure; and last, "*judgment*, or *good sense*, which is indeed the principal thing, and may . . . be said to comprehend all the rest" (44–45). In other words, the person of taste is equipped with several faculties—imagination, method, perception, sympathy, and judgment—all which, when working together in harmony, allow him or her to perceive and evaluate the aesthetic and moral worth of scenes or objects surely and quickly, if not instantaneously.

According to Newman, taste aids us in evaluating that which is presented to our emotions. Experience with beautiful or ugly things produces emotions; the capacity to judge or evaluate these experiences, that is, our capacity for taste, is founded on, and grows with, emotional experience. There are three sorts of emotions: moral emotions, emotions of passion, and emotions of beauty. Moral emotions are excited by actions that are vicious or virtuous; passion is generated by objects of desire or aversion; and beauty by experiences of grandeur or sublimity, such as glorious sunsets or moving stories.

As you can see, these accounts are characteristic of 19th-century rhetorical theory, where faculty psychology was used quite uncritically to develop a rather mechanical theory of human response. On this view, persons have sensations and experiences; these are stored in memory and simultaneously worked on by a variety of higher faculties, such as reason, emotion, or imagination. Persons who wished to develop their rational and imaginative capacities were encouraged to have more and better experiences, and to think about them harder and more carefully. Boyd, for example, counseled his readers to improve their faculties of taste by "studying Nature and the best performances in art" (44). He also encouraged them to keep "at a distance from every thing gross and indelicate, in books and conversation, in manners and in language."

TASTE AS DISCRIMINATION AND EXCLUSION

Newman and company advised their students that *taste*—the ability to discriminate the bad from the good, the beautiful from the ugly—is also a sign of excellence that allows discrimination among persons. Someone who receives no pleasure from nature or art, according to Boyd, "is said to be a man of no taste" (43). On the other hand, he or she who is gratified with that which is faulty in works of art is a person of bad taste; and he or she who is pleased or displeased, according to the degree of excellence or faultiness, is a person of good taste. Because taste is natural, all people display it in some degree; Quackenbos pointed out that "savages . . . by their ornaments, their songs, and the rude eloquence of their harangues, show that along with reason and speech they have received the faculty of appreciating beauty" (171).

Obviously, though, this natural capacity does not manifest itself in the same way or to the same degree in all people or peoples. Newman generously read this difference as a difference in education and class privilege: Persons who have leisure and occasion to exercise their emotional responses to beautiful scenes or objects will be able to strengthen that response, whereas the ability to respond emotionally will be stunted in persons who do not enjoy such opportunities. He illustrated:

> Addison, when he went forth in the evening, and gazed upon the starry heavens and the moon walking in her majesty, felt emotions of sublimity. In accounting for the rise of these emotions, we might say, that he was a man of sensibility—from the original constitution of his mind he was susceptible of emotions of taste to a high degree. His intellectual habits also, and the circumstances of his life, were such as to cherish and strengthen these original tendencies of his mind. Astronomy had taught him something of the size and number and uses of these heavenly bodies; and in this way, or in other ways, many associations were connected with them. On the same evening, perhaps, and in the same neighbourhood, the laborer returning from his daily toil, looked upon the same starry and moon-lit firmament, but felt no emotion of beauty or sublimity. Still this individual might have been originally constituted with as much sensibility as Addison; but such has been his lot in life, that this sensibility has been lost, and he thinks of the moon and stars only as lighting him homewards from his toil. (48–49)

The subtext of this passage cannot have been lost on Newman's young readers: If you wish to be included among the cultural elite, you cannot fail to notice nature or art. Indeed, you will find much in both to be stimulated by and to comment on. To put this another way: The first use of art and natural beauty in modern aesthetics is neither political nor religious, as was the case in former times; rather, the point of observing art and natural beauty is to find fodder for criticism.

Coppee and Quackenbos were unwilling to assign disparities in taste to different kinds of education or circumstance, as Newman did. Coppee associated the capacity of taste not with education or experience, but with "the finer powers with which some minds are endued, by which they are permitted to discern beauties and delicacies which are not seen by commoner intellects" (68). And Quackenbos went so far as to classify people according to the delicacy of their tastes: There are some "endowed with feelings so blunt, and tempers so cold and phlegmatic," that they are nearly insensible to the world around them; others "are capable of appreciating only the coarsest kind of beauties"; whereas in yet a third class of men "pleasurable emotions are excited by the most delicate graces" (171). It would be disastrous if reason were so thinly dispersed among men, Quackenbos remarked, but because taste has to do only with "the ornamental part of life," nature has wisely limited its distribution (172).

In these accounts, peoples who exhibit inadequate taste are inevitably non-Anglo or non-European. Coppee asked us to compare "a hut of reeds with a gorgeous palace; an Indian canoe with the floating palaces which cross the

Atlantic; an Indian village with one of our great cities—Philadelphia or New York; the barbarous and inadequate dialect of the Hottentot with the copiousness of the English or the graces of the Spanish language" (64–65). Now it would seem that, because taste is natural to some extent, this copious display of natural taste, this diversity of home and boat designs and among languages should be accepted, if not welcomed. Coppee himself wrote: "Since we are all gifted with taste by God, each man's taste must be as good as his neighbour's; and therefore there can be no standard" of taste (64). But he abruptly withdrew from this generous insight. In the very next sentence he posited flatly, without explanation or support, that "there is a standard." In other words, the standard of taste is so important to Coppee that he maintained it in the face of Christian magnanimity. He announced the existence of "a union, a concurrence of Taste, not only among the refined, but among the barbarous, as far as they can comprehend these things," a unity of taste that "will establish the necessity and existence of a standard of taste" (65). I guess he meant that even peoples whose tastes are defined as barbarous by the standard will nonetheless agree that such a standard ought to exist.

Newman defined the standard of taste as "the agreeing voice of such as are susceptible of emotions of beauty, both of those who lived in past ages, and of those now existing" (50). The historical aspect of the standard guarantees its worth for Newman, because works of art that have always been accepted as beautiful can serve as "models of excellence in the fine arts" (51). Ironically, his example of enduring beauty is a statue of George Washington that depicts the American commander bedecked in a Roman toga. Newman reasoned that classical drapery "at all times, and to all men, appears graceful and excites emotions of beauty." It follows that this example "both proves, that there is a standard of taste, and illustrates what is meant by it." Newman apparently did not notice that this argument begs the question.

Coppee and Quackenbos, on the other hand, located the standard in "the concurrence of the right judgment of many well ordered and duly cultivated minds," rather than in a history of expressions of good taste (Coppee 64). In other words, the standard is set by the preferences of those persons whose tastes are widely acknowledged to be accurate and penetrating. Quackenbos explained why only cultivated tastes can set the standard:

> When we speak of the concurrent Tastes of men as the universal standard, it must be understood that we mean men placed in situations favorable to the proper development of this faculty. Such loose notions as may be entertained during ages of ignorance and darkness, or among rude and uncivilized nations, carry with them no authority. In such states of society, Taste is either totally suppressed or appears in its worst form. By the common sentiments of men, therefore, we mean the concurrent opinions of refined men in civilized nations, by whom the arts are cultivated, works of genius are freely discussed, and Taste is improved by science and philosophy. (180)

And so we see that the universal standard is actually set by quite a small group, and a familiar group it is, too: "men" living in "civilized nations" who cultivate the arts and who read science and philosophy. In other words, people just like the people who wrote these textbooks.

As I suggested a moment ago, some specious reasoning is at work here. To define taste, as these textbook authors do, in terms of the values or standards held by their group is to create a partial definition. To universalize such a definition is to mistake the part for the whole. To argue that the standard exists because we say it does, and to locate that standard in what we say is good, is to engage in pretty vicious circular reasoning as well. Feminist scholar Elizabeth Minnich called such argumentative moves "hierarchical invidious monisms" (the acronym for which, conveniently enough, is HIM). A HIM is any "system in which one category is taken to be not literally all there is, but the highest, most significant, most valuable, and, critically, the most real category—which sets up all others to be defined and judged solely with reference to that hegemonic category" (53). The hegemonic category soon comes to be seen as controlling the evaluative center, thus relegating other kinds of tastes to the margins, portraying them as coarse, crude, or savage, carefully fenced off, existing altogether beyond the pale.

BOURGEOIS SUBJECTIVITY AND THE PEDAGOGY OF TASTE

I hope that my analysis has indicated the extent to which the pedagogy of taste was articulated as an exclusionary discourse. It is easy enough to deconstruct the exclusions that go on in these discussions, particularly the us/them thinking that operates among classes and across cultural and racial boundaries. What is less easy to see is why this pedagogy emerged at all, and why it emerged within rhetorical education. There seems to be no obvious explanation for the stunning contradiction that informs modern rhetorical instruction in taste: Taste is innate, but it must be taught.

So why did modern teachers of rhetoric develop and promulgate a pedagogy of taste? The easy answer is that they inherited it from Blair. But this does not explain why Blair gave taste such a prominent position in his text, nor does it explain the 19th-century departure from his connection of taste to a more traditional rhetorical project—the cultivation of civic virtue. I think the answer lies elsewhere.

I take it as axiomatic that any successful rhetorical theory will reflect the dominant subjectivity of its era, and that any successful rhetorical education will develop and discipline that subjectivity. Just as ancient rhetorical education was constructed to discipline its students in the practice of civic responsibility, then, modern rhetorical education was constructed to invent and discipline the bourgeois individual.

In *The Ideology of the Aesthetic*, Eagleton argued persuasively that the subjectivity of modern aesthetics—the subjectivity manifested as a person of taste—is at least analogous to, if not synonymous with, the bourgeois subject whose emergence marks the modern period. As he said:

> From the depths of a benighted late feudal autocracy, a vision could be projected of a universal order of free, equal, autonomous human subjects, obeying no laws but those which they gave to themselves. This bourgeois public sphere breaks decisively with the privilege and particularism of the *ancien regime*, installing the middle class, in image if not in reality, as a truly universal subject, and compensating with the grandeur of this dream for its politically supine status. What is at stake here is nothing less than the production of an entirely new kind of human subject—one which, like the work of art itself, discovers the laws in the depths of its own free identity, rather than in some oppressive external power. (19)

As Eagleton was careful to note, this new form of subjectivity is always already inhabited by contradictions: In the face of its loss of external law, of external sources of authority, the bourgeois subject celebrates its freedom. At the very same moment, however, it internalizes the rule of law, agrees to police itself, to produce from out of itself the rules by which it will govern and restrain itself.

The pedagogy of taste, I would argue, is such a policing mechanism. It is the means through which young men were taught to internalize the marks and limits of bourgeois subjectivity (read "white, straight, male, comfortable, Christian" subjectivity). The ability to discriminate the bad from the good, in concert with their fellows, marks the bourgeois subjects for membership in the community. Just as surely, this mark distinguishes them from those others who are not so disciplined, those who are so roughened by toil and hard circumstance that they ignore beauty altogether, like Newman's laborer, or those, like Quackenbos' barbarians, who revel in the coarse or the bizarre.

Like all ideologies, the ideology of taste works to naturalize that which is culturally instituted. As Eagleton remarked, the bourgeois conflation of taste, morality, and "the natural" entitles its subjects to the claim that "we just know what is right and wrong, as we know that Homer is superb or that someone is standing on our foot" (64). The ideology of taste assigns socially constructed differences to nature, thus rendering its judgments true, right, and inevitable; at the same time it covers over the real social work it performs, which is to maintain and harden class distinctions. Early 19th-century school rhetoric texts teach not so much what, but who, to avoid. The pedagogy of taste helps students to internalize a set of rules that mark their inclusion in bourgeois subjectivity at the same time as it sets them off from members of other classes.

And so the paradox that seems inherent in the pedagogy of taste—taste is innate, but it can be learned—is not a paradox, really, but a coverup. The pedagogy of taste is a sham, or a scam, a promise made by teachers to students that instruction in rhetoric will quickly and readily inculcate the subjectivity necessary to mark them as members of a hegemonic class. This work is only partly a scam because bourgeois tastes, like working-class or aristocratic tastes, are learned through lifetimes of association with members of those classes. Teachers' real work, of course, is not to inculcate taste, but to rationalize the preferences of the hegemonic class. Teachers make categories and hierarchical distinctions; in the case of the pedagogy of taste, they turn class-bound preferences into knowledge. It is this work that is crucial to the maintenance and continuing dominance of the dominant class.

I suggest that the ideological impulse of the pedagogy of taste lingers on in the required introductory course in rhetoric or composition that is in place in most American colleges and universities.[4] Indeed, its required status testifies to the special disciplinary work performed by the course—the maintenance and promulgation of bourgeois subjectivity. During the first half of the 19th century, all of the students who worked with Professors Boyd, Coppee, Newman, and Quackenbos shared the subjectivity that was adumbrated in their pedagogy of taste. For such students, the pedagogy of taste simply confirmed and enlarged the tastes they already possessed and preferred. These days, however, the course enrolls many students who do not grow up sharing that subjectivity. If my historical analysis holds for the contemporary setting, it follows that such students will find their differences continually remarked by such instruction.

ENDNOTES

1. Nineteenth-century American school rhetoric resonates with this paradox: Its teachers regularly offer instruction in facilities, such as invention or taste, that they nevertheless posit to be natural to all reasonable people. To put such paradoxical thinking in historical perspective, consider the classical attitude toward the acquisition of arts or skills. Isocrates, and Quintilian after him, posited that the achievement of any art required a combination of three things: talent, education, and practice.

2. Gregory Clark traced the influence of this tradition of taste on American Calvinist rhetoric in "The Oratorical Poetic of Timothy Dwight."

3. The belles-lettres tradition can be opposed to the scientific-empirical tradition of American school rhetoric, a tradition carried forward by writers such as Alexander Bain and Henry Noble Day, who were inspired by Campbell's *Philosophy of Rhetoric* (1776) more than by Blair. It was this tradition that spawned current-traditional rhetoric (see my *The Methodical Memory*). However, as I posit in the conclusion to this chapter, attitudes associated with the pedagogy of taste also lingered on in composition instruction well into the 20th century.

4. Susan Miller makes this argument in different terms in *Textual Carnivals*.

WORKS CITED

Blair, Hugh. *Lectures on Rhetoric and Belles-Lettres*. Ed. Harold Harding. Carbondale: Southern Illinois UP, 1965. 2 vols.

Bourdieu, Pierre. *Distinction: A Social Critique of the Judgement of Taste*. Trans. Richard Nice. Cambridge, MA: Harvard UP, 1984.

Boyd, James R. *Elements of English Composition, Grammar, Rhetoric, Logic, and Practice,*

Preparatory for Academies and Schools. New York: Barnes, 1867.

Clark, Gregory. "The Oratorical Poetic of Timothy Dwight." *Oratorical Culture in Nineteenth-Century America: Transformations in the Theory and Practice of Rhetoric*. Eds. Gregory Clark and S. Michael Halloran. Carbondale: Southern Illinois UP, 1993. 57–77.

Coppee, Henry. *Elements of Rhetoric*. Philadelphia: Butler, 1860.

Crowley, Sharon. *The Methodical Memory: Invention in Current-Traditional Rhetoric*. Carbondale: Southern Illinois UP, 1990.

Eagleton, Terry. *The Ideology of the Aesthetic*. Oxford: Blackwell, 1990.

Johnson, Nan. *Nineteenth-Century Rhetoric in North America*. Carbondale: Southern Illinois UP, 1991.

Miller, Susan. *Textual Carnivals: The Politics of Composition*. Carbondale: Southern Illinois UP, 1990.

Minnich, Elizabeth. *Transforming Knowledge*. Philadelphia: Temple UP, 1990.

Newman, Samuel. *A Practical System of Rhetoric*. Boston: Newman, 1851.

Quackenbos, George Payn. *Advanced Course of Composition and Rhetoric*. New York: Appleton, 1864.

3 Intellectuals and the Place of Cultural Critique

Edward Schiappa
Purdue University

As the Rhetoric Society of America focuses on Cultural Studies for the second time in as many conferences, I want to take the occasion of the Charles Kneupper Memorial Address to talk about the place of cultural critique. My thesis is simple and hardly novel, but worth repeating at this juncture: The place for cultural critique by teachers and scholars of rhetorical studies is not only the classroom or academic books and journals, but also "in the streets" and in other nonacademic public and private forums.

My presentation's title is "Intellectuals and the place of Cultural Critique." I use the term *intellectual* in the same sense used by Russell Jacoby in his book, *The Last Intellectuals: American Culture in the Age of Academe*, and it is to this text I now turn. Jacoby bemoans the demise of the public intellectual in the second half of the 20th century. To be more specific, he laments the cultural transformation of the independent, nonacademic, urban, public critic into the academic professor. Jacoby attributes this transformation in part to gentrification, to suburbanization, and to the tremendous growth of colleges and universities after World War II. For the generation born around and after 1940, intellectual life and university life became coterminous: "To be an intellectual entailed being a professor" (16):

> To put it sharply: the habitat, manners, and idiom of intellectuals have been transformed within the past fifty years. Younger intellectuals no longer need or want a larger public; they are almost exclusively professors. Campuses are their homes; colleagues their audience; monographs and specialized journals their media. Unlike past intellectuals they situate themselves within fields and disciplines—for good

reason. Their jobs, advancement, and salaries depend on the evaluation of specialists, and this dependence affects the issues broached and the language employed. (6)

Jacoby's concern is that American culture in general and political discourse in particular are diminished by the professionalization of intellectual life.

[Academics] write for professional journals that . . . create insular societies. . . . Gathering in annual conferences to compare notes, they constitute their own universe. A "famous" sociologist or art historian means famous to other sociologists or art historians, not to anyone else. As intellectuals became academics, they had no need to write in a public prose; they did not, and finally they could not. (7)

The cost, Jacoby argued, is in social impact. As our studies become more specialized, jargon-filled, and esoteric, the audience addressed narrows, and our ability to change the world around us shrinks accordingly.

Critiques of contemporary scholarship such as Jacoby's are well known in academe. The most socially conscious of us typically respond by trying to invest more of ourselves into our teaching. Pedagogy that enacts cultural critique is vitally important, but it is not enough. A variety of scholars have done a thorough job of documenting the inescapable ideological work that happens in every classroom, regardless of the topic. Teacher-scholars in rhetoric and composition, in particular, have made great strides to see and to act on the interconnections among rhetorical theory, cultural studies, and classroom pedagogy. Those of us in communication have much to learn in this area.

But cultural critique in the classroom has a limited audience and its influence is indirect at best. We should not allow ourselves the easy out of believing that being "political" in the classroom is a substitute for our direct civic participation. Cultural critique in the classroom reaches a handful of students, whereas a column in the student newspaper reaches thousands, and a column in the hometown newspaper can reach even more. Denouncing homophobia in a classroom is important, but it is not the same as denouncing homophobia before a city council or state assembly. We certainly should take pride in the values and critical tools with which we equip our students, but if they do not *also* see us in the trenches, so to speak, then they know our values and critical tools are *merely* academic. Many of us want to teach "critical literacy" in the classroom to "help students gain a voice and connection to their learning" such that they see "the connection between knowledge and power" (Carbone). But the connection between knowledge and power that they learn most of the time is that they have to do what we tell them to get a good grade. The power relationships found in the classroom are often inimical to the goal of empowerment. There is a tension between fostering individual freedom and maintaining direction in the classroom, between "discovery learning versus transmissional teaching, the realization of personal potential versus the exercise of social power and determination" (Billig et al. 62).

The problem is not solvable on a theoretical level; it can only be worked out minute by minute, day by day, in the concrete practices of each of our classrooms (Billig et al.). The lesson we want them to learn—that skills learned in the classroom can empower them beyond the classroom—can be enhanced if we *show* by our example what critical literacy in nonacademic settings means and not just *tell* them about it in theory. Whether we encourage our students to be "technical experts" trained to ignore the social and political consequences of their expertise (Burke 30), or whether we produce what Michel Foucault (1980) calls the socially conscious "specific intellectual" (126–33) depends, in large measure, on *how we see ourselves* and whether we practice what we preach. In short: We should not rely on our classrooms to provide "trickle-down" citizen participation.

There has been a great deal of discussion about the ancient Greek Sophists as models for contemporary pedagogy and writing. But while we are busy appropriating "Sophistic epistemologies" and developing "neo-Sophistic theory," let us not forget that the original Sophists were directly involved in the politics of their time. Gorgias and Hippias were ambassadors. Protagoras advised Pericles and drafted the laws of Thurii. They directly engaged the great philosophical, political, and social issues of fifth-century Greece.

The first permanent school of higher learning in Greece, we are told, was opened by Isocrates. His texts typically are assumed to have been composed for the sole purpose of providing his students with appropriate models to emulate. Such a view is mistaken, for many of his compositions addressed actual, not hypothetical, audiences and were intended to move them toward specific actions. His essays were political and moral not only in content, but also in their objectives. Following the ill-conceived "Social War" he tried to persuade his fellow Athenians to reverse the policy of aggression. After the Thebans destroyed Plataea, Isocrates encouraged Athenians to help their long-time ally to rebuild. A persistent opponent of the anti-Macedonian war party, he hailed the peace between Philip and Athens in 346 BCE. He wrote to encourage Timotheus to continue to pursue a milder and more democratic course of leadership than Timotheus's father had shown. His several discourses on behalf of panhellenic unity, urging that Greek city-states cease warring against each other, became famous in his own time and remains his best known theme.

Although Isocrates certainly was not as influential as active orators such as Demosthenes, Georges Mathieu argued that Isocrates, in fact, did influence Greek politics far more than did other philosophers and many orators of his own time (222–23). Mathieu rejected the belief that Isocrates' orations were merely the idealist dreams of an armchair critic. Instead, he contended that Isocrates directly influenced certain policy choices by the Athenian *polis* and played an important role in shaping public opinion for later reorganization of the Greek world (189–99, 208–24). Jacqueline de Romilly pointed out that the second Athenian Confederation was created in 377 BCE, "two years after Isocrates had written his

Panegyricus, and it follows several of the suggestions he had made in that treatise" (11). Some years later, Philip created the League of Corinth in which "Isocrates' influence is even more conspicuous" (11). As we all know, Isocrates was not a traditional politician or public speaker; instead he found new ways to contribute to the political life of the community in which he found himself. Perhaps the most important lesson provided by Isocrates' and other Sophists' texts is that our own role in society is limited only by our ingenuity.

Of course we need not go back 2,500 years for examples of socially engaged intellectuals. Jacoby identified the golden age of intellectuals as the decades between the two World Wars. Richard Rorty argued that during this time both academic and nonacademic philosophers often functioned as important cultural critics of their time, and suggested that their influence was not inconsequential: "Lots of Deweyans wrote all over the map. And lots of officials in the Roosevelt Administration cared what those thinkers were saying" ("What are?" 49). As Rorty noted, "There are all kinds of ways, apart from university course contents and the professional journals, in which an academic discipline can be influential in society as a whole" (49). One example Rorty developed at some length is the missed opportunity by academic economists and professors of banking, business, and law to draw early national attention to the impending savings and loan disaster in the early 1980s ("Intellectuals" 485–86). Had such academicians seen themselves not just as privileged members of the sheltered ivory tower, but as responsible citizens—members of a polity—then Rorty hypothesized that enormous damage might have been prevented.

Socially engaged cultural critique need not be national in scope, as Rorty's example is. Allow me a brief local example. In the fall of 1992, a city council member of the town of Lafayette, IN, proposed an amendment to the city's human relations ordinance that would add "sexual orientation" to the list of categories protected against discrimination. The public debate was heated, to say the least. A very few Purdue University faculty and graduate students joined the public dialogue. The number was embarrassingly low, given that most academic intellectuals would agree that gay rights is *the* civil rights issue of the 1990s. Nonetheless, a few brought together their respective areas of expertise and argumentative ability to weigh in on the side of civil rights. They spoke before city council meetings, sometimes to be jeered publicly and harassed privately by the opposition. They wrote columns for the town newspaper and agreed to be interviewed by the media. They wrote position papers on specific issues for the media and for the city council. When an attorney on the city council expressed certain misgivings about the legal aspects of the ordinance, a position paper was written that was devoted exclusively to that topic. When the local paper ran a phone-in poll that showed vast opposition to the ordinance, they conducted a far more accurate poll using appropriate randomized data-gathering techniques that generated more representative results that showed majority support. Members of the Women's Studies Program at Purdue organized a teach-in about gay rights at the Lafayette public library. In short, a few faculty and graduate students acted as cultural critics who were *also* fellow concerned citizens.

I wouldn't tell this story if it did not have a happy ending. The city council member who is an attorney eventually switched and voted *for* the proposed ordinance. In the spring of 1993 the city of Lafayette approved the gay-rights proposal by a vote of 5 to 4, becoming the first city in the entire state of Indiana to do so. A few months later the city of West Lafayette followed suit. I honestly cannot tell you how *much* of a difference those ordinances will make, but I can assure you that they will. And while it may be hubris on my part, I remain convinced that the participation of those dedicated few faculty and graduate students was decisive.

The idea that there should be no bright line between "political" and "scholarly" activism is old hat in some corners—particularly in sociology and anthropology. Nearly a hundred years ago, Jane Addams's efforts as a pioneering sociologist at Hull House working with Chicago's immigrants, and W. E. B. Du Bois's efforts as a social scientist and political activist documenting the social conditions of black Americans, provide shining exemplars of socially engaged scholars. Their legacy survives today in various forms and settings, but especially in Women's Studies and African-American Studies programs. Such programs often encourage connections with local community programs and services. Typically their faculty and graduate students are among the first to plan and organize local political action when the occasion demands it. I shared the local success story I told earlier because it was an example with which I am familiar. That example could be multiplied many times over thanks to the efforts of dedicated scholar-activists all over the country. The key feminist insight that "the personal is political" calls our attention to the social and power dimensions of our private relationships, actions, and experiences. Scholar-activists have learned to resist the temptation to define their "professional" or "scholarly" life as somehow apart from the personal and the political. Thus, to "the personal is political" they would add that "the professional is political." Those of us interested in cultural studies need to take a lesson from those for whom such expressions as "the personal is political" is a way of life, not just a slogan.

The point of these stories is that when intellectuals choose to get involved, we can make a difference. All too often we do not get involved for one of several reasons. More often than not, we feel we just do not have the time or energy for such "extra" efforts. Typically we disenfranchise ourselves from the so-called "outside world" in order to concentrate on the problems facing us *within* academe. Or even if we are willing to get involved, we figure we lack the appropriate expertise to say anything important. I think we need to reconsider these reasons.

Each of us must make the decision of what is important enough to devote our time and effort to. Institutionally, we need to rethink how we evaluate faculty contributions and how we determine what *counts* as "scholarship," "teaching," and "service." Individually, we need to recognize that we do not live apart from the "real" world "outside" of academe. We are positioned in both. Although it is true that universities are "privileged enclave[s]" (Rorty, "Humanistic"), the fact is that the world outside universities keeps on moving—with or without us. We are simultaneously positioned as members of university communities and as citizens of local, state, and national polities. We have the right, and the obligation, to speak and act on the issues that concern us. No one can deny us of that right to participate.

Ironically, it is often *we* ourselves who censor our participation. Too often we see an issue as outside of our "expertise." This sort of *self*-disciplining and turf sensitivity is dangerous enough *within* academe, but it is *deadly* to a democracy. First of all, no one needs special credentials to be a cultural critic (just ask Rush Limbaugh). The fact is that graduate students and faculty members are typically pretty darn smart and have better-than-average educated views. And we're pretty quick to learn. Most of us speak and write well. Our research skills, analytical abilities, and argumentative prowess make us formidable public intellectuals. The sort of work involved in cultural studies is particularly valuable: media criticism, the ability to trace the ideological work of texts, the ability to argue that categories taken as "natural" or "normal" are better understood as "constructed" and historically contingent, the ability to situate an individual sign or group of signs into a larger context of meaning—these are some of the specific skills that cultural critics bring to bear. The point is not that we have some sort of special sight that allows us to understand culture "more clearly" than mere mortals. The point is that to the extent that we do not share our insights and abilities, public discourse is correspondingly impoverished.

There is lots to do. Our ability to interpret and to critique public discourse has never been needed more. RSA is my favorite academic organization because it is committed to tearing down artificial walls between academic disciplines so that we can work together on issues of common concern. It is in that spirit that I urge you to think about tearing down other artificial walls that deprive your community of your contributions.

The critical practices enacted through cultural studies must be more than merely academic. We cannot afford to give up, in Rorty's words, "on the idea of democratic politics, of mobilizing moral outrage in defense of the weak, of drawing upon a moral vocabulary common to the well educated and the badly educated, to those who get paid for analyzing symbols" and those who work in the so-called "real world" ("Intellectuals" 489). So let us take the occasion of this conference to celebrate our scholarship, to learn from each other about the cultural work of various rhetorical practices, and—last but not least—to commit ourselves to the task of cultural critique in and out of academe.

ACKNOWLEDGMENTS

The author is grateful for suggestions from Roxanne Mountford and Cynthia Stohl.

WORKS CITED

Billig, M., S. Condor, D. Edwards, M. Gane, D. Middleton, and A. Radley. *Ideological Dilemmas*. Beverly Hills: Sage, 1988.

Burke, Kenneth. *A Rhetoric of Motives*. Berkeley: U of California P, 1950/1969.

Carbone, M. J. "Empowering the Liberal Arts: Analysis and Paradigms from Critical Theory." *Quarterly Journal of Ideology*, 12 (1988): 1–14.

Foucault, Michel. *Power/Knowledge*. New York: Pantheon Books, 1980.

Jacoby, Russell. *The Last Intellectuals: American Culture in the Age of Academe*. New York: Noonday Press, 1987.

Mathieu, Georges. *Les Idées Politiques d'Isocrate*. Paris: Les Belles Lettres, 1925.

Rorty, Richard. "The Humanistic Intellectual: Eleven Theses." *ACLS Occasional Papers* 11 (1989): 9–12.

–––––. "Intellectuals in Politics." *Dissent* (Fall, 1991): 483–90.

–––––. "What Are Philosophers For?" *The Center Magazine* (Sept./Oct. 1983): 40–44.

4

Rhetoric, Cultural Studies, and Literacy: An Overview of the 1994 Rhetoric Society of America Meeting

Robert L. McDonald
Virginia Military Institute
Christina G. Russell
James Madison University

As even a brief examination of the 1994 Rhetoric Society of America (RSA) program attests, the Norfolk meeting, with its timely theme of "Rhetoric, Cultural Studies, and Literacy," showcased a truly remarkable range of work, much of it interdisciplinary and nearly all of it immediately applicable to further research and teaching in rhetoric and composition.

We enjoyed reading all the eligible submissions, but in considering them for publication in these proceedings, we have done our very best to observe the criteria set by the editor. Briefly, he asked us to observe three principles in recommending the papers to be included: *quality*, *diversity*, and *usefulness*. We read, then, for essays that demonstrated careful scholarship on the fullest breadth of topics related to the conference theme, and that might ultimately be of use and/ or interest to the RSA membership. We also exercised our preference for papers that communicated economically, without falling prey to what Jacoby recently called "the obscurity fetish."

We should note that our original plan for making a "balanced" selection for this volume—roughly, recommending so many essays emphasizing "rhetoric," so many on "cultural studies," and perhaps an equal number on "literacy"—simply did not work. As we were pleased to discover, most of the essays defied this type of easy categorization. Our final stack of choices did, however, seem to group themselves naturally into four categories.

HISTORICAL STUDIES

Each of the three historical studies included exemplifies work in completing or correcting inadequate understandings of our past. In "Rereading Aspasia: The

Palimpsest of Her Thoughts," Cheryl Glenn illustrates how studying "the fault line of gender" can help reveal women's true contributions to the history of rhetoric. Looking particularly at the case of Aspasia of Miletus, Glenn reconstructs the intellectual life of a 5th-century BCE Athenian woman by examining her representation in the texts of men who appropriated her ideas over the centuries. John Kimsey similarly attempts to reconstruct history in "Primitives and Pretenders: Blair and Ossian," in which he conjectures an explanation for Blair's support of Macpherson's "alleged translation of the poems of Ossian" in 18th-century Scotland and raises provocative questions about the relationship between authorship and folk culture. Blair championed Ossian as an "epic" poet, Kimsey claims, because he found in the Celt's work "a self-fulfilling prophecy": an historical justification for Romanticism. And finally, Dottie Broaddus maintains that James Russell Lowell, Ralph Waldo Emerson, and Oliver Wendell Holmes—all students of Edward Tyrell Channing at Harvard—in effect "constructed" the 19th-century American "gentleman," primarily through their influence as public intellectuals. According to Broaddus, "The American gentleman composed by these writers became an agent for social exclusion."

PRACTICING THEORIES OF READING AND WRITING

Four of the essays here concern themselves with aspects of one of the most basic concerns of studies in rhetoric and composition: better informing the activities of reading and writing. In "Orwell, Russell, and the Language of Imperialism," William T. Ross confronts the "quandary" we face "when we meet disturbing convictions or distasteful language in a writer we otherwise admire." Examining selected passages from Bertrand Russell and George Orwell, two prolific writers, Ross suggests that readers must learn to recognize and then appreciate "seemingly inconsistent and contradictory rhetorical constructions" as evidence of culture's inescapable influences on writers. Mary Grabar suggests, perhaps, a less critical stance for readers, arguing persuasively that Gadamer's "dialectic of experience" can help recover "reading as 'playful' or pleasurable and meaningful" activity. In "'Truth' as Experience and 'Method' as Dialectic: Gadamer's Hermeneutics and Literacy," Grabar recommends against the prevailing "hermeneutics of suspicion" inherent in fashionable critical schools such as feminism and Marxism, recommending instead the potential of reading informed by "a hermeneutics of trust."

Demonstrating theory in praxis, "Burke *Contra* Jameson on Ideological Criticism: Or How to Read Patricia Hampl Reading Whitman During the Vietnam War," David W. Smit contrasts two apparently oppositional theoretical frameworks for deriving meaning from a text. Offering two speculative readings of Hampl's little-known essay "The Mayflower Moment: Reading Whitman During the Vietnam War"—one as Kenneth Burke might approach the essay and another as Frederic Jameson would—Smit concludes that whereas both theories permit similar "insights" into the essay, finally Burke offers more complete "strategies for dealing with the aspects of form." And Glenda Conway invokes Bakhtin in "Judicial Constructions of Difference: The Supreme Court's Majority Opinions in *Scott v. Sandford* and *Bowers v. Hardwick*" to reveal ways litigants are (mis)represented in published court decisions. Conway analyzes two landmark cases to demonstrate how "'real' litigants become subject to artificial identities in judicial opinions . . . through dialogic voice constructions."

PUBLIC/PRIVATE VOICES

Given the snowballing debates concerning the place of public and private discourses, especially as those debates influence our teaching, it should be no surprise that six of the essays included address facets of this topic. In "Expressive Rhetoric, A Genealogy of Ideas, and a Case for the British Romantics," Rex Veeder provides an historical context for reconsidering the genesis of expressivism. His aim, he says, is twofold: "to reconcile the British Romantics to rhetoric and place expressionist theory in a historical context other than post-1960." Searching even farther back into our histories, Steven B. Katz and T.R. Johnson examine expressivism in similarly contextual terms. In "The Kabbalah as a Theory of Rhetoric: Another Suppressed Epistemology," Katz explains how the Kabbalah—a written text expressing ancient traditions of Judaism—"may provide us with a glimpse into an ancient epistemology in Western culture that connects the subjective with the transcendent, the personal with the universal." Johnson's essay, "Expressivism, Pleasure, and the Magical Medicine of Gorgias," studies Gorgias's *Encomium of Helen* as an example of language's "power to transform reality." Johnson urges us to "reimagine expressivism" in order to "develop a theory of writing-as-magical" that might empower apprehensive or unskilled student writers.

LuMing Mao questions the very terms of the private/public discourse debates—or at least any foundations for their universality—in his essay "'Individualism' or 'Personhood': A Battle of Locution or Rhetoric?" Through an examination of seminal texts in the Chinese rhetorical tradition, primarily *The Analects* of Confucius, Mao claims that "the word *individualism* . . . [and] its 'negative application' not only falls short of adequately describing Chinese rhetorical practices, but imposes on them a different way of thinking." Hephzibah Roskelly also rejects too easy indictments of the "personal." Her essay, "Private Voices and Public Acts: Reform in the Teaching of Literacy," builds a powerful case for resisting the current pedagogical "backlash" that labels personal discourse "as destructive to good academic prose or as merely self-indulgent." Juanita Comfort finds such divisions dangerous not only in the classroom, but also in the academy at large. In "A Rhetoric of 'Cultural Negotiation': Toward an Ethos of Empowerment for African-American Women Graduate Students," Comfort wonders, "Where do we learn how to assert a distinct—yet effective—scholarly presence in our academic writing?"

INSTITUTIONAL CONCERNS

Four of the essays deal directly with the institutional philosophies that drive—or at least complicate—our work. Rolf Norgaard's "The Rhetoric of Writing Requirements" labels writing requirements "an institution's fiction of itself," and uses Brooke's concept of "underlife" to discuss how "[t]he rhetoric we teach and use in the context of required writing courses . . . becomes a way of responding to, and not just representing, institutional norms." Kristine L. Blair and Joyce Neff Magnotto also tackle institutional rhetorics, but on different fronts. In "Resisting and Revising Culture: From Modernist Theory to Postmodernist Pedagogy," Blair explores the pedagogical effects of the "clash between modernist epistemology and postmodernist technology," calling for "more dialogue with students to address the concerns over textuality and culture as well as conflicts over authority and subjectivity" as we plan our writing courses. Magnotto's concern is with how we define "academic literacy" for the larger student population. In "Literacy Among Undergraduates: How We Represent Students as Writers and What It Means When We Don't," she presents the results of an original study indicating that "institutional practices regarding writing have not moved much beyond gate-keeping" because "academic institutions continue to define undergraduate literacy in very narrow terms."

The final essay in this section is Richard C. Gebhardt's most recent installment in his ongoing examination of "Scholarship, Promotion, and Tenure in Composition Studies." Gebhardt elaborates four crucial issues regarding tenure and promotion in the discipline: (a) the difficulty of defining "standards of scholarship" in such a diverse field; (b) the prejudice against teaching and students as topics of research and publication; (c) the conflict between research and teaching as the discipline's central work; and (d) the situation of that same conflict within the "system of American higher education." It is an essay that should prompt some lively coffee-room debates.

The 1994 RSA program exemplifies the impressive quality of scholarship the members of this organization are generating. It is our pleasure to recommend this selection from that program for publication for a larger audience.

WORK CITED

Jacoby, Russell. "The Ivory Tower Obscurity Fetish." *Harper's* (Sept. 1994): 22-28.

Part I

Historical Studies

5 Rereading Aspasia: The Palimpsest of Her Thoughts

Cheryl Glenn
Oregon State University

Like many of you here, I'm working on a history of rhetoric, which means that, like you, I am having problems with both history and writing history,[1] with what Michel de Certeau calls "scriptural construction" (309). In *The Writing of History*, Certeau explains history as "our myth" and tells us that historiography (that is, *history* and *writing*) bears within its own name the paradox of a relation established between two antinomic terms, between the real and discourse. The task of historiography is one of connecting the real and discourse, and at the point where this link cannot be imagined, historiography must work as if the real and discourse were actually being joined (xxvii).

He's right: That's what we're all doing—we're all working as if the real and discourse were actually being joined in our texts. We're all constructing histories of rhetoric under the most paradoxical conditions of postmodernism: We write history knowing that we cannot tell the "truth"; knowing that our traditional foundations are at best shaky and at worst nonexistent; knowing, for a fact, that our historical narratives are neither stable nor necessarily coherent. Still, we simply cannot seem to separate ourselves from these symbols of representation, even if our intelligible histories represent an impenetrable reality, even if the concepts of *writing* and *history* are both suspect.

Thus, we regularly employ postmodern methodologies to interrogate and inform our scriptural constructions—even under those paradoxical conditions. Those of us writing women into the history of rhetoric use three postmodern methodologies in particular—historiography, feminism, and gender theory—to enrich and complicate and make possible our research and writing. And for me, gender theory has served as an exceptionally useful analytical category for rereading rhetoric history to include Aspasia of Miletus.[2] Until I began to view Aspasia's intellectual and social context through the lens of gender studies, she appeared in my view only as a *hetaera* (upper-class courtesan), who successfully and perhaps wisely exploited her sexual access to Pericles to gain access to his intellectual and political circle. But by contextualizing Aspasia within the gendered limits and expectations of her time, I can now explain her political and intellectual influence—and her rhetorical accomplishments—in terms other than erotic.

Well, I can explain her with gender theory, but I can read her only through the palimpsest of her thoughts, for her words and actions have been inscribed and reinscribed by those of men. We know about Aspasia much the same way we know about Socrates—from secondary sources. None of their work exists in primary sources. Although the historical tradition has readily accepted secondary accounts of Socrates's influence, teaching, and beliefs, the same cannot be said about any female counterpart, especially Aspasia, a woman described in so few accounts. But the fact that Aspasia is even mentioned by her male contemporaries is remarkable, for rare is the mention of any intellectual woman. Surviving fragments and references in the work of male authors provide tantalizing indications that the intellectual efforts of Aspasia were, at least occasionally, committed to writing. And every fragment we have about Aspasia comes from those male authors. Perhaps now it's time to piece those fragments together.

In 5th-century BCE, Aspasia emigrated from Miletus—a cultivated, far-eastern, Greek subject-ally, renowned for its literacy and philosophies of moral thought and nature.[3] A non-Athenian, citizen-class Greek, Aspasia arrived in Athens educated, fully conscious of civic rights and responsibilities, and linked with the great statesman Pericles (fl. 442 BCE). As a free woman brought up in the transitional society of Asia Minor, Aspasia was subject to Athenian law, but without citizen rights. That combination freed her from the gendered identity that arose from that fixed role of the aristocratic Athenian woman, whose activity, education, marriage, and rights as property holder were severely circumscribed by her male relatives. Married at an early age, Athenian women neither attended schools nor participated in the *polis*, the public sphere of trade, war, politics—and other men.[4]

When other women were systematically relegated to the domestic sphere, Aspasia seems to have been the only woman in classical Greece to have distinguished herself in the public domain, in the *polis*. Her reputation as both a rhetorician and philosopher was memorialized by Plato (437–328 BC), Xenophon (fl. 450 BC), Cicero (100–43 BC), Athenaeus (fl. AD 200), and Plutarch (AD 46–c.120)—as was, of course, her enduring romantic attachment to Pericles. For those authors, Aspasia clearly represented the intelligentsia of Periclean Athens. Her alleged connection with the courtesan life is only important so far as it explains her intellectual prowess and social attainments—and the surprise of an

Athenian citizenry unaccustomed to (or perhaps jealous or suspicious of) a public woman.[5] Aspasia opened an academy for young women of good families (or a school for *hetaerae*, according to some sources[6]) that soon became a popular salon for the most influential men of the day: Socrates, Plato, Anaxagoras, Sophocles, Phidias, and Pericles. Aspasia's appearance was unprecedented at a time when the construction of gender ensured that women would be praised only for such attributes as their inherent modesty, for their inborn reluctance to join males (even kinsmen) for society or dining, and for their absolute incapacity to participate as educated beings within the *polis*; in addition, Aspasia's appearance was unprecedented at a time when a woman's only political contribution was serving as a nameless channel for the transmission of citizenship from her father to her son (Keuls 90);[7] and at a time when Pericles pronounced that "the greatest glory of a woman is to be least talked about by men, whether they are praising . . . or criticizing" (Thucydides 5.46.2).[8] It is difficult to overemphasize how extraordinary the foreign-born Aspasia—a public woman, philosopher, political influence, and rhetorician—would have been in 5th-century BC Athenian society.

The Athenian *polis* was founded on the exclusion of women, just as, in other respects, it was founded on the exclusion of foreigners and slaves (Vidal-Naquet 145). Although females born of Athenian-citizen parents were citizen class and subjects within the *polis*, they were not actual citizens in any sense. Nor could foreign-born women or men hope for citizenship, regardless of their political influence, civic contributions, or intellectual ties with those in power. Therefore, noncitizens such as Protagoras, Gorgias, Prodicus, Thrasymachus, Anaxagoras, and Aspasia functioned within the *polis*, yet outside its restraints.

If we think of gender as a cultural role, a social rank, "a social category imposed on a sexed body" (Scott 32), or as "a primary way of signifying relations of power" (Laqueur 12), then we can more easily trace Aspasia's movement across gendered boundaries of appropriate roles for women and men in 5th-century BC Athens. She seems to have profited by her excursion into the male domain of politics and intellect, even at the expense of her respectability, reputation, and authority. And even though her contributions to rhetoric are firmly situated and fully realized within the rhetorical tradition, those contributions have been directed through a powerful gendered lens to both refract toward and reflect Socrates and Pericles. Ironically, then, Aspasia's accomplishments and influence—all of which have been enumerated by men and most often attributed to men—come to us in the form of a palimpsest.

Pericles, perhaps the most socially responsible, powerful, and influential of Athenians, was indeed surrounded with the greatest thinkers of his age, with Sophists, philosophers, architects, scientists, and rhetoricians. In his *Mass and Elite in Democratic Athens*, Josiah Ober referred to Pericles's intellectual circle as the "'educated elite' of late 5th-century Athens," "a brain trust"; he described the Sophists as "experts in political manipulation who were flocking to Athens from other Greek poleis" and placed the "educated courtesan Aspasia . . . among

Pericles' closest associates," calling her "the power behind the throne" (89–90).[9] Several centuries later, Philostratus (fl. AD 250) wrote in his *Epistle* 73 that "Aspasia of Miletus is said to have sharpened the tongue of Pericles in imitation of Gorgias," with "the digressions and transitions of Gorgias' speeches [becoming] the fashion" (quoted in Sprague 41–42). Philostratus echoed Plato, the earliest writer to mention Aspasia. In the *Menexenus*, the Platonic Socrates revealed Aspasia to be the author of Pericles's Funeral Oration (*Epitaphios*). But Aspasia became implicated even more in Pericles's education if we consider that the rhetorician most closely associated with Pericles would no doubt have served as his logographer, as logography was commonly the province of rhetoricians. Hence, Aspasia surely must have influenced Pericles in the composition of those speeches that both established him as a persuasive speaker and informed him as the most respected citizen-orator of the age.

According to several ancient authors, all of whom knitted together secondary sources to shape a reliable Socrates, Socrates deeply respected Aspasia's thinking and admired her rhetorical prowess, disregarding, it seems, her status as a woman and a *hetaera*. In Xenophon's *Memorabilia*, for instance, Socrates explained to Critobulus the "art of catching friends" and of using an intermediary:

> I can quote Aspasia. . . . She once told me that good matchmakers are successful only when the good reports they carry to and fro are true; false reports she would not recommend, for the victims of deceptions hate one another and the matchmaker too. I am convinced that this is sound, so I think it is not open to me to say anything in your praise that I cannot say truthfully. (II.36)

In Xenophon's *Oeconomicus*, Socrates ascribed to Aspasia the marital advice he gave to Critobulus: "There's nothing like investigation. I will introduce Aspasia to you, and she will explain the whole matter [of good wives] to you with more knowledge than I possess" (III.15). Plutarch wrote that "Socrates sometimes came to see [Aspasia] with his disciples, and his intimate friends brought their wives to her to hear her discourse as a teacher of rhetoric" (200); Athenaeus called Aspasia "clever . . . to be sure, . . . Socrates' teacher in rhetoric" (V.29). Furthermore, in the *Menexenus*, the Platonic Socrates agreed that were the Council Chamber to elect him to make the recitation over the dead, he "should be able to make the speech . . . for [Aspasia] who is my instructor is by no means weak in the art of rhetoric; on the contrary, she has turned out many fine orators, and amongst them one who surpassed all other Greeks, Pericles" (235–36). But it was Pericles—not Aspasia—who delivered that speech.

Plato's *Menexenus* contains Plato's version of Socrates' version of Aspasia's version of Pericles's Funeral Oration, further recognition of Aspasia's reputation as rhetorician, philosopher and as influential colleague in the Sophistic movement, a movement devoted to the analysis and creation of rhetoric—and truth. Moreover, the Funeral Oration itself held political, philosophical, and rhetorical significance: by its delivery alone, the Funeral Oration played out "rhetoric's important role in shaping community" (Mackin 251). In *The Invention of Athens: The Funeral Oration in the Classical City*, Nicole Loraux clarified the funeral oration as an *"institution—*an institution of speech in which the symbolic constantly encroached upon the functional, since in each oration the codified praise of the dead spilled over into generalized praise of Athens" (2). (We have only to think of Ochs's keynote address, which beautifully explained the epideictic procedure.) Besides conflating praise of the Athenians with praise of Athens, this institutionalized and specialized epideictic was useful for developing "consubstantiality" and creating a "similar rhetorical experience" for everyone present, be they citizens, foreigners, or women related to the dead.[10] The shared experience of this rhetorical ritual linked everyone present even as it connected them "with other audiences in the past" (Mackin 251). As "one of the authorized mouthpieces of classical Athens," the funeral oration translated into "Greek patriotism"—"Athenian eloquence" "adapted to the needs of a given historical situation" (Loraux 5), an adaptation that connected with Sophistic philosophy. No doubt because of her Sophistic training, political capacity, and powerful influence on Pericles' persuasive oratory, Aspasia was alleged to have composed the famous funeral oration delivered by Pericles, just as Socrates told Menexenus:

> I was listening only yesterday to Aspasia going through a funeral speech for [the Athenians]. . . . [S]he rehearsed to me the speech in the form it should take, extemporizing in part, while other parts of it she had previously prepared, . . . at the time when she was composing the funeral oration which Pericles delivered. (236b)

That Aspasia may well have composed Pericles's speech makes sense: After all, being honored by the opportunity to deliver the *Epitaphios*, Pericles would have prepared well, seeking and following the advice of his colleagues, including Aspasia, on points of style and substance. That she wrote it becomes more convincing when we consider Loraux's assurance that "the political orator must have the ascendant over the logographer" (11) and that the Sophists would preserve the "essential features of the civic representations" (107). For reasons of Aspasia's proximity to Pericles and her intellectual training, we can reread the speech as one composed by Aspasia.

Before demonstrating her expertise at composing moving, patriotic epideictic oratory, Aspasia reminded Socrates of the efficacy of rhetoric. In the *Menexenus*, the Platonic Aspasia explained that "it is by means of speech finely spoken that deeds nobly done gain for their doers from the hearers the meed of memory and renown" (236e)—an accurate description of contingent truth. Hence, the author of the *Epitaphios*—whether viewed as Aspasia or Pericles—made clear the power of oratory to influence the public's belief that its history was other than it was. Loraux explained that "a Sophist and a rhetor [would have] used the official oration in order to write a fictitious logos; within the corpus, then, the 'false' follows hard upon the 'true'" (9). Accordingly, the most aggressive exploits of Attic imperialism are represented as "[bringing] freedom [to] all the dwellers of this continent" (240e), as "fighting in defence of the liberties of the BoeOtians" (242b), as "fighting for the freedom of Leontini" (243a), as "setting free . . . friends" (243c), and as "saving their walls from ruin" (244c).

In offering this version of Pericles' Funeral Oration, an exaggerated encomium abounding with historical misstatements and anachronisms, Plato implied his own cynicism about the use of rhetoric. In his opinion, the development of oratory had negative consequences for Athens, the most glaring defect of current oratory being its *in*difference to truth. A rhetorician such as Aspasia was, indeed, interested more in believability than in truth, more interested in constructing than delivering truth, more interested in *nomos* (beliefs, customs, laws) than *physis* (nature, reality), interests leading to Thucydides's claims that such "prose chroniclers . . . are less interested in telling the truth than in catching the attention of their public" (I.21).

Like Aspasia, Plato taught that belief and truth are not necessarily the same, a sentiment he made evident in his *Gorgias* when Gorgias admitted that rhetoric produces "[mere] belief without knowledge" (454). Plato also agreed with Aspasia that rhetoric, which is the daughter of truth-disclosing philosophy, does not always carry on the family tradition; rhetoric can be used to obscure the truth, to control and deceive believers into belief. In the *Gorgias*, his Socrates said, "[R]hetoric seems not to be an artistic pursuit at all, but that of a shrewd, courageous spirit which is naturally clever at dealing with men; and I call the chief part of it flattery" (463). And in the *Phaedrus*, Plato wrote that "in the courts, they say, nobody cares for truth about . . . [things which are just or good], but for that which is convincing; and that is probability" (272e). Like Aspasia, Plato approved of a rhetoric of persuasion; he too saw the political potential of public rhetoric. But Plato's rhetoric is foremost a search for the truth; only truth—not fictive effect over accuracy—should constitute persuasive rhetoric. What Plato could learn, then, from Aspasia is the as-yet uncalibrated potential of rhetoric to create belief.

Although Aspasia was a powerful and exceptional intellectual force in Periclean Athens, and although she seemed to have affected the thinking of Plato and Socrates, few Greek thinkers accepted women as mental equals. Aristotle made no provision for the intellectual woman, except for his nod to Sappho: "Everyone honours the wise. . . . [T]he Mytilenaeans [honour] Sappho, though she was a woman" (*Rhetoric* 1389b.12). Otherwise, Aristotle denied any philosophical or rhetorical contributions of women. For Aristotle, men and women differed in their permanent inequality. In the *Politics*, Aristotle wrote "between the sexes, the male is by nature superior and the female inferior, the male ruler and the female subject" (I.ii.12); in the *Poetics*, he pronounced goodness as possible "even in a woman . . . though [she] is perhaps an inferior

. . .; but it is not appropriate in a female Character to be manly, or clever" (15.1454a.20–24); and in the *Rhetoric*, he wrote that "one quality or action is nobler than another if it is that of a naturally finer being: thus a man's will be nobler than a woman's" (I.9.15).

Reasoning from Aristotle's basic premise, Aspasia could not have become a teacher, much less a rhetorician. By the principle of *entelechy* (the vital force urging one toward fulfilling one's actual essence), she would have naturally followed her predetermined life course, her progress distinctly marked off and limited to a degree of perfection less than that for a man. The power politics of gender, the social category imposed on each sexed body, both gives rise to and then maintains the social creation of ideas about appropriate roles for women and men. Men—those naturally finer beings—were awarded a public voice, which enabled them to participate as speakers, thinkers, and writers in the *polis*, in the "good" of public life. A public voice was the right and privilege of those who were declared to possess reason and goodness to its fullest extent—men only. The *polis*—the public sphere of action, the realm of highest justice—was the world of perfection, the world of men only. "Naturally," then, women were denied the *telos* of perfect maleness, and Athenian women were denied a passport into the gendered intellectual battleground of politics, philosophy, rhetoric. Yet Aspasia had regendered herself—and trespassed into masculine territory. But even the outline of Aspasia's life is difficult to bring into focus, for she appeared only through layers of men's words and lives.

Aspasia of Miletus inscribed her self and her texts on rhetorical history, but her inscriptions were quickly appropriated by males. Although she herself escaped the traditional limitations of her gender, she did not escape those who reinscribed her. Thus, only now are we rereading Aspasia of Miletus as a teacher of rhetoric, as influential to the thinking of Plato, Socrates, and Pericles. Only now are we examining the fault line of gender that reveals that women have, indeed, participated in and contributed to the rhetorical tradition. And only now are we realizing that the fault line reverberates down the corridors of past scholarship to the foundations of the Greek intellectual tradition. The story of Aspasia's contributions to rhetoric, one of gendered expectations and violations, brings to the fore the whole notion of woman's place in the history of rhetoric. And her story also foregrounds our rethinking of that history, for we no longer think of it as a linear narrative chiseled chronologically in stone, but rather as a collection of unstable tellings that have been inscribed and reinscribed on waxen tablets.

ENDNOTES

1. This chapter constitutes part of my forthcoming book-length project, *Rhetoric Retold: Regendering the Tradition from Antiquity through the Renaissance*.
2. See my "sex, lies, and manuscript: Refiguring Aspasia in the History of Rhetoric" for a thorough treatment of this rhetorical woman.

3. Miletus had relatively large numbers of literate citizens, among them the philosophers Anaximander, Anaximenes, and Thales (Harris 63; Vernant, *Origins* 127, *Myth and Thought* 343ff.; Kirk and Raven 73ff.). In *Myth and Society in Ancient Greece*, Vernant wrote that alongside moral thought, "a philosophy of nature starts to develop . . . in the Greek cities of Asia Minor. The theories of these first 'physicists' of Ionia have been hailed as the beginning of rational though as it is understood in the West" (96).

4. Kitto placed Athenian women in Oriental seclusion: "In this pre-eminently masculine society women moved in so restricted a sphere that we may reasonably regard them as a 'depressed area'" (222). He accepted such restrictions as sensible.

5. Just reminded us that "Aspasia's notoriety and the popular resentment her supposed influence aroused should . . . be remembered—a resentment transmuted into mockery by comedy" (21). In the *Acharnians*, Aristophanes wrote that the Megarians "abducted *two* whores from Aspasia's stable in Athens" (523); Plutarch wrote that Cratinus, "in downright terms, calls her a harlot": "To find him a Juno the goddess of lust / Bore that harlot past shame, / Aspasia by name" (201). Flaceliere assured us that "the Athenian comic poets never tired of repeating that Aspasia led a life of debauchery, though apparently she was as well behaved as she was well informed, and even a scholar" (131). And Cantarella wrote, "It is not surprising that many Athenians hated Aspasia. She was not like other women; she was an intellectual" (54–55).

6. Just 144; Pomeroy, *Goddesses* 89. But Hans Licht (a pseudonym for Paul Brandt) explained that: "the preference for Aspasia shown by Pericles afforded a welcome excuse for his opponents to attack him; people would not hear of a woman having anything to say in political life, especially one who was not an Athenian but was brought from abroad, and even from Ionia . . ., which was notorious for the immorality of its women. . . . Hence she was severely criticized by the comic poets. . . . [A]ccording to a statement in Athenaeus . . . she was said to have maintained a regular brothel. . . . When she was accused of *asebeia* (impiety) and procuring, Pericles defended her and secured her acquittal" (352–53).

7. Vidal-Naquet wrote that "the sole civic function of women was to give birth to citizens. The conditions imposed upon them by Pericles' law of 451 was to be the daughter of a citizen and a citizen's daughter" (145).

8. Women of low reputation could be spoken of publicly and freely; for some, Aspasia fit such a category. For others, Aspasia's intellectual and political gifts earned her a measure of public distinction. Schaps asserted that there were three categories of women whose "names could be mentioned freely: disreputable women, opposing women, and dead women" (329).

9. The tautology of Elshtain's argument rightly encompasses Aspasia: "I am not impressed with the claims made for powerful women who influenced men through their private activities—in Athenian society this claim is frequently made for the *hetaera*. . . . Were such 'women-behind-the-men' to have attempted to enter the public arena to speak with their own voices, they would have been roundly jeered, satirized, and condemned" (14-15 n.11).

10. Thucydides wrote, "Everyone who wishes to, both citizens and foreigners, can join in the procession, and the women who are related to the dead are there to make their laments at the tomb" (II.34).

WORKS CITED

Aristophanes. *The Archarnians*. Trans. Douglass Parker. *Four Comedies*. Ed. William Arrowsmith. Ann Arbor: U of Michigan P, 1969. 99–112.

Aristotle. *Politics*. Trans. H. Rackham. Cambridge: Loeb-Harvard UP, 1977.

———. *The Rhetoric and Poetics of Aristotle*. Trans. W. Rhys Roberts and Ingram Bywater. New York: Modern Library, 1984.

Athenaeus. *The Deipnosophists*. Trans. Charles Burton Gulick. Cambridge: Harvard UP, 1967.

Cantarella, Eva. *Pandora's Daughters*. Baltimore: Johns Hopkins UP, 1981/1987.

Certeau, Michel de. *The Writing of History*. Trans. Tom Conley. New York: Columbia UP, 1975/1988.

Elshtain, Jean Bethke. *Public Man, Private Woman*. Princeton: Princeton UP, 1987.

Flaceliere, Robert. *Love in Ancient Greece*. 1960. Trans. James Cleugh. London: Frederick Muller, 1962.

Glenn, Cheryl. *Rhetoric Retold: Regendering the Tradition from Antiquity through the Renaissance*. Carbondale: Southern Illinois UP, forthcoming.

———. "sex, lies, manuscript: Refiguring Aspasia in the History of Rhetoric." *College Composition and Communication* 45 (May 1994): 180–99.

Harris, William V. *Ancient Literacy*. Cambridge: Harvard UP, 1989.

Just, Roger. *Women in Athenian Law and Life*. London: Routledge, 1989.

Keuls, Eva C. *The Reign of the Phallus*. New York: Harper, 1985.

Kirk, G.S., and J.E. Raven. *The Presocratic Philosophers*. Cambridge: Cambridge UP, 1962.

Kitto, H.D.F. *The Greeks*. Middlesex: Penguin, 1951.

Laqueur, Thomas. *Making Sex*. Cambridge: Harvard UP, 1990.

Licht, Hans [Paul Brandt]. *Sexual Life in Ancient Greece*. London: Abbey Library, 1932.

Loraux, Nicole. *The Invention of Athens*. Trans. Alan Sheridan. Cambridge: Harvard UP, 1986.

Mackin, James A., Jr. "Schismogenesis and Community: Pericles' Funeral Oration." *Quarterly Journal of Speech* 77 (1991): 251–62.

Ober, Josiah. *Mass and Elite in Democratic Athens*. Princeton: Princeton UP, 1989.

Plato. *Euthyphro, Apology, Crito, Phaedo, Phaedrus*. Trans. H. N. Fowler. Cambridge: Harvard UP, 1977. 405–579.

———. *Gorgias*. Trans. W. C. Helmbold. Indianapolis: Bobbs-Merrill, 1952.

———. *Timaeus, Critias, Cleitophon, Menexenus, Epistles*. Trans. R. G. Bury. 1929. London: Heinemann-Loeb, 1981.

Plutarch. *The Lives of the Noble Grecians and Romans*. Trans. John Dryden. Rev. Arthur Hugh Clough. New York: Modern Library, 1932.

Pomeroy, Sarah. *Goddesses, Whores, Wives, and Slaves*. New York: Schocken, 1975.

———. *Women's History and Ancient History*. Chapel Hill: U of North Carolina P, 1991.

Schaps, David M. "The Woman Least Mentioned: Etiquette and Women's Names." *Classical Quarterly* 27 (1977): 323–31.

Scott, Joan Wallach. *Gender and the Politics of History*. New York: Columbia UP, 1988.

Sprague, Rosamond Kent, ed. *The Older Sophists*. Columbia: U of South Carolina P, 1972.

Thucydides. *History of the Peloponnesian War*. Trans. Rex Warner. London: Penguin, 1954.

Vernant, Jean-Pierre. *Myth and Society in Ancient Greece*. New York: Zone, 1974/1980.

———. *Myth and Thought among the Greeks*. London: Routledge, 1965/1983.

———. *The Origins of Greek Thought*. Ithaca: Cornell UP, 1962/1982.

Vidal-Naquet, Pierre. *The Black Hunter*. Trans. Andrew Szegedy-Maszak. Baltimore: Johns Hopkins UP, 1986.

Xenophon. *Memorabilia and Oeconomicus*. Trans. E. C. Marchant. Cambridge: Harvard UP, 1988.

6 Primitives and Pretenders: Blair and Ossian

John Kimsey
University of Illinois at Chicago

Although today little more than a literary footnote, in the late 18th century, James Macpherson and his alleged translation of the poems of Ossian were the subject of ardent celebration and heated controversy. At the center of the project and the dispute was Hugh Blair. Blair sponsored Macpherson's efforts and championed Ossian as the Scottish Homer, his "Critical Dissertation Upon the Poems of Ossian" accompanying most editions of the poems. The works of Ossian created an immediate stir. As a dramatic departure from neoclassical canons of refinement, the poems seemed to anticipate romanticism and were beloved by Goethe, Blake, Byron, and Napoleon (Saunders 23). When the taint of forgery began to settle over the affair in the late 1700s, the popularity of Ossian and the reputation of Macpherson began a slow decline. Although Blair's involvement and his "Dissertation" were forgotten along with Macpherson, Blair's reputation survived the scandal.

Investigation of the matter and Blair's involvement in it reveals it to be more than a simple case of misprision or con-artistry. The Ossianic controversy is shaped by issues central to Blair's rhetorical theory and tensions peculiar to 18th-century British cultural debate. When Blair's role in the controversy is seen in cultural context, these issues—and the contradictions with which they are bound up—are thrown into high relief.

The affair began in 1760 when Blair was presented with some fragments of verse that had been translated into English from Gaelic, the language of the Scottish Highlands (74). The translations were in the possession of John Home, one of the Edinburgh literati, who had obtained them from James Macpherson, a 25-year-old schoolmaster and aspiring poet whom Home had met on European holiday. At their meeting, Macpherson, a native Highlander, had recited some traditional Highland verse, which he had translated into English. At Home's request, Macpherson wrote down a fragment of a poem called "The Death of Oscar," reputed to be the work of the ancient Scottish bard Ossian (Smart 88–90).

No more came of the matter until the piece came to Blair's attention. Blair and his circle were in some ways primed for such a discovery, as interest in the Highlands as a cultural region and in the Gaelic dialect spoken there was at a peak (Saunders 97).

To some extent this interest was of a piece with the *volkische* and antiquarian enthusiasms sweeping Europe generally at this time, such interests themselves being a by-product of the rising ideology of nationalism. But issues specific to Scottish politics of the period also played an important role. At this time the Highlands were being officially disciplined by British rule. The Jacobite risings of 1715 and 1745 had been based in the Highlands, and their failures brought the full wrath of British justice down on the northwest of Scotland. Among other things, this resulted in the outlawing of native customs such as the wearing of the belted plaid (Trevor-Roper 21). It also meant a ban on the speaking of Gaelic.

Like most Lowlanders, the literati of Edinburgh knew little directly of Highland life. And further south, in England and its intellectual center London, the west of Scotland was viewed as a mountainous wasteland populated by grunting brutes. Although they did not take quite so dim a view as this, the Edinburgh crowd too saw the Highlands and its residents as distant, exotic, and primitive.

Two traditional English prejudices no doubt played a role here as well: namely, hatred of Catholics and hatred of Celts. The Jacobite cause was, of course, that of the Stuart—that is, Catholic—pretenders to the British throne. To complicate matters further, the Highlands were also identified with Ireland, a British colony with its own long history of degradation and oppression:

> From the late fifth century, when the Scots of Ulster landed in Argyll, until the mid-eighteenth century, when it was "opened up" after the Jacobite revolts, the West of Scotland, cut off by mountains from the East, was always linked rather to Ireland than to the Saxon Lowlands. Racially and culturally, it was a colony of Ireland. (MacDougall 15)

In other words, the Highlands were the colony of a colony, and a particularly despised colony at that. In the 18th century, English historical thought was very much in the grip of the Anglo-Saxon myth. According to the myth, Anglo-Saxon domination of British civilization was a function of the racial superiority of the Anglo-Saxons who were, it was believed, descended from the Teutons, supposedly the only pure racial group in Europe. According to the myth, it was the Teutons who had bequeathed modern Europe such progressive institutions as parliamentary democracy and Protestant religion and who were the hope of humanity (MacDougall 31–70). From the conventional English viewpoint, the Highlands were a hotbed of Papish apostasy, Stuart insurrection, and Celtic backwardness, lower even than Ireland in the scheme of things.

In addition to these specific political factors, broader cultural trends such as Rousseau's notion of the noble savage and interest in the sublime as an aesthetic category no doubt conditioned the reception by Blair and his circle of the Ossianic material.

Blair was initially impressed by what he regarded as the verse's rude, natural vigor (Blair 101). He was also aware of the poignancy of such a discovery at a time when the Gaelic language was being rendered extinct. He got in touch with Macpherson and requested more material. When Macpherson expressed reluctance, Blair suggested that Macpherson owed it to his homeland to try to preserve its linguistic heritage (Saunders 76–77).

Less than a year later, in June 1760, Macpherson responded with a group of 16 poems that he claimed to have collected in the Highlands and translated. These were published in Edinburgh under the title *Fragments of Ancient Poetry collected in the Highlands of Scotland and translated from the Gaelic or Erse Language*. The volume included a preface by Blair (78–79), and its publication caught the attention of the Edinburgh intellectuals, particularly Hume and Gray, who expressed interest in seeing more such material.

Although all anyone had seen by this point were fragments of the type suggested by Macpherson's title, Blair began at this time to speak of an "epic" (90). It was his suspicion that the fragments were the bones of one great literary dinosaur. Blair was probably led to this assumption by a few factors: (a) Since at least the 1750s, there had been rumors of Highlanders who recited Gaelic verse concerning the wars of Fingal, which, legend had it, had been experienced and duly recorded by Ossian, the prince of poets; and (b) the Finn cycle (the name folklorists gave to the mythos) was already known to possess the loose unity of a group of folktales involving common personages and their heroic deeds.

A third factor could well have been the nationalistic implications of the epic as a genre. The epic can be formulated as the literary expression of empire. In this view, an epic is a work that encyclopedically sums up a particular culture at a particular time, cataloguing its customs, inscribing its history, and legitimizing its claims to importance on the world stage, all through the medium of the national language. In the 18th century, Scottish national culture was embattled and endangered, and Blair may well have felt that it could use the support of a literary performative utterance that would at a stroke establish its importance.

But in speaking of an epic, Blair was jumping to conclusions and inadvertently laying the groundwork for the controversy. Although Macpherson was eventually accused of forgery on all sorts of bases (including Dr. Johnson's axiom that Scotsmen are born liars), the largest and most persistent question concerned what Hume called the "regular plan" and unity of the Ossianic poems (quoted in Saunders 203).

This issue is knotty, though. In his preface to *Temora* (1763), Macpherson flatly admitted that he organized the poem into chapters with titles and moved passages around to make for easier reading. And the 18th century was not unacquainted with liberal translation and heavy-handed adaptation; Pope had spun Homer into perfectly rhymed iambic couplets.

At any rate, when Blair called on Macpherson to search out the remaining fragments of the supposed epic, Macpherson again expressed reluctance. Blair responded by forming a scholarship committee (which included Hume and Gray) and raising a stipend to support an expedition by Macpherson (91). Macpherson accepted the offer and undertook an expedition to the Highlands.

When it was completed, Macpherson came to stay in the house below Blair to work under Blair's supervision. In 1761, he produced *Fingal: An Ancient Epic Poem in 6 Books; together with several other Poems, composed by Ossian, the son of Fingal. Translated from the Gaelic Language by James Macpherson*, published in London and in Edinburgh in December 1761. Smollett greeted it with great favor in the *Critical Review* and by January 1763, Ossian was the talk of London (172).

The poems soon became the talk of Europe as well. Goethe was taken by Ossian, translating him into German and making him the favorite poet of young Werther, who echoed the sentiment, popular at the time, that the Scotsman was superior to Homer (Smart 13).

In March 1763, a second epic similar to *Fingal* appeared, called *Temora*. Two months earlier, Blair had published his "Critical Dissertation." In the "Dissertation," Blair's project was threefold: (a) to establish the poem as ancient and as an epic; (b) to prove Ossian the equal and, in some ways, the superior of Homer; and (c) to point out, in detail, Ossian's literary skills and merits.

In 1763, the question of authenticity had already been raised, and Blair began by trying to answer it. Although Hume would later advocate collecting testimony from Highlanders in support of the poems' antiquity, Blair's method in the "Dissertation" was to make inferences from the text based on certain axiomatic first premises. In other words, rather than empirically substantiating authenticity, Blair deduced it.

He began with a Vico-like notion of "rude historical ages." From these, he said, we can expect little abstraction but much figuration, little analysis but much action, little understanding but much imagination. In each of these binarisms, the second term is associated with youth, whether of persons or societies. This is the literary version of the biological principle that ontogeny recapitulates phylogeny—that is, that the life of both individual and species are structured by the same developmental stages. Because *Fingal* exhibits so strongly the features of an early stage of social development, it must date from an early age.

Further evidence of Ossian's antiquity derived from another developmental scheme: societies pass through four stages—hunting, pasturage, agriculture, and commerce. Ossian spoke mostly of hunting, a little of pasturage, never of cities or art; in other words, just as one would expect a Celt of the third century to speak (Blair 103).

The notion of the state of society supported Blair's next major topic—the equation of Homer and Ossian. Although Ossian lived centuries after Homer, the society he knew was at the same stage of development as Ionian Greece. Hence, the two can be equated. Blair then proceeded to a discussion of the relative merits of the two bards, in which Homer was cast roughly as Henry James and Ossian as Hemingway. That is, where Homer had great compass, Ossian was concise; where Homer displayed variety and cheer, Ossian was grave and solemn. These differences did not diminish the poets' respective greatness, and were accounted for again by recourse to the society and the environment. That is, Homer was more varied because the physical environment in which he lived was more various, a fact that worked in Ossian's favor because the spare environment inclined a poet to close analysis and intense contemplation (109).

This deductive method also informed Blair's discussion of the controversial epic plan. It is no more surprising that Ossian's work should exhibit Aristotelian unity than that Homer's should. Aristotle derived his canons of epic unity from his study of Homer; Homer, however, did not study Aristotle or any other critic. He drew his ideas directly from nature, and so did Ossian (111).

This narrowly mimetic conception of invention, although an Augustan commonplace (Golden 106), was not well equipped to deal with a possible forgery of "primitive" art. In the manner of the theological argument from design, Blair reasoned from the condition of the artifact back to its ancient artificer. He seemed incapable of conceiving that the features he read as *prima facie* archaic might simply be conventional; nor did he consider that if they could be catalogued by a professor, perhaps they could be imitated by a poet. No, said Blair, he had seen Macpherson's own work and he was not up to authoring Ossian (Saunders 207).

Others, Samuel Johnson chief among them, argued much the opposite. Johnson withheld the brunt of his criticism until the 1770s, when the poems were peaking in popularity, but then, as readers of Boswell's *Life* know, he went on a campaign to expose fraud.

In response to Johnson's challenge and the growing doubts of initial supporters such as Hume, Macpherson produced, in 1763, what he called his originals— Gaelic manuscripts placed with his London publisher, who made them available by subscription. There was no interest (there were few if any readers of Gaelic in London's literary community), and the manuscripts were withdrawn after six months. When it was suggested the manuscripts might be fakes too, Macpherson seemed to have washed his hands of the matter (Saunders 205).

This prompted Hume to call for an expedition to the Highlands to collect testimony in support of Macpherson's claims. When Macpherson refused to participate, Hume turned to Blair, who proceeded to collect the reports of numerous Highlanders attesting to Macpherson's actually having collected Highland poetry and verifying the resemblance of passages of *Fingal* to verses long recited in the region (210–11).

However, Johnson conducted his own expedition to the Highlands in 1772 and attempted to confound Blair and his witnesses. When he met with witnesses who refused to recant, Johnson, an enthusiastic Celtophobe, attributed the phenomenon to Scottish chauvinism: "A Scotchman must be a very sturdy moralist who does not love Scotland better than truth" (243). Johnson also dismissed all manuscript evidence, asserting that Gaelic had never been a written language, a claim that was inaccurate. Although it had never had a stable orthography, Gaelic had been written (255). Despite these lapses, Johnson's view carried the day, and the perception of forgery began to overshadow Ossian's popularity in the waning years of the century.

The sneers of Johnson aside, it seems clear that Blair was somehow mistaken. The question of precisely how is a vexed one though, given that no disinterested investigation was conducted at the time, and none of the principals (i.e., Blair, Johnson, Hume) could read Gaelic. Moreover, these points are linked to larger factors: the problematic nature of authorship as a category applied to folk culture, and the relative inaccessibility of and pervasive ignorance about the native culture in question. Did Macpherson work from actual Gaelic sources? From a modern distance, the question seems undecidable.

It seems safe to say, however, that something about the affair stinks. Whether Macpherson was a cynical hoaxer or just an overbearing adaptor, Ossian was not what Blair thought him to be—an epic poet. Poetry contemporaneous with and culturally similar to that of Ossian—the *Book of Taliesin*, for example, unknown in Blair's day—did not, whatever its virtues, exhibit the sort of narrative scope or dramatic flair one finds in *Temora* or *Fingal*. In his zeal to find a Highland epic—at the precise cultural moment when one was most needed—Blair may have enacted a self-fulfilling prophecy.

Indeed, Ossian's misty Celtic past seems just what the late Augustan doctor ordered. In literary terms, Blair found in Ossian what was missing from his own moment. Neither hidebound classic nor trendy innovation, Ossian was the tertium quid in the battle of the ancients and the moderns. In this sense, Ossian was a romantic requirement: If he did not exist, it was indeed necessary to invent him. If the neoclassical paradigm were to be displaced, then romanticism needed a founder—an originary figure whose looming presence in the bardic past legitimized its departures in the present. Such a figure was something all great religions require and which some (consider the case of Hermes Trismegistus) simply invented. Romanticism, which T.E. Hulme called "spilt religion," would seem to be no exception. And although he may have failed at affirming Scottish national culture, Ossian definitely succeeded in empowering Sir Walter Scott (Trevor-Roper 17–18).

The practice of projecting the needs of the present into the past is key to what Marianna Torgovnick has called primitivist discourse—"a generalized notion of the primitive . . . embodied in . . . multiple, and often contradictory tropes" (22), which is "fundamental to the Western sense of self and Other" (8):

[The] world [of the "primitive"] is structured by sets of images and ideas that have slipped from their original metaphoric status to control perceptions of primitives. . . . Primitives are like children, the tropes say. Primitives are our untamed selves. . . . Primitives are mystics, in tune with nature. . . . Primitives exist at the "lowest cultural levels" [while] we occupy the "highest." (8)

This is the framework of Blair's "Dissertation." And the notion of such tropes slipping "from their original metaphoric status to control perceptions" may explain a great deal about Blair's inadequate handling of the controversy.

This point gives rise to another speculation: Could it be that Macpherson was aware of the primitivist paradigm in a way that Blair was not? Might he, a native Highlander, have recognized these ossified analogies for the metaphors—the fictions—that they were? Might he have sensed Blair and company's investment in the primitivist myth and sat down to write, more or less, to its requirements? In the *Predicament of Culture*, James Clifford documented numerous instances of so-called savages shrewdly exploiting the primitivist myth to their own advantage, a double movement that suggested acquiescence on one level and resistance on another. "Primitives," it would seem, care little for the myth of the primitive. But one way for such people to mock the system—and advance their own interests—is to themselves exploit the myth meant to exploit them.

Did Macpherson, then, decide to give the authorities what they wanted? And furthermore, might he have done so not simply out of a desire for personal gain but from a sense of cultural politics? More than just a hoaxer, might he have been a subversive?

There was the political predicament of the Highlands, the ban on Gaelic, the rampant anti-Scots sentiment of those who wielded cultural power, the Anglo-Saxon racial fiction that supported that power, and the contention of the dominant culture that this myth was simply the truth. Might this have moved a young Scotsman—poor, literary, ambitious, and badgered—to elide, conveniently, the line between transcription and invention?

"Why not?," he may have thought. It would serve them right. Anyway, they already had the gall to refer to the royal house of Scotland—the rightful kings of Britain—as pretenders.

WORKS CITED

Blair, Hugh. "A Critical Dissertation Upon the Poems of Ossian." *The Poems of Ossian*. Trans. James Macpherson. St. Clair Shores, MI: Scholarly Press, 1970. 87–180.

Boswell, James. "Johnson and Macpherson." *The Life of Samuel Johnson*. New York: Doubleday, 1946. 288–97.

Clifford, James. *The Predicament of Culture*. Cambridge: Harvard UP, 1988.

Golden, James, Goodwin F. Berquist and William E. Coleman. "NeoClassicism and Belles Lettres." *The Rhetoric of Western Thought*. 3rd ed. Dubuque, IA: Kendall/Hunt, 1978. 105–25.

MacDougall, Hugh. *Racial Myth in English History: Trojans, Teutons, and Anglo-Saxons*. Hanover: UP of New England, 1982.

Saunders, Bailey. *The Life and Letters of James Macpherson*. New York: Haskell House, 1968.

Smart, J.S. *James Macpherson: An Episode in Literature*. London: David Nutt, Long Acre, 1905.

Torgovnick, Marianna. "Defining the Primitive/Reimagining Modernity." *Gone Primitive: Savage Intellects, Modern Lives*. Chicago: U of Chicago P, 1991. 3–41.

Trevor-Roper, Hugh. "The Invention of Tradition: The Highland Tradition of Scotland." *The Invention of Tradition*. Ed. Eric Hobsbawm and Terence Ranger. New York: Cambridge UP, 1983. 15–41.

7 Composing the Gentleman Writer in America

Dottie Broaddus
Arizona State University West

When Emerson visited Wordsworth in 1833, he recorded in his journal Wordsworth's attack on American culture. Americans "are too much given to making of money & secondly to politics," Wordsworth said. "And I fear they lack a class of men of leisure—in short of gentlemen to give a tone of honor to the community" (quoted in Leverenz 12). Wordsworth was right that America lacked "men of leisure," but he was wrong in assuming that "leisure" was a necessary condition for an American gentleman. On the contrary, 19th-century American gentility comprised several factors, among them a late version of Puritan calling, the notion that one serves God by serving the community. This idea fit well with the more secular notion of republican virtue, the idea that public good should be placed above private gain. The ethical content of these two notions ensured that work was a moral matter, and abundant leisure, if not an actual sin, was at least a social vice (Thornton 2). In 1847, when Emerson republished his essay "Self-Reliance," he had changed "do your thing" to "do your work."

Although leisure was not a significant factor in American gentility, the idea of high culture emerged in the 19th century when the Eastern intelligentsia began to distinguish cultural activities. In the process the genteel class became aware of itself; that is, its members started performing as genteel and began considering themselves arbiters of high culture. Especially in America's cities, as Levine and Rubin documented, culture was becoming divided into highbrow and lowbrow, the culture of the elite and the culture of the masses (see Levine and Rubin). Nowhere was the emergence of cultural hierarchy more pronounced than at Boston, where the elite, those who created high culture, were primarily

Unitarians, a highly literate group who in the years preceding the Civil War supported and controlled Harvard College, the Boston Athenaeum, the Lowell Institute, the Boston Public Library, as well as numerous learned societies, publishing houses, and magazines (Howe 10). The control of these cultural institutions meant that in and around Boston high culture became defined and performed according to Unitarian tastes.

Although Unitarianism never really took hold except in and around Boston, students at Harvard were imbued with the Unitarian ethos that connected gentility with learning. Graduates of Harvard essentially defined American gentility, a topic that by the end of the Civil War became a New England obsession, but one that had been pondered for several generations. For example, the Boston patrician Whig Edward Everett—orator, professor, president at Harvard—wrote that the gentleman must have character, integrity, and intelligence as well as manners (quoted in Persons 38). Thus the emerging idea of the American gentleman was based both on inherited or accidental factors of family and place and on performance. *Good breeding* referred to more than mere genetics; it carried with it the notion of *cultivation*—what William Ellery Channing called *self-culture*. I examine the notion of 19th-century male gentility by first looking at the rhetorical theory of Harvard's Edward T. Channing as well as the Unitarian philosophy of his brother William Ellery Channing. Together the Channings' rhetoric serves as a cultural backdrop to the essays of Ralph Waldo Emerson, James Russell Lowell, and Oliver Wendell Holmes, whose writing, I argue, helped create and institutionalize a genteel rhetoric that composed the writers themselves as gentlemen and perpetuated the ideal 19th-century American gentleman as also a man of letters.

Scholars in the history of American rhetoric agree that Edward T. Channing's rhetorical theory is heavily influenced by 18th-century Scottish Enlightenment philosophy. Practitioners of faculty psychology, the Scottish philosophers argued that God gave humans certain faculties that should be cultivated or improved lest they waste away. According to the Scots, human beings have an obligation, an implicit contract with God, to cultivate or strengthen their faculties. The philosopher Francis Hutcheson posited the moral sense as such a faculty, and the rhetorician Hugh Blair discussed the faculty of taste as incorporating moral and intellectual qualities. Blair argued that the cultivation of taste will improve the "understanding" by leading men to reflect on the operations of their own "refined feelings," and this reflection will result in the "will" being directed in the "proper pursuit of the good" (Blair 13).

Hutcheson, Blair, Thomas Reid, and George Campbell, members of the Scottish Enlightenment, were also Moderate Calvinist ministers. These men successfully revised orthodox Calvinism by discounting the doctrines of total depravity and predestination and arguing that, whereas God provides the raw material, a person could and should "improve" himself. After Blair's highly influential rhetorical and aesthetic theory, cultivating proper taste was considered both an intellectual and a moral activity. People with good taste were simply better in every respect. The old Calvinist notion of the *elect*, those people selected by God, became the elite, those who had cultivated proper taste.

Nineteenth-century American colleges taught Scottish Enlightenment thought both in moral philosophy classes and in rhetoric classes, with Blair's text *Lectures on Rhetoric and Belles Lettres* becoming the single most popular rhetoric text in American colleges in the first half of the 19th century. Blair's text was especially popular at Harvard, with Albert Kitzhaber recording that, in 1953, Harvard had on its shelves 26 separate printings issued between 1789 and 1832 (Kitzhaber 50). According to the editors of Edward Channing's *Lectures*, Harvard students read Blair during their sophomore year (xviii).

That Blair's conception of taste greatly influenced American oratory and writing is well known and well documented. Equally as important to American rhetorical history is the Unitarian control of Harvard that occurred with the 1805 appointment of Henry Ware as Hollis Professor of Divinity (Howe 4; Morison 189). *Unitarianism*, an ultraliberal Protestantism, took ideas from liberal Christian cultures such as Arminianism and merged them with the Moderate Calvinism of the 18th-century Scots. Even before they called themselves *Unitarians*, New England liberal Christians attached significance to human conduct, believing that people could help the operation of grace by placing themselves in the proper attitude for its reception. As important as *proper attitude* was *benevolence*, working to help one's neighbors. Practitioners of liberal Christianity dominated religious and cultural life in Boston and Cambridge. The sons of well-known liberal ministers, Ralph Waldo Emerson, James Russell Lowell, and Oliver Wendell Holmes became New England's best known poets, lecturers, and essayists. All were Harvard graduates, all studied Blair, all were students of Edward T. Channing.

In 1819, the same year Edward Channing became Harvard's Boylston Professor of Rhetoric and Oratory, his brother William Ellery Channing preached his famous "Baltimore Sermon," the sermon that defined American Unitarianism. According to William Ellery Channing, Unitarians stressed reason in religious practice, ethical activity rather than Calvinist piety, and, most important, Christ's humanity (Robinson 70–102). That the Unitarian Christ was a mere man with a "sublime purpose" opened opportunities for American men, especially those trained at Unitarian Harvard, to become Christ-like; that is, at the same time, a man and more than a man, a gentle man, a man engaged in ethical activity directed toward what he considers public good. Unitarianism's Christ, no longer a deity, provided a model for the American gentleman, and Blair's rhetorical theory, particularly as it blended with the Unitarian ethos of Edward T. Channing's *Lectures*, provided the vocabulary and the method: cultivation of taste with its defining characteristics delicacy and correctness, and improvement of intellectual and moral faculties through reading, writing, and ennobling conversations with like-minded individuals.

In his *Lectures Read to the Seniors at Harvard College*, Edward Channing argued that if a modern American man holds powerful influence, he must subordinate his personal ambition to the "solid good of a country." Instead of operating in a despotic manner, he should work "in more quiet ways," using the "power of just sentiments" to create a "growing and permanent influence over the character and opinions, even where it does not produce, at once, an obvious effect on the decisions and conduct of men" (16–19). Channing's "quiet ways" operate more effectively in a written rather than an oral culture, in a culture in which writing is esteemed, and indeed, the first half of the 19th century witnessed a shift in public communication when the high oratorical skills of, for example, Daniel Webster and Edward Everett became less valued as written discourse gained prestige. Edward Channing, recognizing the power of writing, argued that a "work of genius" must be studied "patiently and long, if we would possess ourselves of the greater part of its highest merits, and make it a pleasure and blessing all our lives" (156). After William Ellery Channing preached his carefully worded compositions from the pulpit on Sunday, his faithful, unpaid scribe Elizabeth Peabody copied them to make them legible and took them to the printer so they could be read, reread, studied.

Although Edward Channing admitted that common readers can adequately judge good writing, they often cannot understand writers of the "highest genius" whose work must be interpreted by "disciples" (154–59). We "leave the highest criticism," Channing maintained, "in very few hands; not, however, in the hands of monopolists or exclusives, but of the only true radicals—the men who aim at realizing great ideas" (160). Elsewhere in his *Lectures*, Channing called for a "prophetic reasoner," who "binds the truths and the wisdom of today to those of all past time, and to those that will be the fruit of a still larger experience in the ages to come." This "prophetic reasoner" should give "right direction to public opinion" (81). In his lectures, Channing thus suggested that for the Harvard man, the activity of writing may become an ethical enterprise in two ways. The writer may be either a "prophetic reasoner" or a critic who interprets the works of the prophet for common readers. Either activity serves the public good by uplifting the masses; and writing, rather than speaking, has the extra advantage of allowing the writer to remain detached from the masses. Channing's "prophetic reasoner" or "writer of genius" is the 19th-century secularized priest or minister, with "disciples" or critics as interpreters. Both prophet/genius and disciple/critic are spokesmen for high, genteel culture.

Emerson, who studied under both Channing brothers, was the first Harvard graduate to accept Edward Channing's call for a "prophetic reasoner," composing himself in his most famous essays as an American prophet. But Emerson also helped to define the American gentleman. In his essay "Manners," Emerson envisioned a natural aristocracy, a "select society" or "fraternity of the best," comprised of gentlemen who are good-natured, benevolent, energetic (283–85). They are "doers" with a "broad sympathy which puts them in fellowship with crowds, and makes their actions popular" (287). According to Emerson, of all the "points of good breeding" the highest is "deference," which he explained thusly:

> Let us not be too much acquainted. . . . We should meet each morning, as from foreign countries, and spending the day together, should depart at night, as into foreign countries. In all things I would have the island of a man inviolate. Let us sit apart as the gods, talking from peak to peak all around Olympus. (292)

The meeting of the gods that Emerson envisioned became reality when a group of men began to meet at Boston's Parker House to discuss launching a new magazine. Among others at the meetings were Emerson, Lowell, and Holmes. Holmes named the magazine the *Atlantic Monthly*, and Lowell became its first editor in 1857. The magazine became an instant success with its list of subscribers rising from 20,000 in its first year to 30,000 in its second. Lowell felt from the beginning that Oliver Wendell Holmes's writing would give the magazine a distinctive gentlemanly style, and Holmes's was the only writing that went into the magazine unedited (Cyganowski 43–44).

Both Lowell and Holmes taught at Harvard, Lowell as Smith Professor of French and Spanish Languages and Literature, and Holmes as Parkman Professor of Anatomy and, for 6 years, Dean taught at Harvard Medical School. After giving up the editorship of the *Atlantic Monthly* in 1861, Lowell became associated with the *North American Review*. He continued to publish essays in both magazines, even while he served as United States Minister to Spain and to the Court of St. James. Because both Lowell and Holmes were prolific, well-published, highly visible, and well-connected public men, these two writers became the most influential men of letters in New England until well after the Civil War. Together they extended what Emerson had begun in "Manners" as a working definition of the American gentleman.

Oliver Wendell Holmes named and characterized Boston gentility in his novel *Elsie Venner*, first published in 1861. In the first chapter entitled "The Brahmin Caste of New England," Holmes described two students—the first "inelegant" with an "unmusical" voice who treats words as "coarse castings, instead of fine carvings." The second student has "delicate" features, a "bright and quick" eye, with lips that "play over the thought he utters as a pianist's fingers dance over their music" (3). The first youth is a "common country boy, whose race has been bred to bodily labor," and whose "organs of thought and expression" have not been properly exercised. His "finer instincts," Holmes says, "are latent and must be developed." The second youth comes from the "Brahmin caste of New England" and therefore belongs to a "race of scholars" in which "aptitude for learning . . . are congenital and hereditary." Although Holmes admitted there are "families who refine themselves," their refinement results from a "series of felicitous crosses" that develop an "improved strain of blood." Holmes called this rare phenomenon "Nature's republicanism" (5). But the rule, according to

Holmes, is that "our scholars come chiefly from a privileged order, just as our best fruits come from well-known grafts" (6).

In *The Autocrat of the Breakfast Table*, Holmes deprecated what he called the "self-made man" by using the analogy of an Irishman's "self-made house" that, although it took him several years to build, was a "little out of plumb, and a little wavy in outline, and a little queer and uncertain in general aspect" (20). "I prefer," Holmes wrote, "a man of family"—that is, a man who has inherited "family traditions and the cumulative humanities of at least four or five generations." Above all, the true gentleman "as a child . . . should have tumbled about in a library" because all men "are afraid of books, who have not handled them from infancy" (20–23).

In addition to Holmes describing the "Brahmin" gentleman in explicit terms, he also touched on the link between the gentleman and language. "Life and language are alike sacred," he argued. "Homicide and verbicide—that is, violent treatment of a word with fatal results to its legitimate meaning, which is its life—are alike forbidden" (11).

During the time Holmes and Lowell were writing, those people who considered themselves members of New England gentility were trying to come to terms with democracy, and they worried deeply about such issues as whether women should have the vote and about the role of the newly freed African Americans. Before the Civil War, Lowell suggested Frederick Douglass as a potential member of an exclusive men's club, but withdrew his name when it became apparent that Douglass would not be voted in. Lowell believed that Emerson would blackball Douglass (Duberman 185). Of the three writers, Lowell tried hardest to grapple with democratic egalitarianism while maintaining the essentializing features of gentility. His ambiguity and even anxiety are evident in his essay, "On a Certain Condescension in Foreigners."

In this essay, Lowell intended to provide an answer to remarks such as those that Wordsworth made to Emerson: that because America has no real aristocracy, it has no gentlemen, and indeed, no high culture. Foreigners believe, according to Lowell, that America's greatness lies in its "barbarian mass only," or in its "material prosperity." They accuse Americans of vulgarity, "one of those horribly vague accusations" against which the "victim has no defence." Although we're as "clean, morally and physically," we haven't developed enough, they think. Even though with the Civil War, the "young giant had certainly got out of long clothes," the world still looks on us as young and treats us accordingly. But "libraries," Lowell argued, make "all nations equally old." Lowell's argument against foreigners' condescension is that cultivation and even gentility are possible in a democracy if one has the proper books and associations.

Lowell, Emerson, and Holmes constructed gentility socially through associations, through institutions, and, as I have argued, through their writing. The American gentleman composed by these writers became an agent for social exclusion. Frederick Douglass, for example, was excluded, as was Holmes's

Irishman of the "self-made house." Yet the culture constructed by these writers also served as a cohesive force, an agent for inclusion.

When young Howells first came to Boston as a young writer, he sought out Lowell, who as editor of the *Atlantic Monthly* had published some of Howells's work. Lowell invited Howells to dine with him and Holmes. During dinner, Howells recorded Holmes as saying,"Well, James, this is something like the apostolic succession; this is the laying on of hands." Whether Holmes actually made the remark is irrelevant; the significance lies in Howells's belief that he could become the successor, the disciple, another gentleman-writer. Howells wrote,"[T]he charm of it went to my head long before any drop of wine" (36).

WORKS CITED

Blair, Hugh. *Lectures on Rhetoric and Belles Lettres.* Halifax: William Milner, 1842.

Channing, Edward T. *Lectures Read to the Seniors in Harvard College.* Carbondale: Southern Illinois UP, 1968.

Cyganowski, Carol Klimick. *Magazine Editors and Professional Authors in Nineteenth-Century America.* New York: Garland, 1988.

Duberman, Martin. *James Russell Lowell.* Boston: Houghton Mifflin, 1966.

Emerson, Ralph Waldo. *Essays: First and Second Series.* New York: Vintage, 1990.

Holmes, Oliver Wendell. *The Autocrat of the Breakfast Table.* Boston: Houghton Mifflin, 1890.

———. *Elsie Venner: A Romance of Destiny.* Cambridge: Riverside P, 1892.

Howe, Daniel Walker. *The Unitarian Conscience: Harvard Moral Philosophy, 1805–1861.* Cambridge: Harvard UP, 1970.

Howells, W. D. *Literary Friends and Acquaintance.* Eds. David F. Hiatt and Edwin H. Cady. Bloomington: Indiana UP, 1968.

Kitzhaber, Albert R. "Rhetoric in American Colleges, 1850–1900." Diss. U of Washington, 1953.

Leverenz, David. *Manhood and the American Renaissance.* Ithaca: Cornell UP, 1989.

Levine, Lawrence W. *Highbrow/Lowbrow: The Emergency of Cultural Hierarchy in America.* Cambridge: Harvard UP, 1988.

Lowell, James Russell. *Literary Essays III.* Boston: Houghton Mifflin, 1892.

Morison, Samuel Eliot. *Three Centuries of Harvard, 1636–1936.* Cambridge: Belknap P, 1964.

Persons, Stow. *The Decline of American Gentility.* New York: Columbia UP, 1973.

Robinson, David, ed. *William Ellery Channing: Selected Writings.* New York: Paulist P., 1985.

Rubin, Joan Shelley. *The Making of Middlebrow Culture.* Chapel Hill: U of North Carolina P, 1992.

Thornton, Tamara Plakins. *Cultivating Gentlemen: The Meaning of Country Life Among the Boston Elite, 1785–1860.* New Haven: Yale UP, 1989.

Part II

Practicing Theories of Reading and Writing

8 Orwell, Russell, and the Language of Imperialism

William T. Ross
University of South Florida

When we meet disturbing convictions or distasteful language in a writer we otherwise admire, we are left in a quandary, especially when what disturbs us seems to run counter to the very basic positions we find so attractive. As readers, we usually have three choices. We can attempt to rationalize the passages away. How many times have we heard, for example, that T.S. Eliot was not really antisemitic? Or, we can simply revise—even reverse—our overall assessment of the individual, which is what Daphne Patai attempted to do in her *Orwell Mystique*, in which she discovers that Orwell was actually antifeminist. Such wholesale rejections, however, make us suspect that shifting intellectual and moral tides will eventually put any historical figure beyond the pale. And, as Rodden pointed out, the consequences of this maneuver "for literary criticism and scholarship are impoverishing" (222). The third choice is to avoid both rationalization and rejection, at the same time devising an explanation of how seemingly inconsistent and contradictory rhetorical constructions can be imbedded in a larger pattern of discourse.

My attempt at an explanation involves selected passages from Bertrand Russell and George Orwell. My explanatory machinery is dependent on Morse Peckham's *Explanation and Power: The Control of Human Behavior*. Before looking at some of the examples, however, I note that Peckham defined *rhetoric* as "redundancy" in discourse, which is really an explanation of how language can persuade or at least make us aware of a point of view (42). In other words, both Russell and Orwell left enough discourse on the subject of anti-imperialism that the presence of passages that are counter to those redundancies (but in some way pro-

63

imperialist and hence replicating other redundancies present in the culture) creates our sense of conflict.

In 1918, Russell, on the eve of going to prison for pacifist activities during the First World War, wrote *Roads to Freedom: Socialism, Anarchism and Syndicalism*, an exposition of three radical political doctrines. Establishing a peaceful civilization after the war was much on his mind, and this popularization of political theory ended with reflections on the necessity for democratic world government. It is therefore somewhat surprising to see this foe of imperialism frequently using racist epithets that betray a decidedly Eurocentric mindset. When he pointed out, for example, that English workers "have a share in the benefit accruing from the exploitation of inferior races," we are struck not only by the anti-imperialist observation, but by the participation in the denigration of the colonized non-Europeans (104). And later when he discussed the dangers of disproportionately increasing birth rates between "civilized" countries and others, he admitted that

> Negroes may continue to increase in the tropics, but are not likely to be a serious menace to the white inhabitants of temperate regions. There remains, of course, the Yellow Peril; but by the time that begins to be serious, it is quite likely that the birth-rate will also have begun to decline among the races of Asia. If not, there are other means of dealing with the question. (137)

What those other means are is not clear, but it is not as ominous as it may sound, because no matter what else, Russell was not a warmonger.

But he was capable of repeated racist comments or redundancies throughout his long career as an intellectual popularizer. In *Marriage and Morals*, his most popular book, this amazing sentence occurred:

> It seems on the whole fair to regard negroes as on the average inferior to white men, although for work in the tropics they are indispensable, so that their extermination (apart from questions of humanity) would be highly undesirable. (267)

Ironically enough this passage occurs in a paragraph devoted primarily to debunking the "mass of bad science," which at that moment was trying to discriminate "among the races of Europe." Between the time Russell wrote *Roads to Freedom* and *Marriage and Morals*, he had visited China and Japan and been impressed by Chinese civilization and Japanese industriousness. Thus, he could then assure his readers that he did not "see any valid reason for regarding the yellow races as in any degree inferior to our noble selves" (267).

There is another passage in *Marriage and Morals* that also reveals a less-than-internationalist perspective. Russell had been discussing how the rise of the welfare state would diminish the role of the father. The results of this diminishment are complex, but one of the effects would be to reduce the father's interest in the legitimacy of his wife's offspring—because he would not, in any case, be responsible for their well being. (This responsibility, Russell felt, was one of the principal causes of male jealousy.) Such diminishment, he continued to speculate, would have one good effect: it would "eliminate the most fierce and savage passion to which civilized men are liable, namely, the fury which is felt in defending wives and children from attacks of coloured populations" (188). The opposition between *civilized* and *coloured* is worthy of an Old India Hand, a type Russell should have hated, but the assurance that such passion can exist is not based on a reading of history but on personal experience, as one can find by reading the autobiography published 39 years after *Marriage and Morals*.

The experience occurred during a trip Russell and Dora Black made to China and Japan in 1920–21. (Russell was waiting for his first marriage to be dissolved to marry the already pregnant Dora.) He was already a public figure and was the object of a great deal of press attention during his stay in Japan:

> We made a ten hours' journey in great heat from Kyoto to Yokohama. We arrived there just after dark, and were received by a series of magnesium explosions, each of which made Dora jump, and increased my fear of a miscarriage. I became blind with rage, the only time I have been so since I tried to strangle Fitzgerald [an incident from his pre-university days]. I pursued the boys with flashlights, but being lame, was unable to catch them, which was fortunate, as I should certainly have committed murder. An enterprising photographer succeeded in photographing me with my eyes blazing. I should not have known that I could have looked so completely insane. This photograph was my introduction to Tokyo. I felt at that moment the same type of passion as must have been felt by Anglo-Indians during the Mutiny, or by white men surrounded by a rebel coloured population. (193)

What is striking here is not just the stark contrast between Anglo-Indians or white men and "coloured[s]," but the way a somewhat less-than-genteel reception in a foreign country conjures up the experience of a full-blown rebellion or a threatened massacre. Furthermore, there would seem to be deliberate obfuscation. The "magnesium explosions" are really nothing more than the photographers' flashes, and the "boys" are not Japanese juvenile delinquents, but press photographers.

None of this would be very intriguing if these passages and these attitudes did not seem to be having a rhetorical effect, exactly the opposite of what one would expect Bertrand Russell to be aiming for. After all, Russell inherited his anti-imperialism from his grandfather, Lord John Russell, pursued his notion of world government for over 50 years, and insisted in the opening sentences of his autobiography that an "unbearable pity for the suffering of mankind" had been one of the three passions of his life. Yet, clearly, throughout his life he did not mind adding to the suffering of part of that audience through his demeaning rhetoric.

The more one is disturbed by these examples of Russell's verbal behavior, the more he or she is likely to hold an essentialist view of personality or persona. For Peckham, any such essentialist view of the "self" cannot be true, because the brain is capable of random activity. That is, no internal control exists to render an individual incapable of producing random (i.e., unpredictable) behavior, including verbal behavior (245–46). It is this capacity for randomness that makes innovation possible. Orwell, for example, innovated his own anti-imperialist views out of his experience, in early manhood, in the Burma police.

This innovation did not make him as enamored of internationalism (nor for the majority of his life of pacifism) as Russell was. In fact, on at least one occasion he referred to both internationalism and pacifism as "half-baked antinomian opinions" (*Wigan Pier* 140). But he did become anti-imperialist, as he took pains to tell us in *The Road to Wigan Pier*. And this anti-imperialism came not from family tradition or intellectual principles, but from guilt in his own participation in the dirty work of the empire as a policeman in Burma. After five years of service he "hated imperialism with a bitterness which I probably cannot make clear" (*Wigan Pier* 145). Indeed, that bitterness led to one of the most famous (if overwrought) passages in *Wigan Pier*, in which Orwell recounted passing the night with another servant of the Empire on a train traveling across India:

> It was too hot to sleep and we spent the night talking. Half an hour's cautious questioning decided each of us that the other was "safe"; and then for hours, while the train jolted slowly through the pitch-black night, sitting up in our bunks with bottles of beer handy, we damned the British Empire—damned it from the inside, intelligently and intimately. It did us both good. But we had been speaking forbidden things, and in the haggard morning light when the train crawled into Mandalay, we parted as guilty as any adulterous couple. (147)

Yet for all this guilt, as Daphne Patai pointed out in her excessively unsympathetic study of Orwell, he nevertheless adopted an imperialist perspective toward the Burmese in two of his most famous essays "A Hanging" and "Shooting an Elephant."

In "A Hanging," Orwell, as a witness to the execution of a Burmese prisoner, only recognized the humanity of the victim when he stepped aside to avoid a puddle on the way to the gallows. As Patai said, the conclusion Orwell wanted to draw had to do with the barbarity of taking human life. But it is hard to resist Patai's conclusion that there is another (she would call it "primary") meaning: "an inferiorized human being has for an instant become a genuine person in the eyes of one of his masters. That this master is the proper model of human life and authentic awareness goes without saying" (106). In other words, until this moment Orwell took for granted the "otherness" of the victim. It is difficult indeed to imagine the same narrative being written about Constable Orwell following a European to the gallows and having this revelation spring on him so late.

In "Shooting an Elephant," as Patai again pointed out, the crowd of Burmese who force the colonial policeman to shoot a formerly enraged but now docile elephant (or else lose face) are depicted as rambunctious "children on an outing, a quite traditional expression of imperialist ideology." Orwell's point is that the colonialist is the victim of this crowd, forced to act against his will—thus reversing the usual master/servant trope of colonialism (49). But it is all too evident that what he would prefer is not equality with this manifestation of the "other," but, in Patai's words, "superiority, centrality, and domination" (50). (Patai, of course, made these masculine *and* colonial imperatives.)

If space permitted one could find many other examples in both Russell and Orwell of these imperialist and racist moments. But it is important to note that they are moments. Orwell and Russell *were* anti-imperialists; neither secretly joined Churchill in hoping the dissolution of the British Empire would never occur. Still, we are left with these moments, and to return briefly to Russell, it should be pointed out that his remarks cannot be blamed on a popularizer's sense of audience. That is, they did not grow out of a need to satisfy audience expectations. None of the reviews I have examined mentions these items for either praise or condemnation. Both *Roads to Freedom* and *Marriage and Morals* went through many reprintings. In 1948, Russell wrote a preface to the third edition of *Roads to Freedom*, but made no apology for the passages cited, and he did not edit them out of the reprinted text. But in 1963, he wrote to his publisher Stanley Unwin:

> it has been drawn to my attention that [in] "Marriage and Morals" I say "it seems on the whole fair to regard negroes as on the average inferior to white men." I wish in any future reprint to substitute for the words: "It seems on the whole fair," the words "There is no sound reason." (quoted in Clark 431)

As far as I am able to determine, the change was never made, and with good reason. Russell, who by this time had no high regard for the book as a whole, had apparently relied on a correspondent's word and not checked it against the text. Clearly his substitution, given the whole of the original sentence and not the shortened one quoted in his letter, would have resulted in nonsense.

Both the absence of cultural feedback before this correspondent's comment and the effect it had on Russell remind us that human verbal behavior takes place in the context of the writers' culture. For Peckham, culture exists precisely to control that behavior. Rhetoric, which, as we have seen, Peckham defined as redundancy in discourse, is one of the tools culture uses to channel that behavior. Rhetoric is employed through the institutions of culture—government, churches, universities, belief and value systems, and so on. Thus, repeated verbal messages from the institutions of a culture tend to channel the verbal behavior of individuals (183–84).

But, of course, culture and its institutions do not speak with a single voice—the proof of the randomness of response. Thus, an individual is conflicted, the recipient of mixed signals. This certainly makes his or her behavior even less predictable. Furthermore, the individual is not just the passive recipient of conflicting redundancies. He or she is still capable of random response that does not just parrot the available redundancies of the regnant institutions, but actually innovates (272–74). Innovation explains arguments generated in favor of imperialism in the 19th century, but it also explains the generally anti-imperial response of individuals such as Russell. It is our ability to innovate that guarantees that culture will never be a seamless web, that there will always be conflict and contradiction.

But there is also conflict and contradiction within the individual, for he (or she) is a social dyad (163–64, 189–90). That is, individuals view themselves from the outside just as much as members view an institution—criticizing, changing their value systems, and innovating their verbal behavior in response to this self-scrutiny.

If we see Russell and Orwell as social dyads, then we can begin to see the source of their discontinuities. In the context of their time, much of what they said was against the grain—that is, it lacked validation by some of the most important and indeed coercive institutions of their time. In this they were culturally innovative. But if verbal behavior is not unitary but rather a bundle of discrete redundancies, then innovation is never total. For whatever reason, their view of their own personae did not impel them to change the verbal behaviors demonstrated earlier, or did not impel them to make them consistent with their innovative behavior. And, more to the point, they were not coerced into doing so by their cultural institutions. Apparently it was not until 1963 that Russell's racism in *Marriage and Morals* was even partially and ineffectively called into question. Orwell's case is even worse, because Patai's anti-imperialist critique was first raised a half-century after the initial publication of the essays and years after they had become favorites of college textbook anthologists. Both men were controversial, but the points of controversy seldom, if ever, during their lifetime revolved around the verbal behaviors exhibited earlier. Thus, there were insufficient cultural redundancies to control (i.e., change) these particular behaviors. Or, to put it another way, the older, more conservative redundancies responsible for their presence were unchallenged.

If Peckham is right in his theories of culture and the individual, then both rationalization and rejection (two of the strategies mentioned at the beginning of this chapter) seem self-defeating. Given a large enough collection of discourse and the penchant to innovate new redundancies and revalue old ones, no writer is going to escape inconsistency. But if his insights rule out essentializing and totalizing strategies, they also open new perspectives. We can, for example, more fully appreciate the sometimes heroic efforts to counter prevailing cultural redundancies. And we can certainly get a better sense of cultural processes at work.

WORKS CITED

Clark, Ronald W. *The Life of Bertrand Russell*. New York: Knopf, 1976.

Orwell, George. Vol. 1 of *The Collected Essays, Journalism, and Letters of George Orwell*. 4 vols. Ed. Sonia Orwell and Ian Angus. London: Secker and Warburg, 1968.

———. *The Road To Wigan Pier*. London: Secker and Warburg, 1937/1959.

Patai, Daphne. *The Orwell Mystique*. Amherst: U of Massachusetts P, 1984.

Peckham, Morse. *Explanation and Power: The Control of Human Behavior*. Minneapolis: U of Minnesota P, 1972/1988.

Rodden, John. *The Politics of Literary Reputation: The Making and Claiming of "St. George" Orwell*. New York: Oxford UP, 1989.

Russell, Bertrand. Vol. 2 of *The Autobiography of Bertrand Russell*. 3 vols. Boston: Little, Brown, 1968.

———. *Marriage and Morals*. Boston: Liveright, 1929.

———. *Roads to Freedom: Socialism, Anarchism and Syndicalism*. London: Unwin, 1918/1966.

9

"Truth" as Experience and "Method" as Dialectic: Gadamer's Hermeneutics and Literacy

Mary Grabar
Georgia State University

Hans-Georg Gadamer's call for a return of hermeneutics to its original speculative origin from Platonic dialectic has relevance, I think, in the wake of the current accusations of deconstruction or poststructuralism as nihilistic, ahistorical, elitist, and conservative (Miller, "Derrida's Topographies" 2),[1] as well as in debates about the loss of literacy in the classroom and in the public sphere. The problem of modern scholarship, as Gadamer sees it in *Truth and Method*, is that it is "scientific . . . [in] that it objectifies tradition and methodically eliminates the influence of the interpreter and his time on understanding" (333). Gadamer's later contention that "methodical science" has been extended to the humanities ("Rhetoric" 280) has been borne out in the schools of interpretation that have gained a foothold since the publication of *Truth and Method*. The structuralist school of deconstruction, as well as new historicism, feminist criticism, and Marxist criticism, share the limitations of method. They may have had the effect of alienating the reader and of reducing literacy in my extended sense as meaningful reading.

Gadamer's phenomenological approach offers an alternative or supplement to such methods that, as Dickstein (passim) recently noted, have taken the enjoyment out of reading. Gadamer's hermeneutics, based on the dialectic of experience, might offer a more fluid and relevant approach than method that attempts definitive knowledge:

> Experience stands in an ineluctable opposition to knowledge and to the kind of instruction that follows from general theoretical or technical knowledge. The truth of experience always implies an orientation toward new experience. . . . The

71

experienced person proves to be . . . someone who is radically undogmatic. (*Truth* 355)

This is not "knowledge as domination" (311) or "technical virtuosity" (489) of a scientific method, but the play of dialectic. Gadamer extended the idea of experience to art, which is "a self-encounter . . . an encounter with the authentic, as a familiarity that includes surprise"; the task becomes one of "integrating it into the whole of one's own orientation to a world and one's own self-understanding" ("Aesthetics" 101–102). Such understanding "goes beyond what we can bring to the understanding of the other person's words through methodical effort and critical self-control" ("On the Problem of Self-Understanding" 58). Instead, the interpreter loses her- or himself in the "play of language itself, which addresses us, proposes and withdraws, asks and fulfills itself in the answer" (*Truth* 490).

The idea of reading as "playful" or pleasurable and meaningful is disappearing, notes Dickstein (1993) in the PMLA publication, *Profession 93*. He attributes this "damaged literacy" to the fact that interpretation has been consigned to experts who speak an increasingly "specialized" language (36). Specialized language, in that it is cut off from a community of meaning, resembles the artificial language of science. Gadamer's insistence on the concept of *sensus communis* (*Truth* 21–27) and its resulting task in hermeneutics "to clarify [the] miracle of understanding, which is . . . a sharing in common meaning" (292) can provide a remedy to what Dickstein sees as academic "professional readers" reading "against the grain of the text, against common sense" (36). The "hermeneutics of suspicion" criticized by Dickstein as another factor behind "damaged literacy" can be countered with what Dostal described as Gadamer's "hermeneutics of trust" that does not deny repression that is hidden ideologically or neurotically, but operates under the assumption that in a dialogue of understanding there must be "as much interest in the good as there is in the truth" (433).[2]

The interest in the good and a view of truth that is neither subjective nor objective, but based on experience, can provide an alternative to methods based on a hermeneutics of suspicion, such as deconstruction. An experiential approach to interpretation can be applied to the classroom to supplement the method of deconstruction promoted by such theorists as J. Hillis Miller. Although Miller advocates combining the studies of reading and writing, he curiously contradicts this idea of unity by promoting reading not as the "synthesis" he claims writing should be, but as "decomposition, deconstruction, the analysis or untying of the links that bind a piece of language together so that the reader can see how it works and make sure he has grasped its meaning correctly" (230). Although such close reading is necessary to an extent, as Gadamer admitted, such an approach by itself fails to provide the sense of "participation" or the "enrichment in the inner store of our lives" that results from an experiential encounter with literature ("Hermeneutics of Suspicion" 64).

Certainly the standard of "correctly" grasping the meaning of a literary text has led to many anxious moments in the classroom. Dialectic, conversely, leads not to "definitive knowledge," but to openness and meaning for the individual interpreter:

> The reader before whose eyes the great book of world history simply lies open does not exist. But neither does the reader exist who, when he has his text before him simply reads what is there. Rather, all reading involves application, so that a person reading a text is himself part of the meaning he apprehends. (*Truth* 340)

The hermeneutics of suspicion that assumes that the reader *can* objectively discern the psychological and ideological "truths" lurking beneath the apparent meaning from the advantage of a historically objective position in a sense assumes that the "great book of world history" does lie before the reader. It ignores the influence of the interpreter, including his or her prejudices and history.

The "hermeneutics of suspicion" of Marx, Freud, and Derrida that celebrates the "untrustworthiness of historical speech" is described as an "enlightenment strategy" by Dostal (430). The strategy of the enlightenment is essentially the method of science based on Cartesian doubt criticized by Gadamer. "Cartesian doubt, accepting nothing as certain that can in any way be doubted, and adopting the idea of method that follows from this rule" (*Truth* 271) has perhaps found its fulfillment in deconstruction, which doubts the ability of language to access meaning outside itself and suspects the text itself. Its method involves a search for a moment when the text reverses the meaning of its own argument, when the binary opposition of priority is overturned. It suspiciously seeks the discrepancy between an author's discourse and its subtext.

The scientific view of language is inherited from Saussure's view of language as a differential network based on an arbitrary relation between signifier and signified. This view is reflected in Derrida's concepts of *differance*: the differing of distinctive oppositions and the constant deferring of meaning "perhaps to the point of endless supplementarity, by the play of signification" (Norris 32). Like structuralism, deconstruction in Derrida's hands relies on a binary logic, of the constant opposition of sign and signified: "The opposition is part of the system, along with the reduction" ("Structure" 962). The model of structuralism constantly reasserts itself, although in movement: a "decentering" or "absence of the transcendental signified" that "extends the domain and the interplay of signification *ad infinitum*" (961). Language is not ground in being, but is a system of elusive phonemes and graphemes that can refer only to each other. Language constantly refers to itself. In Derrida's description, "the presence of an element is always a signifying and substitutive reference inscribed in a system of differences and the movement of a chain" (969). Or, as John Caputo puts it: "Deconstruction is a way of writing from below, of insisting that we never get access to things except by way of a maze of markings" (263). By default, deconstruction, in not respecting that meaning can become thematic through dialogue, relies on aesthetics and abstraction, reverting back to formalism.

An alternative to a formalist view of language is one of presence based on ambiguity, or language as a medium for experience. Rather than the constant replacement of codes, language, in Gadamer's phenomenological view, goes beyond code or conventionalism and similarity theory (*Truth* 406) to a recognition of the "contingency of the historical languages and the vagueness of their concepts" (415). Word and subject matter are united (403) to the extent that language and thinking are bound together (417); language arises from community (435). Language is not mere form, but grounded in being.

Gadamer's view of language as ambiguous calls for a hermeneutics of trust and respect for the claim of the other. In opposition to it is the hermeneutics of suspicion, which has been noted by Armstrong as a possible tool of oppression: "Unmasking a text's deceptions can be an assertion of power which denies mutuality by refusing to hear the claim it would make on us." Such "claims" can be heard in what Gadamer describes as a true conversation, and it is in this speculative aspect of the "tireless constitution of meaning" that Gadamer sees the essential difference between himself and Derrida:

> [Decoding] represents merely a precondition for hermeneutic attention to what is said in the words. In this regard, I am fully in agreement with the critique of structuralism. But it seems to me that I go beyond Derrida's deconstruction, since a word exists only in conversation and never exists there as an isolated word but as the totality of a way of accounting by means of speaking and answering. ("*Destruktion*" 112)

Claims for the ambiguity of language are evidenced in a true conversation, in the mutually respectful "I–Thou" relationship in which each person is open to the claims of the other. The alternative, as Gadamer presents it, is the master–slave relationship in which the master assumes to completely know the other.

Deconstruction has been appropriated by other schools of criticism, such as Marxism, new historicism, and feminism; these schools also have a scientific basis, which is twofold. They have as their basis a hermeneutics of suspicion: taking their cues from Marx and Freud, they attempt to establish a science that would uncover the truth beneath ideology and rationalization (Dostal 430).[3] They also impose the method of the natural sciences by interpreting human nature on the basis of regularities, a charge Gadamer levels at John Stuart Mill and 19th-century analytic philosophy in the opening pages of *Truth and Method*. In these sociologically oriented schools, literature too is interpreted on the basis of group dynamics—as a product of economic, social, political, and gender classes. Gadamer's ethical misgivings about viewing humans as groups is based on a notion of intersubjectivity that has its ground and its metaphysical definition in precisely the communicative relationship:

There is a kind of experience of the Thou that tries to discover typical behavior in one's fellowmen and can make predictions about others on the basis of experience. . . . We understand the other person in the same way that we understand any other typical event in our experiential field—i.e., he is predictable. His behavior is as much a means to our end as any other means. From the moral point of view this orientation toward the Thou is purely self-regarding and contradicts the moral definition of man. (358)

Gadamer extended this idea of the I–Thou relationship to the hermeneutical problem; seeing tradition in an objective way makes the interpreter "[detach] himself from the continuing effect of the tradition in which he himself has historical reality" (359).

In criticism that relies on judgments made according to group dynamics, the individual is subordinated to the class to which he or she belongs, to the "superstructure" to use Marx's metaphor. As Sandra Gilbert and Susan Gubar stated in their Preface to *No Man's Land*, their task is to "reimagine the author as a gendered human being whose text reflects key cultural conditions, [and to] conflate and collate individual literary narratives so that they constitute one possible metastory" (xiv). They made two assumptions: "that there is a knowable history" and "that texts are authored by people whose lives and minds are affected by the material conditions of that history" (xiii). They then adopted Marx's idea that the "production of ideas, of conceptions, of consciousness" (Marx 568) is premised on "real individuals, their activity, and the material conditions under which they live" that can be verified in "a purely empirical way" (565). Their interpretation of T. S. Eliot's *The Family Reunion* thus became "the tale of a man who may have killed (and certainly believes he has killed) a hard-drinking, New Womanly Delilaesque wife," a tale written by an author who had abandoned his own wife (37). The interpretation was reduced to the biographical description of a man who displayed "typical behavior" of the men of his time and society and who was therefore threatened by women's political, social, and literary advances. It is a suspicious reading that denies any claim outside of one typical of the group to which the author belongs, which can be exposed with the support of historical evidence. Although such evidence as history and biography can certainly assist in interpretation, too often the larger *human* questions of authenticity brought up in such a text—questions that would require granting the claims of the individual work, as well as self-application and self-understanding—are overlooked.

Similarly, Dickstein assessed that "the new historicists of the eighties pitted writers against themselves. . . . These critics looked for the little gaps and contradictions that would reveal what the writer had repressed, . . . they saw these subtexts as ideological formations, the unconscious assumption by which a society propagates its values" (37). The interpreter given these assumptions becomes the scrutinizer, backing away from the text, imposing paradigms, searching not for self-relevant meanings, but for evidence in order to indict.

As an alternative, Dickstein suggested that "a naive reading anchored in wonder must remain an indispensable moment of a more self-conscious reading" (40). This is paralleled by Gadamer's view that in the humanities the interpretation of the common world through methodical thinking may be included, but is not the

> raison d'etre of our activity. . . . The intention is to understand *this* love poem, on its own and in its unique relation to the common structure of love poems. It is an absolutely individualized particular form, so that one participates in the utterance or message which is there embodied by the poet. ("The Hermeneutics of Suspicion" 64)

In this view, a work of art is not simply a product of a member of a group, but is unique in itself. One should be as open to its claims as one is open to the claims of the "Thou." The openness of a true conversation, furthermore, is productive and enriching. It does not end in the aporia of deconstruction, but leads to an increasing amount of understanding through interpretation and reinterpretation: "When I know a good poem by heart, when I know it inside and out, it even says more to me; it does not become poorer but richer" ("Philosophy and Literature" 250). Such a view recognizes the finiteness of one's ability to understand, but in recognition of this finiteness comes a greater appreciation for the "wonder"-ful aspect of literature.

Ultimately, what separates Gadamer from many other contemporary theorists is an ethical concern (*Destruktion* passim). Unlike such objectivist theorists such as E.D. Hirsch, Gadamer recognizes the "play" of language; therein lie his affinities with the poststructuralists. However, Gadamer's view of language as grounded in community and common human tradition leads to the recognition of the possibility of qualities and virtues generated by the activities and expressions of the other. Conversely, a hermeneutics of suspicion, which on the one hand can be employed to disrupt power structures, can also by its suspicion exclude or deny the legitimate claims of others.

The debate between Gadamer and Derrida has been political and ultimately reverts to a question of ethics. On one side are positioned such defenders of deconstruction as Caputo, who suspiciously sees Gadamer as a defender of the status quo, although having "a very liberal, non-teleological, non-hierarchal version of a fundamentally conservative, traditionalist, essentialist idea" (260). Although Gadamer's own prejudice is toward neoclassicism, I think his idea of tradition is inclusive: Tradition can be open to our whole history, including recent positive liberal movements and developments. A recognition of tradition can reveal the positive, as well as the negative. The alternative is to destroy tradition or, more accurately, attempt to ignore it. But this alternative presents the question that once tradition has been destroyed to allow marginalized voices to come to the fore, what is to prevent these voices, unacknowledged as having any claim, from being swept away in the relativistic tide of mere difference?

My question is extended from Gadamer's question posed to Derrida in the midst of what Gadamer describes as the "nihilism" of our "technological era":

On the one side stands the bewildering richness of facets and the endless play of masks in which Nietzsche's bold experiments in thinking appear to disperse themselves into an ungraspable multiplicity. On the other side, there is the question one may put to Nietzsche of what all the play in this enterprise might mean. (*"Destruktion"* 113)

This is a question that I think all readers and teachers of readers must ultimately ask themselves. It should be the concern of hermeneutics.

ENDNOTES

1. Miller, of course, asserted that these accusations are false.
2. Caputo, on the other hand, viewed what he described as Gadamer's "hermeneutics of trust" suspiciously (262).
3. I extend Dostal's description of a hermeneutics of suspicion to these schools of criticism.

WORKS CITED

Armstrong, Paul. "The Politics of Reading." Department of English, Georgia State University. Atlanta, 17 Feb. 1994.

Caputo, John D. "Gadamer's Closet Essentialism: A Derridian Critique." *Dialogue and Deconstruction: The Gadamer–Derrida Encounter*. Ed. Diane P. Michelfelder and Richard E. Palmer. Albany: State U of New York P, 1989. 258–64.

Derrida, Jacques. "Structure, Sign, and Play in the Discourse of the Human Sciences." *The Critical Tradition: Classic Texts and Contemporary Trends*. Ed. David H. Richter. New York: St. Martin's Press, 1989. 959–71.

Dickstein, Morris. "Damaged Literacy: The Decay of Reading." *Profession*. New York: MLA, 1993. 34–40.

Dostal, Robert J. "The World Never Lost: The Hermeneutics of Trust." *Philosophy and Phenomenological Research* 47, No. 3 (1987): 413–34.

Gadamer, Hans-Georg. "Aesthetics and Hermeneutics." *Philosophical Hermeneutics*. Trans. and Ed. David E. Linge. Berkeley: U of California P, 1976. 95–104.

———. *"Destruktion* and Deconstruction." *Dialogue and Deconstruction: The Gadamer–Derrida Encounter*. Ed. Diane P. Michelfelder and Richard E. Palmer. Albany: State U of New York P, 1989. 102–13.

———. "The Hermeneutics of Suspicion." *Hermeneutics: Questions and Prospects*. Eds. Gary Shapiro and Alan Sica. Amherst: U of Massachusetts P, 1984.

———. "On the Problem of Self-Understanding." *Philosophical Hermeneutics*. Trans. and Ed. David E. Linge. Berkeley: U of California P, 1976. 44–58.

———. "Philosophy and Literature." Trans. Anthony J. Steinbock. *Man and World* 18 (1985): 241–59.

———. "Rhetoric, Hermeneutics, and the Critique of Ideology: Metacritical Comments on *Truth and Method*." *The Hermeneutics Reader: Texts of the German Tradition from the Enlightenment to the Present*. Ed. Kurt Mueller-Vollmer. New York: Continuum, 1989. 274–92.

———. *Truth and Method*. Trans. Weinsheimer, Joel, and Donald G. Marshall. 2nd revised ed. New York: Continuum, 1993.

Gilbert, Sandra, and Susan Gubar. Vol. 1 of *No Man's Land: The Place of the Woman Writer in the Twentieth Century*. 2 vols. New Haven: Yale UP, 1988.

Marx, Karl. "'Consciousness Derived from Material Conditions' from *The German Ideology*." *The Critical Tradition: Classic Texts and Contemporary Trends*. Ed. David H. Richter. New York: St. Martin's Press, 1989. 565–71.

Miller, J. Hillis. "Composition and Decomposition: Deconstruction and the Teaching of Writing." *Composition and Literature*. Ed. Winifred B. Hoarner. Chicago: U of Chicago, 1983. Rpt. in *Theory Now and Then*. J. Hillis Miller. Durham: Duke UP, 1991, 227–43.

———. "Derrida's Topographies." *South Atlantic Review* 59, No. 1 (1994): 2–25.

Norris, Christopher. *Deconstruction: Theory and Practice*. London: Methuen, 1982.

10

Burke *Contra* Jameson on Ideological Criticism; or How to Read Patricia Hampl Reading Whitman During the Vietnam War

David W. Smit
Kansas State University

> *[The literary work or cultural object] articulates its own situation and textualizes it, encouraging the illusion that the very situation itself did not exist before, that there is nothing but a text, that there never was any extra- or con-textual reality before the text itself generated it.*
>
> —Fredric Jameson, "Symbolic Inference," 512

> *But magic, in the sense of novelty, is seen to exist normally, in some degree, as an ingredient of every human act; for each act contains some measure of motivation that cannot be explained simply in terms of the past, being to an extent, however tiny,* a new thing.
>
> —Kenneth Burke, *Grammar of Motives*, 65

The question that haunts Cultural Studies, as it has haunted Rhetoric long before, is the old question, perhaps the most important question, and like all important questions it has many forms. Put it this way: To what degree does knowledge matter? Or put it another way: Can we transcend the limits of our experience, the limits of our consciousness, the limits of history? Or in terms of the things human beings create: Can we create something, say a work of art, that seems to exist above and beyond the givens of its social condition?

The question is especially acute for Cultural Studies and its study of ideology, for the primary assumption of many ideological critics is that, as Fredric Jameson put it, "There is nothing that is not social and historical—indeed, that everything is 'in the last analysis' political" (*Political* 20). Jameson put his claim to absolute determinism in the strongest terms:

> To imagine that, sheltered from the omnipresence of history and the implacable influence of the social, there already exists a realm of freedom—whether it be that of the microscopic experience of words in a text or the ecstasies and intensities of the various private religions—is only to strengthen the grip of Necessity over all such blind zones in which the individual subject seeks refuge, in pursuit of a purely individual, a merely psychological, project of salvation. (*Political* 20)

Of course, Jameson's assertion of the implacable necessity of history is paradoxical for Cultural Studies, for if even cultural critique is determined by "the omnipresence of history and the implacable influence of the social," if there is no freedom at all to see and act, then cultural critique itself is just another social determination in "the grip of Necessity," without a claim to unique insight or special consideration.

So it would seem natural, not to say inevitable, that sooner or later scholars in Cultural Studies would have to confront the work of Kenneth Burke, with his reputation for being an independent social critic in the 1930s and 1940s, long before the advent of Cultural Studies in the academy. Thus, in 1978, Jameson published a long analysis and critique of Burke in the pages of *Critical Inquiry*, entitled "The Symbolic Inference." In that piece, Jameson affirmed his critical principles: that ideological analysis is a rewriting of a literary text as a function of its social, historical, and political context; that history itself is only accessible to us in a textual form; that textual uniqueness is an illusion (511–12).

With this as a background Jameson went on to praise Burke for emphasizing art as a form of action, as *praxis*; and he found especially useful Burke's notion of art as a strategy for encompassing situations in terms of "dream," "prayer," and "chart," and the Pentad, with its possibilities for locating the scene of artistic production. But in Burke's application of these critical terms and principles, Jameson saw a dark purpose, a strategy of "containment," by which Burke used the language of social analysis to restrict ideological analysis to the aesthetic, to privilege "virtuoso reading" over history, "to furnish aid and comfort to those who want to limit our work to texts whose autonomy has been carefully secured in advance, all the blackout curtains drawn before the lights are turned back on" (518). In short, according to Jameson, in locating the scene of a literary work, Burke too often ignored larger social and ideological purposes. Indeed, Burke most often inferred the purpose of an artwork from act and agent and agency rather than from scene. Thus, to Jameson, Burke was too focused on the "inner logic" of an act rather than on other possible acts that were ignored or on reconstituting the situation to which the act was a response. In addition, Jameson found Burke too accepting of the notion of the ego/self and believed he did not take seriously enough the ways in which ideology could mystify the ways we think and understand.

Burke's response to Jameson's charges came three issues later in *Critical Inquiry* in an article entitled "Methodological Repression and/or Strategies of

Containment." Basically, Burke accused Jameson of repressing the historical aspects of Burke's theory and criticism. He went on to argue that his life's work had been to account for the human disposition to impose symbolism on nature. To Burke, such symbolism could not just be derived from material conditions; symbolic acts also create material conditions, so that ideas of history and class will never be enough to account for human symbolization. To reduce human acts to their supposed causes is, Burke said, the "genetic fallacy," "whereby overstress upon the *origins* of some manifestation can deflect attention from what it *is*, regardless of what it came from" (415).

Burke also defended his concept of identification, which he equated with Jameson's notion of ideology, by listing the many occasions on which he had dealt with the two terms and by arguing that his various methods of analysis were "designed to strike a balance between the New Critic's stress upon the particular work in itself and Jameson's 'ideological' stress upon 'the ultimate horizon of every cultural artifact'" (411).[1]

In his reply to Burke's rebuttal in the same issue of *Critical Inquiry*, Jameson referred to an argument he made in *Marxism and Form*, that the objects of a particular ideology are a function of the "dynamic praxis of a given social group or class," and he asserted that it is the practice of particular social groups that Burke tends to ignore ("Ideology" 419). Jameson sums up his differences with Burke this way: For Burke, ideology dramatizes symbolic action; for Jameson, symbolic action demonstrates "the ideological function of culture" (421).

In the exchange between Jameson and Burke, we have the paradox of cultural critique put in its strongest terms. One way of dealing with this paradox is to argue that any particular cultural critique may be at the moment of its historically determined formulation or at the later moment of our historically determined reading of it more or less helpful to us in our understanding of the personal, social, and political relationships inherent in a literary work and in our own lives. The question we may rightfully ask of Jameson and Burke then is the degree to which their terms and methods of analysis tend to promote possible insights, which promote our understanding of these things. In order to hypothetically test their usefulness, I describe an essay I admire a great deal as I imagine both Jameson and Burke would have interpreted it.

HAMPL'S ESSAY

In 1981, Patricia Hampl—poet, essayist, travel writer—wrote an essay entitled "The Mayflower Moment: Reading Whitman During the Vietnam War" for *Walt Whitman: The Measure of his Song*, a collection of essays by poets celebrating the 100th anniversary of Whitman's writing *Leaves of Grass*. Hampl's essay is a complex reflection on her reading of Whitman and the influence Whitman and his heirs among contemporary poets had on her sense of what it means to have a "national self," especially in the 1960s during the height of the Vietnam War. It is also an excellent example of a writer reflecting on her own experience, an experience with direct political consequences, and achieving an epiphany that may be either an "illusion that the very situation itself did not exist before" or "to an extent, however tiny, a new thing."

Hampl begins her essay in 1968, when she is reading Whitman as the apostle of personal freedom, and under his influence she celebrates her own freedom: the freedom of birth control pills; the freedom to choose her long-haired, marijuana-smoking friends, even though her family disapproves of them; the freedom to confront her father with her refusal to go to Catholic mass; the freedom to read the poets of her choice; the freedom to identify with her own generation as the only larger group that matters:

> The only thing I belonged to was my generation—hardly a permanent address, although I tried to make it home for a long time. But reading Whitman I belonged: to what I felt was the true nation, to those who lived the magic of the possible, in mourning for America, the pure idea. (306)

In all this Hampl recognizes her romanticism, her idealism, her self-righteousness, her longing for innocence; and she knows that she is reading Whitman "ahistorically as if 'Democratic Vistas' had not been written in 1861 but yesterday": "I wanted, in a self-righteous way as well as helplessly, the only American birthright I could imagine: to step off the Mayflower onto undefiled land, unlimited possibility, unwritten history" (308).

Many of Hampl's friends go to prison for refusing to serve in the army during the war: They are following, she thinks, Whitman's advice—"Dismiss whatever insults your own soul" (308). Gradually Hampl comes to realize the price they have paid for following Whitman's advice: the broken marriages, the prolonged depressions, the sense that they have wasted their lives, that their actions were gestures of political futility. After all, despite their going to prison the war went on and on: "The test of dismissing whatever insults your own soul turned out to be the ability to hold in balance all the foolishness and contradictions that followed in the wake of a real gesture" (310).

Cut to 1973. Hampl is not reading Whitman anymore. She has learned that birth control pills cause blood clots and other side effects, and the difficulties of using a diaphragm—they tend to spring out of her hand, fly across the room, and land behind the radiator, where they pick up dust "like a mushroom covered with fresh mold"—make her feel as if she is back in the 19th century. Her friends are out of prison, but the war goes on. And now America no longer seems like an idea, but just a country with a history of slave ships and soon-to-be boat people, "its national self—that personality Whitman tried to identify so passionately—was emerging as national identity always does: out of history, out of circumstances and experience" (312).

In a final epiphany Hampl thinks that she "leaned too hard" on Whitman, had not recognized his contradictions, but now going over her old copy of *Leaves of Grass* she realizes that Whitman's real influence on her was that "he made *himself* a book," that "although he says he sings himself, that is a 'kosmos,' even so these assertions are the opposite, in fact the denial, of self-absorption," "that his invitation was really to my own self, my own book" (312–13). So like a father releasing his children from his custody and control, Whitman sends Hampl, his daughter and comrade, "out of the ashram" and into the world to "grow up," to write her own book.

How then might Jameson's terms and methods give us an insight into the workings of Hampl's essay? In *The Political Unconscious*, Jameson develops the concept of the *fantasm*, an "unconscious master narrative" of daydream and wish fulfillment. At its most complex a fantasm provides a writer with a set of ideological narrative strategies that not only allow for personal wish fulfillment but also for confronting reality "with the utmost representable density," for positing "the most elaborate and systematic difficulties and obstacles, in order the more surely to overcome them" (183). However, "it then sometimes happens that the objections are irrefutable, and that the wish-fulfilling imagination does its preparatory work so well that the wish, the desire itself, are confounded by the unanswerable resistance of the Real" (183). In short, master narrative strategies, what Jameson elsewhere called the Ideology of Form, can sometimes force a writer to articulate the contradiction between his or her desires and the nature of history, the Real.

Thus, we might interpret "The Mayflower Moment" as Hampl's attempt to deal with more than Whitman: She is also confronting her contradictory desires for both total freedom and for political efficacy. The ideological form of the essay allows her to explore her own contradictory desires, to articulate the hard realities she has had to face, and to come to terms with her response. Hampl asserts her freedom from family and tradition and society in the name of Walt Whitman, only to realize that freedom has a price: Her sexual liberation has bad side effects; her break with tradition provides no comfort; and, a final irony, because her friends express their individual freedom by refusing to be drafted, they go to jail. Hampl confronts this contradiction and articulates it eloquently, but she does not try to resolve it. Instead, she develops one of the standard conventions of the essay form itself: She again settles for irony and paradox. If she cannot have both freedom and political efficacy, she will write about her struggles, and the writing about it will be justification enough. In Jameson's terms she substitutes Utopian gratification and compensation for genuine political struggle.

Jameson attributes the modernist preoccupation with the more self-conscious and personal forms of art as the response of people to a capitalist society that has separated them and their artistic expression from an "older concrete social situation" in which art was more organic to everyday life. Capitalism makes literature a thing, a product, something to be packaged and sold—in short, capitalism reifies literary works—and in response to this phenomenon, as well as other alienating aspects of capitalist life, writers use their art to substitute Utopian gratification and compensation for the ugly realities of social life. This "libidinal transformation of an increasingly desiccated and repressive reality" came to the forefront in the counterculture the 1960s, when "the reminder of the accompanying 'ideological' value of the perceptual as the expression of psychic fragmentation is once more politically timely" (*Political Unconscious* 236–37). In short, we can also read Hampl's essay as part of a larger movement during a particular historical moment—the 1960s—to assert both individual and group forms of expression and identity as a response to societal repression: the pressure to support the Vietnam War, but also to support the larger consumer and nationalist ideals of late-capitalist society. Thus, an ideological critique inspired by Jameson might emphasize that Hampl is a member of the university-educated middle class, and that her essay reproduces the collective concerns of that class—its preoccupation with its own individual consciousness and morality—in the face of larger social forces.

In contrast, how might Burke's terms and methods lead us to read Hampl's essay? Rueckert summarized Burke's most well-known critical strategy this way:

> Burke's four-part methodology—which he calls indexing—is designed to permit one to locate, describe, analyze, and interpret the four kinds of structure one finds in verbal works. These are structures of identifications, or what goes with what; structures of opposition and polarization, or what versus what; structures of progression, or what follows what; and structures of transformation, or what becomes what. (235)

In using these categories we can reach many conclusions similar to those Jameson might draw and thereby see Hampl's work as the result of "the praxis of a given social group." Clearly in "The Mayflower Moment," Hampl identifies with Whitman and contemporary antiwar poets as apostles of freedom, an identification she continues, even after her epiphany: She simply shifts the basis of her identification with Whitman from worshiping him as a hero to accepting his blessing as a kind father. She also clearly identifies with the idea of a natural self, who enters into free association with like-minded souls in a kind of communitarian ideal. It is this ideal of community that cannot survive the batterings of the political establishment. When her friends go to jail, her community breaks up. What Hampl very pointedly does *not* identify with is a social or political group or class organized by common interests with the purpose of accomplishing political action.

Thus, in the essay Hampl's vision of personal freedom and her communitarian ideal are opposed by the law, the political system, and the larger society symbolized by draft boards and judges. And when her friend goes to jail for dismissing what insults his soul, Hampl's vision of personal freedom has to be reconstructed. In the process she abandons her communitarian ideal, and because she identifies with no other social or political groups, she is left with her own individualism, her own consciousness, as her primary resource in dealing with the repressions of society.

However, confronted by the limitations of her old views, she does undergo a kind of transformation to a higher order of her god term: freedom. Hampl always privileges freedom, but when she is restricted by her own biology and the limitations of science, and when her friends are physically restricted by being put in jail for their political beliefs, she resorts to a higher *spiritual* freedom, to write her own book. She never confronts the opposition—the law, the political system—on its own terms because to do so would mean sacrificing to some extent the personal and the communitarian ideal for group political work, the drudgery of political action, the compromises with people she may not like.

But whereas Burke's indexing may help us reach many of the same insights as Jameson—if we are so inclined—Burke also offers us a number of other strategies for capturing the complexity of what Hampl has accomplished, strategies for dealing with the rhetorical aspects of form. Burke defined *form* as the "arousing and fulfillment of desires" (*Counter-Statement* 124), and over the course of his career he gave us a host of terms and strategies for contemplating how a literary work "encompasses a situation": his taxonomy of forms; perspective by incongruity; literature as chart, prayer, and dream; the Pentad—to name only the most popularly known. But let me use just one—"representative anecdotes"—to illustrate how Burke's approach to form gets at an aspect of literary art that Jameson's may not.

To Burke, a *representative anecdote* is a "selection of reality," which is both a reflection and a necessary reduction of that reality, the basis for a terminological structure from which a point of view, a set of terms, and even certain conclusions naturally follow (*Grammar* 59–61). A critic may focus on a representative anecdote of a literary work as the key to how the writer may be trying to encompass a certain situation.

Rather curiously, Hampl devotes the most dramatic detail in her essay to two episodes that are seemingly tangential to her main concerns. She opens with a scene in a doctor's office, in which she blushingly asks the doctor for birth control pills, sitting there in her "large blue Kleenex" while he wears a $200 suit. She ends with a funny scene in which she is unable to control her diaphragm, which has the "habit of springing wildly, perversely out of [her] hand," all lathered in goo, landing behind the radiator. Clearly neither of these episodes is directly related to Hampl's response to the Vietnam War or her search for a "national self." But these two episodes do become dramatic metaphors for her situation, for how she perceives her situation and how she resolves her conflict. If we look closely at these two episodes we can see a measure of novelty, of paradox and dialectic, which Jameson's terms do not account for.

Indeed, these episodes capture the ambiguity of freedom in ways that undercut the neat distinction between free will and historical determinism. Note that when Hampl achieves her newfound freedom, it is at the hands of a man who is very much in control: the doctor in a $200 suit, who has the authority to grant her request for birth control pills or not; she is the supplicant dressed in a large blue Kleenex. Paradoxically, Hampl achieves her sexual freedom by acting like a supplicant before a symbol of the social order. And after her epiphany, after she has realized the limitations of that freedom, the springing diaphragm also becomes a symbol of the uncontrollable nature of her new reality. Like her diaphragm, her new freedom is messy, complex, hard to get a grip on, and not nearly as neat as her closing image implies: her guru/father releasing her into the world. In short, whether she realizes it or not, Hampl has encompassed the complexities of her situation in novel ways which are the stuff of art and which may be beyond the neat conclusions of a great deal of ideological criticism. Such paradoxes and dialectics may be beyond our ability to understand, according to Burke, because they are "inherent in the very germ-plasm" of human beings (*Counter-Statement* 46).

In the last analysis then, in dealing with the political and historical, Burke is just as helpful as Jameson in giving us the terms and strategies we need to do ideological criticism. But because Burke pays more attention to form and develops more useful strategies for dealing with form, his terms and strategies may help us to account for more aspects of the literary act than Jameson's terms and strategies do.

Literary art may reflect the praxis of a particular social group, but it is not only that. Undoubtedly Hampl was in some sense and to some degree historically conditioned in writing "The Mayflower Moment." But there is also magic and novelty in what she has wrought. And in her art we have the irony, the paradox, the dialectic, of what it means to write well and of what it means to be free. Now at this historically conditioned moment in my own experience, Burke helps me to understand this irony, this paradox, this dialectic, in Hampl's essay more than Jameson does.

ENDNOTE

1. Other ideological critics have subsequently come to Burke's defense. Both Frank Lentricchia and Stephen Bygrave have defended Burke against the charge of essentialism, the charge that Burke's methods imply an ontological status for literary work and critical judgment outside the constraints of history. See especially Lentricchia, "Reading History," for an analysis of how Burke's readings of the "Medieval synthesis" and Darwin's *Origin of Species* reflect larger cultural factors.

WORKS CITED

Burke, Kenneth. *Counter-Statement*. 2nd ed. Berkeley: U of California P, 1968.
———. *A Grammar of Motives*. Berkeley and Los Angeles: U of California P, 1969.
———. "Methodological Repression and/or Strategies of Containment." *Critical Inquiry* 5, No. 2

(Winter 1978): 401–416.

Bygrave, Stephen. *Kenneth Burke: Rhetoric and Ideology*. New York: Routledge, 1993.

Hampl, Patricia. "The Mayflower Moment: Reading Whitman During the Vietnam War." *Walt Whitman: The Measure of His Song*. Ed. Jim Perlman, Ed Folsom, Dan Campion. Minneapolis: Holy Cow! Press, 1981. 300–13.

Jameson, Fredric R. "Ideology and Symbolic Action." *Critical Inquiry* 5, No. 2 (Winter 1978): 417–22.

———. *Marxism and Form*. Princeton: Princeton UP, 1972.

———. *The Political Unconscious: Narrative as a Socially Symbolic Act*. Ithaca, NY: Cornell UP, 1981.

———. "The Symbolic Inference; or, Kenneth Burke and Ideological Analysis." *Critical Inquiry* 4, No. 3 (Spring 1978): 507–23.

Lentricchia, Frank. *Criticism and Social Change*. Chicago: U of Chicago P, 1983.

———. "Reading History with Kenneth Burke." *Landmark Essays on Kenneth Burke*. Ed. Barry Brummett. Davis, CA: Hermagoras Press, 1993. 221–41. Reprinted from *Representing Kenneth Burke*. Ed. Hayden White and Margaret Brose. Baltimore: Johns Hopkins UP, 1982.

Rueckert, William H. *Encounters with Kenneth Burke*. Urbana and Chicago: U of Illinois P, 1994.

11 Judicial Constructions of Difference: The Supreme Court's Majority Opinions in *Scott v. Sandford* and *Bowers v. Hardwick*

Glenda Conway
University of Louisville

"Neglect of persons," wrote John T. Noonan in *Persons and Masks of the Law*, has "led to the worst sins for which American law . . . [is] accountable" (vii). Although many progressive law critics argue that the case opinions written by judges tend to dehumanize litigants (see, for example, Irons and West), my own claim is that litigants actually are *re*humanized in opinions. Specifically, opinions give litigants character (or lack of character, as the case may be) by constructing implied voices and personalities for them. The constructed voices provide not only utterances of litigants' arguments, they also convey distinct ideological values and attitudes.

This chapter uses theories of dialogism first proposed by Russian literary theorist and linguist M. M. Bakhtin as a means of identifying and analyzing the voices ascribed to key individuals in two highly controversial U.S. Supreme Court majority opinions, *Scott v. Sandford* (1857) and *Bowers v. Hardwick* (1986). The opinions issued in these cases depict the Court as a resistant body, unsympathetic and repulsed by two seemingly aberrant individuals—one an African American, the other a homosexual—who asked to have their legal rights broadened. My purpose in this examination is not to indict the Court for insensitivity; our Supreme Court justices, after all, deserve ultimate credit for extending and protecting some of our country's most precious individual rights. But who is entitled to these rights is not always as egalitarian as the Declaration of Independence and Constitution might appear to avow.

The plaintiff in *Scott v. Sandford* was Dred Scott, a slave who challenged his status on the basis of his residence in parts of the United States where slavery was outlawed. The respondent in *Bowers v. Hardwick* was Michael Hardwick, a gay male who challenged Georgia's antisodomy law on the basis of its violation of the Fourteenth Amendment.

Both Scott and Hardwick lost their cases, ostensibly because their claims did not rely on explicit Constitutional authority. In the opinion of a majority of the nine members of the Supreme Court who decided the Dred Scott case, "the class of persons described" in Scott's plea "[were] not included, and were not intended to be included, under the word 'citizens' in the constitution, and can therefore claim none of the rights and privileges which that instrument provides for and secures to citizens of the United States" (404). The most immediate of these privileges concerning the Court was the right to file a lawsuit—a right belonging exclusively to citizens. Scott's arguments, therefore, were moot. But that does not mean they were insignificant. As my analysis of several dialogic constructions in the Court's majority opinion shows, Dred Scott's arguments were perceived by the justices as an affront and a threat to the very documents that guarantee life and liberty to those who can rightfully call themselves American citizens.

Michael Hardwick, much like Dred Scott 130 years before him, was determined by the Court to have brought a case that was not only without Constitutional merit, but that advocated conduct offensive to the traditional American way of life. "The Constitution does not confer a fundamental right upon homosexuals to engage in sodomy," wrote Justice Byron White in the majority opinion (186). Any claim otherwise, according to White, was "at best, facetious" (194). My dialogic analysis of the *Bowers* opinion locates several constructions in which Hardwick's arguments (along with his "conduct," a word used repeatedly in the opinion) are portrayed as facetious, misguided, and forceful.

Milner S. Ball, in *The Promise of American Law: A Theological, Humanistic View of Legal Process*, described the people represented in judicial opinions as "artificial persons" (82). Not surprisingly, the "real" persons represented by these artificial ones tend to feel that court opinions inaccurately portray their legal stories and claims (Conley and O'Barr 1; Schlepple 2077). But, as judicial handbooks and law school texts invariably attest, opinions are not supposed to be about people; rather, they are supposed to be about judicial reasoning (see, for example, George xxii; Golding v). It makes sense that, from a psychoanalytic standpoint, as Stewart theorized in *Crimes of Writing: Problems in the Containment of Representation*, the law serves to position individual litigants as subjects within the judicial realm.

One way "real" litigants become subject to artificial identities in judicial opinions is through dialogic voice constructions. Within texts, according to Bakhtin, dialogism is a straightforward matter of the presentation of "another's speech in another's language" ("Discourse in the Novel" 304). Ideological representations in language are inevitable, in Bakhtin's understanding, given language's capacity to create places for both speakers and subjects. And in the case of judicial opinions, speakers represent ruling groups, while their subjects are, quite literally, their subjects. Thus, in a Bakhtinian sense, the language of judicial opinions, like the language of political domination, "becomes strictly repressive" (Hirschkop 104).

Direct quotations from litigants appear rarely in opinion texts, and when they do, that appearance is usually only in footnotes. But litigants still have a definite existence in most opinions, usually through characterizations implied by dialogic constructions. Dialogic constructions are especially prevalent in the *Scott* and *Bowers* opinions, both of which offer only a few words of direct information about the key individuals under scrutiny.

A character's discourse, whether "real" or contrived, conveys the author's version of that character's values and thinking processes. In "Discourse in the Novel," Bakhtin expressed the radical view that all characters in narratives function as "ideologues," and that their "words are always ideologemes" supporting "a particular way of viewing the world" (333). White, who has been looking rhetorically at legal writing for the past 20 years, argues that a similar form of privileging occurs in judicial opinions. He believes that every opinion issued by a court of law "validates or authorizes one form of life—one kind of reasoning, one kind of response to argument, one way of looking at the world." (*Justice as Translation* 101).

From the Supreme Court's view, it would seem that Dred Scott was far more than a person with a weak case; he was an inferior alien with seditious goals that would have destroyed this country at its foundations. He appears to not even have been perceived as human. The opinion never refers to him as a man—among the various terms used to describe him instead are "[t]he plaintiff in error" (400); "a negro" (403); a "descendant . . . of Africans" (403); a member of "a subordinate and inferior class of beings" (404–405); a representative of "that unfortunate race" (407); "an article of property" (408); a victim of "the degraded condition of this unhappy race" (409); and one of "a separate class of persons" (411) not intended to be protected by the U.S. Constitution.

Critics of the Dred Scott opinion have long observed that its effect was to construe Scott, along with every other African American residing in the country at that time, as a nonhuman being, a piece of property subject to the whims of its owner. His desires did not count; his presence was of no importance; he was, in effect, nonexistent in the eyes of the law. So it is more than just semantically interesting that the Court's voicing of Scott's threat gets attributed to a being described as "No one." In five separate passages of the majority opinion, the only possible objector to Taney's white supremacist vision of America is described as "no one." For instance, Taney made an appeal to history to support what he described as a "naturally impressed" (408) opinion among American people that African Americans are "beings of an inferior order . . . altogether unfit to associate with the white race" (407). Significantly, he concluded this appeal by adding that "*no one* seems to have doubted the correctness of the prevailing opinion of the time" (408, emphasis added). No one, that is, except the dreaded

Dred Scott—apparently his dissent in the face of prevailing opinion serves to further underline the correctness of his exclusion from civilized American society.

Curiously, whereas Taney purported to hold a sort of reverence for the opinions of the Constitutional framers, any opinions formed in the 75 years since their work were of no concern to him. Again, "no one" would think enlightened values related to slavery should influence a legal decision:

> No one, we presume, supposes that any change in public opinion or feeling, in relation to this unfortunate race, in the civilized nations of Europe or in this country, should induce the court to give to the words of the constitution a more liberal construction in their favor than they were intended to bear when the instrument was framed and adopted. (426)

No one, except, of course, Dred Scott.

In defending the property laws governing slavery, Taney shifted his "no one" defense into a veiled accusation that Scott would repudiate people's property rights—"No one . . . would think a moment of depriving the power of congress to make needful rules and regulations in relation to property of this kind from this clause of the constitution" (437). What is being said here, essentially, is that Scott's desire is take away the security that people have when they own property. And what else would he do? He would support the destruction of the Bill of Rights:

> no one, we presume, will contend that congress can make any law in a territory respecting the establishment of religion, or the free exercise thereof, or abridging the freedom of speech or of the press, or the right of the people of the territory peaceably to assemble, and to petition the government for the redress of grievances. (450)

In this last reference to what "no one" would contend, America's whole democratic system is nearly overthrown. It is probably more than coincidence that each of "no one's" arguments becomes progressively more threatening than the one preceding it.

Gillerman, chairman of the *Boston Bar Journal*'s Board of Editors, observed a basic philosophical similarity between the *Scott* and *Bowers* cases almost immediately after the Supreme Court issued its ruling against Michael Hardwick. The *Bowers* opinion, Gillerman wrote, exhibits "a deep and virulent prejudice against homosexuals fully equal to the prejudice against blacks" shown in *Scott* (4). Gillerman believes that the Court discounted Hardwick's rights of citizenship on his alleged "moral inferiority" just as Scott lost his case due to alleged racial inferiority (7). The abjection with which Justice Byron White viewed Hardwick seems evident from his opinion's first words: He used Hardwick's name once, followed by a parenthetical notation that "hereafter" the appellation will be simply "respondent" (187). Hardwick, like Scott, got deprived of a name and a valid right to be heard. The Court's opinion characterized his arguments, accordingly, as originating from an alien way of thinking whose very existence disturbs the justices' vision of appropriate sexual behavior. White seemed amazed in his fourth sentence, in which he stated that Hardwick "*asserted* that he was a *practicing* homosexual" (188, emphasis added). Further, he seemed appalled that Hardwick had sought endorsement for his "conduct" from the Supreme Court. That White saw Hardwick's goal as presumptuous is evident from his particular choice of words: "[R]espondent would have us announce . . . a fundamental right to engage in homosexual sodomy. That," White continues, "we are quite unwilling to do" (191).

In outlining the Court's argument in favor of antisodomy laws, White appeared to incorporate Hardwick's claims. Close analysis, however, shows that the opinion actually construes Hardwick's voice within a context that exaggerates, invalidates, or parodies his meanings. In this sense, Hardwick's voice, like his name, is never truly allowed to enter the opinion. This is similar to the way in which Dred Scott was denied a valid presence in the *Scott v. Sandford* opinion.

Throughout the *Bowers* opinion, Hardwick's argument is mocked and ridiculed through embedded fragments of what superficially appears to be his language. In his theories related to characterization in novels, Bakhtin devised a term—hybrid constructions—to describe discourse that "belongs . . . to a single speaker, but that actually contains mixed within it two utterances, two speech manners, two styles, two 'languages,' two semantic and axiological belief systems" ("Discourse in the Novel" 304). All utterances, Bakhtin wrote in "The Problem of Speech Genres," have "dialogic overtones." Accordingly, readers can discover through close study of discourse "many half-concealed or completely concealed words of others with varying degrees of foreignness" (92–93). Hybrid constructions, not surprisingly, are usually structured in such a way that the author's view is favored ("Discourse in the Novel" 306). With this understanding, it becomes evident that the issue statement for the case presents a skewed and parodic view of Hardwick's main argument:

> The issue presented is whether the Federal Constitution confers a fundamental right upon homosexuals to engage in sodomy and hence invalidates the laws of the many States that still make such conduct illegal and have done so for a very long time. (190)

In this phrasing, it sounds as if Hardwick, like Dred Scott before him, was actually arguing against the total American system of law as well as all the moral traditions it upholds.

In a second parody of Hardwick's case, White "registers" the Court's "disagreement . . . with respondent that the Court's prior cases have construed the Constitution to confer a right of privacy that extends to homosexual sodomy and for all intents and purposes have decided this case" (190). Hardwick is portrayed in this statement as believing that cases "construe . . . the Constitution," a backward reasoning from traditional constructionist legal viewpoints. He also is implicated for his alleged assumption that he has the interpretive capability to understand and decide his own case. The banal phrase "for all intents and purposes," attributed as it is to Hardwick, implies he made hasty and simplistic leaps in judgment in order to link precedents to his argument.

Probably the justices' most emphatic use of dialogism to underscore their rejection of Hardwick's claims is present in a statement that concludes their discussion of what the previous cases cited by Hardwick really mean. This statement reads as follows: "Moreover, any claim that any kind of private sexual conduct between consenting adults is constitutionally insulated from state proscription is unsupportable" (191). The base structure in this statement is "any claim . . . is unsupportable." Its inclusive wording suggests that what the justices really mean is that any claim from Hardwick would be unsupportable. Besides this blanket negation, the other language event in this statement is the appearance once again of a coded version of Hardwick's argument. The embedded clause distinctly implies that Hardwick advocates "any kind of private sexual conduct." "Any kind of" could mean an infinite number of possibilities, which could certainly conjure up a world of feared sexual practices, most probably having no connection to homosexuality. The idea that attempts to decriminalize sodomy are intended to increase its frequency continually haunts homosexuals and others interested in reform. I know that in Kentucky last year, while our state considered a challenge to antisodomy legislation, conservative church and community leaders regularly warned that if sodomy were legalized, it would then have to be taught in schools. White's implication that Hardwick was advocating "any kind of sexual activity" is just another version of this scare tactic.

An ideal judicial opinion, according to James Boyd White, would demonstrate that the judge

> had listened to the side he voted against and that he had felt the pull of the arguments both ways. The [decision] that was made . . . would comprise two opposing voices, those of the parties, in a work made by another, by the judge who had listened to both and had faced the conflict between them in an honest way. ("Rhetoric" 315)

This ideal sounds much like a conscious Bakhtinian-style dialogism. It is not enough, White implied, for judges to just *say* they have considered both sides of a case; they should also make overt efforts in the opinion to *show* they heard both sides. Still, what White did not deal with is the problem that people hear arguments through their own ideological frameworks. And when they reiterate these arguments, as the Supreme Court justices did in *Scott v. Sandford* and *Bowers v. Hardwick*, they construct versions that will keep their frameworks intact. Although I cannot say whether it is possible for a court opinion to convey a losing litigant's argument without some degree of distortion, I am nearly certain that the two opinions I have discussed in this chapter do not convey the full messages Dred Scott and Michael Hardwick wanted the Supreme Court justices and the rest of the nation to hear.

WORKS CITED

Bakhtin, M. M. "Discourse in the Novel." *The Dialogic Imagination*. Ed. Michael Holquist. Trans. Caryl Emerson and Michael Holquist. Austin: U Texas P, 1981. 259–422.

———. "The Problem of Speech Genres." *Speech Genres and Other Late Essays*. Ed. Caryl Emerson and Michael Holquist. Trans. Vern W. McGee. Austin: U Texas P, 1986. 60–102.

Ball, Milner S. *The Promise of American Law: A Theological, Humanistic View of Legal Process*. Athens: U of Georgia P, 1981.

Bowers v. Hardwick, 478 U.S. 186 (1986).

Conley, John M., and William M. O'Barr. *Rules versus Relationships: The Ethnography of Legal Discourse*. Chicago: U of Chicago P, 1990.

George, Joyce J. *Judicial Opinion Writing Handbook*. 2nd ed. Buffalo: William S. Hein & Co., 1986.

Gillerman, Gerald. "Dred Scott Revisited: A Comment on *Bowers v. Hardwick*." *Boston Bar Journal* (September/October 1986): 4–11.

Golding, Martin. *Legal Reasoning*. New York: Alfred A. Knopf, 1984.

Irons, Peter. *The Courage of Their Convictions*. New York: The Free Press, 1988.

Noonan, John T. *Persons and Masks of the Law: Cardozo, Holmes, Jefferson, and Wythe as Makers of the Masks*. New York: Farrar, Straus and Giroux, 1976.

Schlepple, Kim Lane. "Telling Stories." *Michigan Law Review* 87 (August 1989): 2073–98.

Scott v. Sandford, 19 How. 393 (1857).

Stewart, Susan. *Crimes of Writing: Problems in the Containment of Representation*. New York: Oxford UP, 1991.

West, Robin. *Narrative, Authority, and Law*. Ann Arbor: U of Michigan P, 1993.

White, James Boyd. *Justice as Translation: An Essay in Cultural and Legal Criticism*. Chicago: U of Chicago P, 1990.

———. "Rhetoric and Law: The Arts of Cultural and Communal Life." *The Rhetoric of the Human Sciences: Language and Argument in Scholarship and Public Affairs*. Ed. John S. Nelson, Allan Megill, and Donald N. McCloskey. Madison: U of Wisconsin P, 1987. 298–318.

Part III

Public/Private Voices

12 Expressive Rhetoric, a Genealogy of Ideas, and a Case for the British Romantics

Rex L. Veeder
St. Cloud State University

The central tenets of expression are echoed in a broad rhetorical tradition. Current source studies of expressionist theory (Burnham; McCarthy and Fishman), reflect philosophical and theoretical concerns of past rhetorics, but our discussion of expressionist theory is tethered to the present and near present. One reason for this is that we are too often arguing with theorists about the dominance of expression or social construction in composition. Instead, we need to concentrate on the relationship between private discourse and public discourse, what Reed Way Dasenbrock calls "concord" individualism ("The Myth of the Subjective" 23). If we look at expression as a broad-based movement to identify a personal voice and then to establish a relationship between private and public discourse, we begin to notice the spectral image of an expressive rhetoric throughout history. That rhetoric is defined by much of what is familiar to us as rhetoricians: Homeric rhetorics and dialectics, ecclesiastic or pulpit rhetoric, Renaissance rhetoric (especially Vico and Ramus), and the Romantic or Transcendental rhetorics of the British Romantics, Emerson, and Thoreau.

I examine the historical contexts of a germinal influence on expression, the British Romantics. By doing so, I hope to reconcile the British Romantics to rhetoric and place expressionist theory in a historical context other than post-1960.

I define *British Romantic rhetoric* as the rhetorics practiced and described by William Blake, Samuel Coleridge, John Keats, Percy Shelley, and William Wordsworth. In addition, I include the circle of their associates in education and politics: William Godwin, William Hazlitt, Charles Lamb, Thomas De Quincey, Joseph Priestley, and Mary Wollstonecraft.

THE RHETORICAL CONTEXT OF THE
BRITISH ROMANTICS

The World has had Treatises of Rhetoric enough to strike it dumb . . . much labour hath been employed in cultivating the powers of language; but it has, for the most part, been employed in vain; and while the Authors of such Treatises pretend to reach the Arts of Persuasion, they have, in general, been unable to persuade their Readers to attention.

—John Langhorne, *Eloquence of the Pulpit*, 1765

Langhorne's description of rhetoric illustrates the confusion about the definition of rhetoric, but also suggests the rich confluence of definitions during the 18th and 19th centuries. The British Romantics have been studied primarily as literary figures, and their rhetorical activities viewed through the lens of literary criticism. The effect of this emphasis is to alienate the Romantics from rhetoricians. Winterowd, for example, found that Samuel Taylor Coleridge is a singular villain, responsible for devaluing the "literature of fact" (59–61). In the same manner, David Russell pointed out that the Romantics served as rallying points for proponents of liberal culture in their arguments against composition studies (*Writing in the Academic Disciplines passim*).

Still, with minor adjustments of the critical lens, we can bring into focus how the British Romantics were directly involved in debates about rhetoric and how they managed, for better or worse, to yoke disparate rhetorical theories into private and subsequent public discourse. In addition, because Coleridge and Wordsworth influenced Edward and Emory Channing, Ralph Waldo Emerson, and James Marsh, they influenced American rhetoric and expressionist theory.

The British Romantics were interested in the same rhetorical issues as Hugh Blair, George Campbell, and Richard Whatley, but the terms they used varied greatly. Winifred Horner and Kerri Barton offered a good description of the circumstances when they argued that 18th-century rhetoric declined in name only. "Rhetoric," they pointed out, "survived under other names, and as the basic concepts changed focus the terminology changed as well" (114). The British Romantics were as much a part of the 18th as the 19th century, and the tendency, perhaps as the result of the Ramist debate, to call rhetoric by many names lasted throughout both centuries.

The three main influences on their rhetoric as well as their literature were the French Revolution, the Royal Society and science, and the Industrial Revolution (Abrams). As a group, they did not develop a detailed and systematic rhetoric, although Coleridge came close in *Aids to Reflection*, *Logic*, and "Essays on the Principles of Method." They did not, however, flinch from arguing about discourse and education—the two primary elements in rhetorical study.

THE RHETORICAL TENETS OF THE
BRITISH ROMANTICS

My system, if I may venture to give it so fine a name, is the only attempt I know ever made to reduce all knowledge into harmony . . . I show to each system that I fully understand and rightly appreciate what that system means; but then I lift up that system to a higher point of view . . . so that the fragment of truth is not only acknowledged, but explained.

—Coleridge, *Table Talk*

Coleridge undertook to organize the systems of philosophy into a synergistic whole. However, the issue for Coleridge was not as much philosophical as rhetorical because he recognized that logic and thought were primarily forms of discourse (*Logic*). Hazlitt and De Quincey wrote on oratory and composition, critiqued speeches from Parliament and pulpit, and offered theoretical commentary on rhetoric (Hazlitt, *The Complete Works*; De Quincey, *Selected Essays on Rhetoric*). Priestley and Godwin contributed discussions on education, rhetoric, and society (Priestley, *Oratory and Criticism*; Godwin, *Political Justice*). The poetic circle contributed discussions about language in discourse and in the creation of knowledge. Wordsworth's preface to the *Lyrical Ballads* is often referred to as a vindication of the language of the people (see most recently Bialostosky). Yet one of the most interesting aspects of the debate between Coleridge and Wordsworth is the issue of how language works in society: Wordsworth takes a vitalist perspective, whereas Coleridge argues for a social constructionist view (*Biographia Literaria* 198).

The central literary and political tropes of the Romantics (the relationship of the one to the many, the relationship between feeling and reasoning, and the relationship between revolution and constancy) dominated their theoretical works on discourse.

Considering the British Romantic writings on discourse, I suggest five basic tenets for British Romantic rhetoric. These tenets are, I think, in harmony with the central philosophy in expressive rhetoric:

1. *Composition is rhetoric in the broadest sense, including in its purview speech, writing, and epistemology*. It was during this time period that writing began to replace speech as the primary form of discourse. The British Romantics are possibly the first compositionists. As such, whatever terminology they used, they thought of rhetoric as print as often as they thought of rhetoric as speech. Along with the shift in emphasis to writing came an increased concern for the formative role language plays in the creation of knowledge.

2. *The keys to social and political change are literature and education*. Literature was one form of political action, and at a time when literary clubs were

popular, most literary clubs were politically affiliated. The relationship among political clubs, education, and literature was strengthened by the haphazard structure of official education (Porter 173–75). Attendance at grammar schools and universities declined, and the dissenting academies challenged the dominance of Oxford and Cambridge. Books often served the public better than formal classrooms, and rhetoric was the business of all people of learning (see Horner and Barton 115). The distinct boundaries between education, politics, and literature became blurred as political clubs, literary journals, and the church served as social adjustment points for a populace struggling to contend with rapid changes in work and government (Porter 175).

Godwin's primary agenda in *Political Justice* was to change government through education. According to Godwin, education was the most accessible means to bring about constant but constructive change. As he put it, "[t]he only method according to which social improvements can be carried on . . . is, when the improvement of our institutions advances, in a just proportion to the illumination of the public understanding" (210; see also "The Characters of Men Originate in their External Circumstances" 1.4).

3. *The purpose of education is to negotiate between private and public discourse in order to create a personal ethos capable of interacting with dynamic social change.* The Romantic interest in a variety of speculative and reflective forms (self-exploration, psychology, and meditation) was commonplace (Stewart 156–62). There was a political and practical need for speculation in a society familiar with rebellion and contending with diversity. Rhetorically, this motivation led the British Romantics to investigate the appropriateness of a personal ethos to contend and negotiate with the public one. In this sense, the idea of ethos as a public description of commonly held values was supplanted by a personal ethos, which habitually defined the character of an individual.

An emphasis on character engendered an accent on style and voice in writing. The writer's voice was an invitation to a set of values and beliefs: a world view that may or may not be the same as a reader's (see Enos; and Ong). Thus, the writer was ironically aware of how the personal ethos is speculative while exercising critical judgment. One description of the voice of British Romantic rhetoric is that it is apologetic and self-defacing. Coleridge, for example, was aware that writing is an act of invitation. The "architect conceals the foundation of his building," he wrote, but "the foundation stones of [the writer's] edifice must lie open to common view, or his friends will hesitate to trust themselves beneath the roof" (*Friend* 14). At the same time, the desire to maintain a confident voice in argument created a situation in which the writer might be at once humble and overbearing.

4. *Personal discourse in journals, notebooks, letters, personal essays, and literature is an essential and primary rhetorical activity.* One of the models for Romantic discourse is Sir Thomas Browne, whose meditative prose in *Urn Burial*

and *Garden of Cyrus* focuses on self-awareness in relation to universal themes. In his essay on rhetoric, De Quincey offered Browne as one of the best examples of English rhetoric. In Browne, he said,

> are two opposite forces of eloquent passion and rhetorical fancy brought together in exquisite equilibrium . . . so as to create a middle species of composition, more various and stimulating to the understanding than pure eloquence, more gratifying to the affections than naked rhetoric. (104)

De Quincey's "middle species of composition" is a description of the kind of rhetoric with which the British Romantics were wrestling, something between the "naked" style of the Royal Academy of Science and the boundaries of poetry. In order to write this kind of prose, the Romantics wrote personal essays, even when they were addressing a diverse public.

5. *Interdependency and identification are the primary purposes of discourse.* The central task of all composition was to embrace and partake of diversity and to bring divergence into a harmonious relationship with the personal ethos or the self. The key element in interdependent thinking and action was "sympathetic imagination," a belief that the way to understand something was to identify with it through imaginative activities (Engell 143–60, 195–208). Shelley's use of the term "identification" in his "Defense" is an example of how the British Romantics used the idea of identification to suggest we are interdependent (1076).

This idea, too, had political implications. Godwin's *Political Justice* described an interdependent universe in which individuals change society through interacting with it. All change must be slow, he said, so that individual differences can be integrated into the whole of society. Coleridge maintained that the relationship of those in power to the populace is one of interdependence, and he warned that not taking care of the poors' physical needs will lead to national disaster. The English public is served best by a consistent discourse between the poor and the rich: "Domestic affections depend upon association" ("On Radicals and Republicans" 508).

The British Romantics maintained that all personal acts are interrelated to public good or ill. Their rhetorical practice and theory reflects this philosophy, and the intricate workings of both poetics and rhetoric is directed toward the interaction of the individual with diversity and, thus, society. Social responsibility is seen as a duty. As Coleridge put it in "Reflections On Having Left a Place of Retirement":

> . . . dear Cot, and Mount sublime!
> I was constrain'd to quit you. Was it right,
> While my unnumber'd brethren toil'd and bled,
> That I should dream away the entrusted hours
> On rose-leaf beds, pampering the coward heart
> With feelings all too delicate for use? (400)

The rhetorical vectors influencing the British Romantics were thus diverse and intense. They struggled to bring together a description of discourse that would reflect a holistic view of their time and discourse practices. The main theorists among them (Coleridge; De Quincey; Hazlitt; and Priestley) wrote about the issue of discourse and composition. They saw rhetoric as the spoken art. When they wrote about writing other than poetry, they used the terms *composition*, *discourse*, *logic*, and *style*, and they generally viewed composition as the holistic act of making meaning and then acting on that meaning in the public world.

Logic rather than rhetoric served as the descriptor for invention and discovery, and they broadened the study of logic to include the study of language and discourse practices. Style became the general rubric for voice and character, and personal forms of writing were considered as important as public ones. Thus, their rhetorical theories were founded on tenets familiar to contemporary rhetoric in general and expressive rhetoric in particular. Principally, the Romantics worked at solving the problem of the relationship between private discourse and public discourse. Their solution, at least in my synthesis of their theoretical works, was to suggest that we are persuaded best and learn the most through our own experience in the company of those we trust.

KENNETH BURKE AND THE BRIDGE
TO EXPRESSIVE RHETORIC

In *Historical Thinking*, Tholfsen Trygve argued that the historical perspective is at once particular and general, that we must focus on the specifics of a culture while recognizing those universal concerns that sustain us as human beings (10). In recognizing how the British Romantics wrestled with the issues expressivists and social constructionist grapple, we are able to keep a bifurcated vision of our past and present that may lead us to a future in which the individual voice more readily transforms public policy.

The British Romantics were concerned with the central issues that dominate the discussion between social construction and expression. Their theoretical and philosophical works demonstrate a keen awareness of the need for action and purpose and a sense of audience. A baseline definition of British Romantic rhetoric includes the desire to validate the private world through the articulation of personal experience. Likewise, expressive models of composition imply that the world can be changed through writing: Writers compose themselves; they create a transcendent character, an ethos, through which they bring private speech into the realm of public action. In this view, world problems are experienced as personal ones, and those who write from the rhetorical stance of the self involve the realms of, spirit, and the mind in "practical" activities.

The historian's task is to find a way to bridge the past and future, perhaps, to predict what may happen in the future. The bridge between the British Romantics and expressionist rhetoric is a familiar one. At first it would seem that the most direct connection between the British Romantics and an expressive rhetoric would be Emerson. However, there are other bridges available. Kenneth Burke, I.A. Richards, and Ann E. Berthoff are modern rhetors who have publicly acknowledged both an interest and a debt to the Romantics. All three have worked to understand the private discourse and the public usefulness of private, speculative writing.

In the preface to *Writing Histories of Rhetoric*, Victor Vitanza argued that "if anyone is going to be concerned with writing *a* history of rhetoric, she or he *must* also 'begin' with Kenneth Burke (KB), who epitomizes the very concept of 'beginnings'" (x). In the same spirit, I propose that expressionists explore the relationship between Burke and the British Romantics, especially Samuel Taylor Coleridge. In letters to Jane Blankenship, Burke commented that people who "snoot" Coleridge are "uninformed," and that his Shedd edition of Coleridge's works are "indexed to the point of morbidity" (144). Blankenship pointed out that Burke had always found Coleridge useful, both in terms of substance and method (128).

Burke understood the way debates over public and private discourse work. His discussion of idealism and materialism echoes our current discussion of expression and social construction. His attitude toward simplified versions of the discussion is that we too easily find rhetorical reasons in a debate to dismiss a relationship in order to make a point. He said,

> [H]ere is the paradigm for the modern rhetorician's shuttling between "idealistic" and "materialistic" motives, as when one imputes "idealistic" motives to one's faction and "materialistic" motives to the adversary; or the adversary can be accursed of "idealistic" motives when they imply ineffectiveness and impracticability. (*A Rhetoric of Motives* 57)

We may agree, with Burke, that there is indeed something useful about "idealistic" motives in composition and recognize them as practical and necessary. This was a chief concern for British Romantic rhetoric and, I take it, for expressionistic rhetoric as well.

WORKS CITED

Abrams, M.H. "English Romanticism: The Spirit of the Age." *Romanticism and Consciousness*. Ed. Harold Bloom. New York: W. W. Norton, 1970. 91–119.

Berthoff, Ann E. "Coleridge, I. A. Richards, and the Imagination." *The Educational Legacy of Romanticism*. Ed. John Willinsky. Waterloo, Ontario: Wilfrid Lauriar UP, 1991. 55–72.

Bialostosky, Don H. *Wordsworth, Dialogics, and the Practice of Criticism*. New York: Cambridge UP, 1992.

Blair, Hugh. *Lectures on Rhetoric and Belles Lettres*. Philadelphia: T. Ellwood Zell, 1862.

Blankenship, Jane. "'Magic' and 'Mystery' in the Works of Kenneth Burke." *The Legacy of Kenneth Burke*. Eds. Herbert W. Simons and Trevor Melia. Madison: U of Wisconsin P, 1989. 128–55.

Brinton, Carne. *The Political Ideas of the English Romantics*. New York: Russell, 1962.

Burke, Kenneth. *A Rhetoric of Motives*. Berkeley: U of California P, 1969.

———. "Rhetoric—Old and New." *Journal of General Education* 5 (April 1951): 202–209.

Burnham, Christopher. "Expressive Rhetoric: A Source Study." *Defining the New Rhetorics*. Eds. Theresa Enos and Stuart C. Brown. Newbury Park: Sage, 1993. 154–70.

Campbell, G. *The Philosophy of Rhetoric*. Ed. L.F. Bitzer. Carbondale: Southern Illinois UP, 1963.

Coleridge, Samuel Taylor. *Aids to Reflection*. Ed. Harold Bloom. New York: Chelsea House, 1983.

———. *Biographia Literaria: or Biographical Sketches of My Literary Life and Opinions*. Ed. George Watson. London: Everyman's Library, 1987.

———. "Essays on the Principles of Method." Vol. 1 of *The Friend*. 2 vols. Ed. Barbara E. Rooke. Vol. 4 of *The Collected Works*. Princeton: Princeton UP, 1969: 409–521.

———. "Reflections on Having Left a Place of Retirement." *English Romantic Writers*. Ed. David Perkins. New York: Harcourt and Brace, 1967. 400–401.

———. *The Friend*. Ed. Barbara E. Rooke. 2 vols. Vol. 4 of *The Collected Works*. Princeton: Princeton UP, 1969.

———. *Logic*. Ed. J. R. de J. Jackson. Vol. 13 of *The Collected Works*. Princeton: Princeton UP, 1981.

———. *Table Talk, &c.* Vol. 6 of *The Complete Works of Samuel Taylor Coleridge*. Ed. W.G.T. Shedd. 7 vols. New York: Harper & Brothers, 1884.

Dasenbrock, Reed Way. "The Myth of the Subjective and the Subject in Composition Studies." *Journal of Advanced Composition* 13 (1993): 21–32.

De Quincey, Thomas. "Rhetoric." *DeQuincey's Works*. Vol. 10 of *The Collected Writings*. Ed. David Masson. London: A. & C. Black, 1897. 81–133.

Downey, James. *The Eighteenth Century Pulpit*. Oxford: Clarendon P, 1969.

Engell, James. *The Creative Imagination: Enlightenment to Romanticism*. Cambridge: Harvard UP, 1981.

Enos, Richard. *Greek Rhetoric Before Aristotle*. Prospect Heights, Illinois: Waveland P, 1993.

Enos, Theresa. "Voice as Echo of Delivery, Ethos as Transforming Process." *Composition in Context: Essays in Honor of Donald C. Stuart*. Eds. W. Ross Winterowd and Vincent Gillespie. Carbondale: Southern Illinois UP, 1994. 180–95.

Godwin, William. "Enquiry Concerning Political Justice and Its Influence on Morals and Happiness." *Backgrounds of Romanticism: English Prose of the Eighteenth Century*. Ed. Leonard M. Trawick. Bloomington: Indiana UP, 1967. 191–221.

———. *Enquiry Concerning Political Justice*. Ed. K. Codell Carter. Oxford: Clarendon P, 1971.

Golden, James L. and Edward P.J. Corbett. *The Rhetoric of Blair, Campbell, and Whately*. Carbondale: Southern Illinois UP, 1990.

Hazlitt, William. *Essays by William Hazlitt*. Ed. Charles Harold Gray. New York: Macmillan, 1924.

Horner, Winifred Bryan and Kerrir Morris Barton. "The Eighteenth Century." *The Present State of Scholarship in Historical and Contemporary Rhetoric*. Ed. Winifred Bryan Horner. Columbia: U of Missouri P, 1990. 114–50.

Howell, Wilbur Samuel. *Eighteenth-Century British Logic and Rhetoric*. Princeton: Princeton UP, 1971.

Kennedy, George. *Classical Rhetoric and Its Christian and Secular Traditions from Ancient to Modern Times*. Chapel Hill: U of North Carolina P, 1980.

Langhorne, John. *Letters on the Eloquence of the Pulpit*. A reprint. New York: Garland, 1970.

McCarthy, Lucille, and Stephen Fishman. "Is Expressivism Dead? Reconsidering Its Romantic Roots and Its Relation to Social Construction." *College English* (1992): 647–61.

Mitchell, Fraser W. *English Pulpit Oratory from Andrewes to Tillotson*. London: Society for Promoting Christian Knowledge, 1932.

Ong, Walter. "Voice as Summons for Belief." *Literature and Belief*. Ed. M.H. Abrams. New York: Columbia UP, 1958. 80–105.

Porter, Roy. *English Society in the Eighteenth Century*. New York: Penguin Books, 1982.

Priestley, Joseph. *A Course of Lectures on Oratory and Criticism*. London: Johnson, 1777.

Ramus, Petrus. *Dialectic*. Ed. Michel Dassonville. Geneva: Librairie Droz, 1964.

Richards, I.A. *Coleridge on Imagination*. London: Kegan Paul, Trench, Trubner & Co. Ltd., 1934.

Russell, David R. *Writing in the Academic Disciplines, 1870–1990: A Curricular History*. Carbondale: Southern Illinois UP, 1991.

Shelley, Percy Bysshe. "A Defense of Poetry." *English Romantic Writers*. Ed. David Perkins. New York: Harcourt Brace & World, 1967. 1972–086.

Stapleton, Laurence. *The Elected Circle: Studies in the Art of Prose*. Princeton: Princeton UP, 1973.

Stephen, Leslie. *English Literature and Society in the Eighteenth Century*. New York: Barnes & Noble, 1962.

Stewart, Donald C. "The Nineteenth Century." *The Present State of Scholarship in Historical and Contemporary Rhetoric*. Ed. Einifred Bryan Horner. Columbia: U of Missouri P, 1990. 151–85.

Trygve, R. Tholfsen. *Historical Thinking*. New York: Harper and Row, 1967.

Vico, Giambattista. *The New Science of Giambattista Vico*. Eds. Thomas Bergin and Max H. Fisch. Ithaca: Cornell UP, 1958.

Vitanza, Victor J. "Editor's Preface, Dedication, and Acknowledgments." *Writing Histories of Rhetoric*. Ed. Victor J. Vitanza. Carbondale: Southern Illinois UP, 1994. vii–xii.

Winterowd, Ross. "I.A. Richards, Literary Theory, and Romantic Composition." *Rhetoric Review* 8 (Fall 1992): 59–78.

Wollstonecraft, Mary. *A Vindication of the Rights of Women*. Ed. Carol H. Poston. New York: W.W. Norton, 1975.

Wordsworth, William. "Preface to the Edition of 1815." *English Romantic Writers*. Ed. David Perkins. New York: Harcourt, Brace, and World, 1967. 333–35.

13 The Kabbalah as a Theory of Rhetoric: Another Suppressed Epistemology

Steven B. Katz
North Carolina State University

> *Identification is affirmed with earnestness precisely because there is division. Identification is compensatory to division. If men were not apart from one another, there would be no need for the rhetorician to proclaim their unity. If men were wholly and truly of one substance, absolute communication would be of man's very essence. It would not be an ideal, as it now is, partly embodied in material conditions and partly frustrated by these same conditions; rather, it would be as natural, spontaneous, and total as with those ideal prototypes of communication, the theologian's angels, or "messengers."*
>
> —Kenneth Burke, *A Rhetoric of Motives*, 22

Burke's vision here of a rhetoric in which all things are connected not only in spirit, or consubstantially, but materially, in substance, perhaps reveals the sublimated desire of rhetoric to be not just referential, a bridge over the gap created by consciousness between mind and reality, or merely eloquent, a harmonious medium paralleling the unity of the universe (Cicero, *De Oratore* III), but rather a transcendent material in which the experience of language *is* the experience of the universe. Operating against the fragmentation of empiricism and the duality of the rational cogito, such a rhetoric would be based on an epistemology in which matter and form are identical, the metaphysical is written in the physical, and language and reality are one. Such a rhetoric, based on an ancient epistemology, exists. I refer not to Platonic or Sophistic rhetorics, although traces of this epistemology *may* be found in these rhetorical philosophies; nor do I refer to deconstruction, but rather to its philosophical opposite which it thus ironically resembles. I refer to the mystical theory of language and knowledge found in the Kabbalah, which Harold Bloom called "a theory of rhetoric" (18).

In addition to the Hebrew Scriptures and centuries of commentary on it in the Talmud and the Midrash in which a whole tradition of hermeneutic theory and practice is developed and contained (Hartman and Burdick), the Kabbalah constitutes an ancient Jewish rhetoric which, although severed from the main trunk of that liturgical tradition, nevertheless continues to inform it. Although when we speak of the Kabbalah we primarily refer to a collection of more or less unrelated texts composed by Moses de Leon, Moses Codovero, Abraham Abulafia, and Isaac Luria between the 12th and 16th centuries (see Scholem, *Origins of the Kabbalah*; *Kabbalah*; *On the Kabbalah and Its Symbolism* for an "archeology"), by *Kabbalah* we also refer to the ancient tradition in Judaism of mysterious pre- or neo-Pythagorean theory, mystical readings of holy texts, and allegorical lore passed down orally to only a few initiates as secret knowledge until the Middle Ages, when it was committed to writing. The word *Kabbalah* literally means "tradition."

Existing outside the main body of Jewish practice (and yet informing that practice), the Kabbalah constitutes among other things a nonrational, nonempirical, yet metaphysical and material theory of language and knowledge that explicitly addresses questions central in rhetoric concerning the relationship between language, thought, and reality. It does so, however, in a way not treated in any other classical rhetoric—certainly not that of Plato, nor even that of the Sophists. Whereas Plato believed that essence existed but could only be apprehended by the rational intellect, thus rendering rhetoric secondary if of any importance in obtaining knowledge, and the Sophists generally denied the possibility of knowing essence, rendering rhetoric a nonrational basis of probable knowledge, these Jewish "rhetoricians" believed that essence is embodied in the material substance of language itself, in the shapes and sounds of Hebrew letters (a position Plato ridicules in the *Cratylus*), rendering *language* the mystical basis of empirical reality and all true knowledge of it.

Thus, Kabbalah as a rhetoric posits a direct connection between the transcendental realm of truth and language; in this tradition, the material substance (shape and sound) of language itself does not attempt to imitate essence, as Plato charged in the *Cratylus*, but *embodies* it. That is, in the mystical tradition of Jewish rhetoric, the Platonic and Sophistic traditions seem to be combined (or not yet separated): The transcendental not only exists, but can be apprehended through language and the senses, although with great difficulty. In fact, the epistemology of the Kabbalah seems to fall exactly between that of the first rationalists—Plato and Aristotle—and their opposition—the first skeptical empiricists, the Sophists— though significantly it shares elements of both and perhaps in the diaspora of Western culture represents an epistemology that is a manifestation of a historical phase in an evolutionary spiral of philosophic thought.

In this chapter I suggest that the Kabbalah represents another nonrational philosophy of rhetoric, one that has been suppressed by rationalist and empiricist philosophies both in Western civilization and in the religion that spawned it. The Kabbalah as a theory of rhetoric may provide us with a glimpse into an ancient epistemology in Western culture that connects the subjective with the transcendent, the personal with the universal—an epistemology in which the individual seeks to experience and know the transcendental directly through the sensory experience of language. Although the Kabbalah actually entails several variations of a philosophy of language (see Idel; Bloom 37–43), my purpose here is to briefly sketch the epistemological thread that unites the various books of the Kabbalah as a theory of rhetoric, its relationship to other theories of rhetoric, and the implications of this rhetoric for understanding a different conception and use of language. To understand the Kabbalah as a theory of rhetoric, I begin with some epistemological considerations.

The dominant assumption in pre-Socratic Greek philosophy was that the word and the thing were one and the same (Kerferd 73). Thus, in the *Cratylus*, Plato explored the theory of origin and nature of language that the shape and/or sound of letters and words were directly related to (or, more accurately, imitated) the objects they represent (423e). However, this is a theory that Plato had Socrates quickly dismiss as inconsistent and ludicrous (esp. 422b–440d). For Plato, there *was* a one-to-one correspondence between word and thing, but it was between *name as visual sign* (logos) and essence (or idea) only, *not shape or sound* (389d–393d).

For Sophists such as Gorgias, on the other hand, there was apparently no correspondence at all between reality and language, either as visual sign or sound (Kerferd 98). For Gorgias and Sophists generally, contradictory statements about phenomena were possible and equally valid (although not necessarily true), precisely because words bear no physical resemblance or direct relationship to the properties of phenomenon they purport to describe or explain. Thus, G. B. Kerferd believed that Gorgias' dictum, "Nothing exists; if it exists it can't be understood; if it is understood, it can't be communicated," is a problem of predication. The problem, Kerferd argued, is not whether some thing is or is not, but what characteristics it possesses, and how we know it. Contrary to Plato, Gorgias believed we do so through language. As Richard Leo Enos demonstrated (78–83), the power of poetic language to create the sensory "illusion" of attributes in a powerfully persuasive simulacrum of reality, not through referential verisimilitude but through subjective response to the metaphorical and musical property of words, is *necessary* for belief, knowledge, and action.

But a direct relationship between letters, names, words, and essence is the basic epistemology of the Kabbalah. In the Sefirotic and Ecstatic Kabbalistic tradition of Codovero and Abulafia, respectively, God in one fashion or another created the world using language (see Idel); because of this fact, through a process of ontic reversal (Katz 31), these "rhetoricians" believed it is possible to directly experience and in some cases affect the metaphysical realm that is real but invisible, hidden, unknowable except through the mystical experience of language. Just as Cassirer claimed that language embodies and contains in its sensuous form the emotional impetus of the original drive that motivated its articulation in consciousness, the Kabbalists claim that all reality, all creation, is a language that bears the imprint of God's will and desire. The universe is what is left, the smoking residue of God having spoken. Turning deconstruction on its head, Kabbalists hold that the whole universe is written—but by God.

The major difference between the Kabbalists and deconstructionists, then, would seem to be the positing of a Final Transcendental Signified. But in the mystical tradition of the Kabbalah, no such notion exists—at least not the way we have understood it. The notion of God as Final Transcendental Signified, at least in part, rests on rational/empirical conceptions of God as anthropomorphic—as having attributes. In fact, in Jewish mysticism, not only can God *only* be named metaphorically, as *Ein-Sof*—that which is infinite—but is often understood as *Ayin*—Nothingness. As Bloom pointed out (24–25), this is an ironic subversion of traditional religious doctrine (which so often is used to clothe mystical experience in canonical garb [Scholem, *Major Trends* 9]). In the Kabbalah, God is not a Final Transcendental Signified, for there is nothing to refer to but more signifiers for God, who remains hidden, invisible in the language of creation—in the "differance," if you will. For Jewish mystics, God is in everything, and thus everything is at once a signifier and a signified in an endless play of signification. And yet for Jewish mystics, this interplay of signifiers, like language itself, constitutes a metaphysical reality, is located in the transcendental realm, which is only apprehended through the *mystical* experience of language.

This philosophy is the result of centuries of speculation that we need to discuss briefly here to make sense of the Kabbalah as a theory of rhetoric. For despite the heightened awareness and attention to the word—both written and oral—throughout the Jewish theological and cultural tradition, and ethnocentric theories concerning the divine origin of the Hebrew alphabet (see Ettisch 1–8; Scholem, *Major Trends* 17), the metaphysical basis for the Kabbalah is perhaps not only the self-conscious literacy we find in contemporary theories of literature and language. Rather, the metaphysical basis for the Kabbalah is also an answer to questions concerning the nature of essences and attributes and their relation to human language and knowledge. For Jewish, Christian, and Muslim philosophers in the Middle Ages confronted with rationalistic Hellenic philosophy, particularly Neoplatonic and Aristotelian, these questions revolved around issues of the "physical" nature of God, and how we can know and describe it.

For the Mutakallimun, an Islamic sect who followed the atomistic philosophy of Democritus, there was no distinction between essences and attributes because everything is composed of material atoms that impinge on each other directly. But if God has the different eternal attributes we ascribe, and essence and attributes are materially related, then there is either more than one God, or God is not of one essence (Husik xxiii). Both possibilities raised unresolvable questions concerning the nature of God because they flew in the face of monotheism—religious and philosophical (Husik xxiii). Although this theosophy was adopted by some Jewish philosophers, it was rejected out of hand by the Medieval Jewish rationalists, most notably Maimonides (Husik xxiii), who followed Aristotle's reasoning concerning the necessity of a prime mover that moves but is itself unmoved. Thus, Maimonides posited the notion of an objective, transcendent God who in essence is different from us, is a pure form, or actuality, whose sphere is external to the universe, and whose being is materially unrelated to the attributes of the sublunar world and is not to be found in it (Husik xxxi–xxxviii).

According to Isaac Husik (xxxvii–xlvi), Aristotle's view was, incorrectly it turns out, supplemented in other Jewish philosophies by a neo-Platonic doctrine of emanations, in which God is identified with the universe and in contact with the material world indirectly through the operation of linked spheres (Husik xxvii–xxviii). In a sense, in the neo-Platonic emanistic theory of Plotinus, the void that is opened in traditional religion (Scholem, *Major Trends* 13) between logos and the material world is filled (and thus replaced) by spheres that are all materially related, one impinging on another from the supralunar to the sublunar. The neo-Platonic emanistic doctrine is similar to the Kabbalah (see Katz 24–32)—*except* in the all-important respect of the primary role of language (Idel 50; Bloom 25).

The question of the nature and relationship of essences and attributes, then, can be understood to hinge on (or entail) different epistemologies of language and knowledge. In the philosophy of the Sophists, Essence either does not exist, is unknowable, or uncommunicable; this makes language all important, for it is the only basis of knowledge, albeit probable, relative, and uncertain. In materialistic philosophies based on Democritus, there is no distinction between essence and attributes, which results in "the multiplication of essence" (Husik xxvi) and so renders language contradictory, problematic, and useless. In the dualistic philosophies of Plato and Aristotle, essences and attributes are separate, and thus essence is knowable through the rational intellect alone (cf. Husik xxxv–xxxvi, xlv). For Plato, rhetoric was therefore rendered unimportant in obtaining "true" knowledge of ideal forms, and only good for communicating that knowledge after the fact (see *Phaedrus*); for Aristotle, style was a "necessary evil" "owing to a defect in our hearers" (*Rhetoric* III, I:8–9).

The major difference between Plato and Aristotle, of course, is that Aristotle did not believe in a transcendental reality that corresponds to universal concepts (Husik xli). That is, Aristotle denied the existence of ideal forms, placing dialectic and rhetoric on equal footing and shifting the ground of certainty to apodictic or scientific knowledge of empirical reality (*Rhetoric* I). But the Kabbalistic understanding of essence and attributes differs considerably from either the atomistic philosophy found in Islamic influences on Jewish philosophy, the Aristotelian view found in rational Jewish philosophies such as Maimonides, or the Sophistic view which, not surprisingly, does not appear to be represented in religious philosophy where the existence of a transcendental realm of experience is more or less assumed. In fact, there is no distinction between essence and attribute for the Kabbalists (Scholem, *Major Trends* 11), for the problem was conceived from an entirely different ontological basis than the atomists: that of the mystical unity of essence and attributes *in* and through the language of the *Sefiroth*, which constitutes a rhetoric of the transcendental.

Found most developed in the *Sefer ha-Zohar*, or the *Book of Splendor*, the "central work of classical Kabbalah" (Bloom 24) written by Moses de Leon in Guadalajara circa 1280–86, the Ten *Sefiroth* "became the divine emanations by which all reality is metaphysically connected and structured" (Bloom 22; cf. Scholem *Major Trends* 10–11; Katz 30–31):

> In [Neo-platonic] Plotinus, emanation is a process *out from* God, but in Kabbalah the process must take place *within* God Himself. An even more crucial difference from Neo-platonism is that all Kabbalistic theories of emanation are also theories of language. As Scholem says, "the God who manifests Himself is the God who expresses Himself," which means that the *Sefirot* are primarily *language*, attributes of God that need to be described by the various names of God when he is at work in creation. The *Sefirot* are complex figurations of God, tropes or turns of language that *substitute* for God. (Bloom 25)

Thus, says Bloom, the *Sefiroth* "are not allegorical personifications, which is what all popular manuals of Kabbalah reduce them to, and though they have extraordinary potency, this is a power of signification rather than what we customarily think of as magic" (25–26). What one gets in the *Sefiroth* is an interplay of signifiers situated in a transcendental realm, everyone reflecting in the other a hint of a divine presence that is hidden in them all (see Bloom 26–32). Language does not refer to a defined Final Transcendental Signified, but to other signs, which are both material and "transcendental" (cf. Katz 8).

A further explication of the Ten *Sefiroth* is not as important here (see Bloom 27–47) as the linguistic philosophy underlying this conception of them in the Kabbalah. If essence and attribute are unified, not atomistically, but metaphysically, linguistically, essence is represented in language not through imitation, but through the actual material substance of language, in the shapes and sounds of letters, names, words, and their numerical equivalents. In the rhetorical philosophy of the Kabbalah, essence and attribute are joined in language, out of which both words and worlds are made (Katz 16). Thus, "the letters are understood to constitute a mesocosmos that enables operations that can bridge the gap between the human—or the material—and the divine" (Idel 43, cf. 47). This metaphysics of letters is also discussed, in a more esoteric way, by Ettisch, who investigated the ancient belief that the Hebrew alphabet physically embodies astronomical knowledge of the stars.

For the Kabbalists in general, language is accorded a special ontological status, at once material and transcendental, at once physical and metaphysical, at once attribute and essence (Idel 44). This is perhaps best illustrated by the practice in ecstatic Kabbalism that centers on God's name in Hebrew, which is literally (physically) unsayable; it thus embodies the unknowableness of God, God's essence (as *Ein-Sof*, infinity, or *Ayin*, nothingness) in the material substance of language itself, which paradoxically expresses the transcendental in the ineffable (cf. Katz 16). As Katz demonstrated, paradoxical language, which was so problematic for Islamic and Jewish philosophers committed to an atomistic philosophy of essence and attributes, is necessary for this kind of mystical experience.

If essence *is* somehow embodied in the paradoxical substance of language, then the transcendental could theoretically be known through the sensory experience of language, although as Katz discussed, mystics always warn of the difficulty of this process (cf. Scholem, *Major Trends* 14–15). The contemplation of sounds, the deconstructing and permutating of words and paradoxical phrases, according to Katz, is supposed to lead the adept to a nonrational knowledge of essences! Through language the mystic as rhetor seeks to know the transcendental subjectively, through personal sense experience. In the mystical philosophy, unlike religion, personal experience within the context of a set of beliefs becomes just as important as doctrinal knowledge (Scholem, *Major Trends* 3–10). But this experience as knowledge is highly problematic and difficult to communicate, prove, or use, precisely because it is highly personal, subjective. Ultimately, this rhetoric is, paradoxically, a philosophy of nonrational, nonreferential experience, a signification of the unknowable.

Perhaps it is for this reason more than any other that the nonreferential, nonrational use of language has been ignored, suppressed, or dismissed in rhetoric by rational and empirical philosophies—despite the fact that certain aspects of mysticism may be retained, for example, in poetry as the affective experience of truth. Mysticism, even Jewish mysticism, may also form part of the foundation for other epistemologies that have influenced rhetoric, for example, the Pythagorean via Plato, although right now this is mere speculation on my part. Perhaps there are also ideological reasons that the nonrational, nonreferential use of language has been excluded from rhetoric. Although knowledge of this use of language is difficult to teach, communicate, or attain, and was meant only for initiates, in this "rhetorical tradition" the function of language is nothing less than the "transformation of consciousness" through the disruption of "the normal categories of thinking" (Katz 6, 7). (It is questionable whether Foucault would think that any language is free enough from any episteme to disrupt consciousness, however, or whether something like a koan would itself set the boundaries that would "institutionalize" and so circumscribe and linguistically limit thought—although perhaps by denying the referential and social functions of language as "commentary," perhaps mystical language escapes this epistemological prison.)

For Jewish mystics, as for the sophists, language is epistemic:

> In that the mechanisms of knowing *necessarily* impinge on, even create, the substantive knowledge gained in mystical experience no less than in the more mundane epistemological contexts, language is a, if not the, key issue in re-forming

those structures required for obtaining mystical awareness. Language creates, when used by the mystical adept . . . the operative process through which the essential epistemic channels that permit mystical forms of knowing and being are accessible. (Katz 8)

But for Jewish mystics, unlike the Sophists, there is a direct, physical connection between a sign and what it represents. And for the mystics, unlike Plato, these essences, as *Ein Sof* or *Ayin*, are knowable only through the language that embodies them, although that knowing is imperfect. The mystical use of language thus undermines and repudiates not only rational but empirical modes of knowledge, whereas it may make other kinds of rhetorical knowing possible, and therefore perhaps deserves closer inspection by rhetoricians.

In this rhetoric, language "does not say something, does not tell something, but it does something" (Katz 12). This, then, is "symbolic action" made material. For in this rhetoric, language is not only about transcendental reality; it is understood as a part of reality, and in some of the more extreme Kabbalistic theories can therefore be used not only to affect the consciousness speaker or hearer, but also to affect the cosmic order itself (Katz 21–24). Unlike the popular understanding of language in magic, however, language in the Kabbalah is not generally understood to evoke a change in physical reality, but rather in metaphysical or "spiritual reality," which (although it may in this regard not be different from "social reality" created by epistemic rhetorics) remains nonempirical, nonrational, and can thus only be intuited and experienced subjectively. Creating or changing physical reality through language is something only a master rhetorician, such as God, would be able to do.

Whether one believes in a metaphysical realm or not, whether God is a transcendental being or socially constructed, created rather than creating, the Kabbalah as a suppressed theory of rhetoric can inform our understanding of another, hidden aspect of the rhetorical tradition. This ancient rhetorical theory, suppressed by rational thinkers both in Judaism and in Western culture generally, shows us a philosophy in which experience rather than referential or rational signification and thought is the focal point and primary concern of its adherents, and reveals an epistemological vision in which all things are connected not only *in spirit* but, as Burke might say, in substance.

WORKS CITED

Aristotle. *The Rhetoric.* Trans. W. Rhys Roberts. Vol. 2 of *The Complete Works of Aristotle.* 2 vols. Ed. Jonathan Barnes. Princeton: Princeton UP, 1984. 2152–69.

Bloom, Harold. *Kabbalah and Criticism.* New York: Seabury P, 1975.

Burke, Kenneth. *A Rhetoric of Motives.* New York: Prentice Hall, 1952.

Cassirer, Ernst. Vol. 1 of *The Philosophy of Symbolic Forms.* 3 vols. *Language.* Trans. Ralph Manheim. New Haven: Yale UP, 1955.

Cicero, Marcus Tullius. *De Oratore* Book III. *De Oratore Book III, De Fato, Paradoxa Stoicorum,*

Partitiones Oratoriae. Trans. E.W. Sutton and H. Rackham. Cambridge, MA: Loeb-Harvard UP, 1942. 1–185.

Enos, Richard Leo. *Greek Rhetoric Before Aristotle.* Prospect Heights, IL: Waveland, 1993.

Ettisch, Ernst. *The Hebrew Vowels and Consonants as Symbols of Ancient Astronomic Concepts.* Trans. Harry Zohn. Boston: Branden, 1987.

Foucault, Michel. "The Discourse on Language." *The Archaeology of Knowledge.* New York: Pantheon, 1972. 215–37.

Hartman, Geoffrey H., and Sanford Budick. *Midrash and Literature.* New Haven, CT: Yale UP, 1986.

Husik, Isaac. *A History of Mediaeval Jewish Philosophy.* New York: Macmillan, 1916.

Idel, Moshe. "Reification of Language in Jewish Mysticism." *Mysticism and Language.* Ed. Steven T. Katz. New York: Oxford UP, 1992. 42–79.

Katz, Steven T. "Mystical Speech and Mystical Meaning." *Mysticism and Language.* Ed. Steven T. Katz. New York: Oxford UP, 1992. 3–41.

Kerferd, G. B. *The Sophistic Movement.* Cambridge: Cambridge UP, 1981.

Plato. *Cratylus.* Trans. Benjamin Jowett. *The Collected Dialogues of Plato.* Eds. Edith Hamilton and Huntington Cairns. New York: Bollingen Foundation-Pantheon, 1961. 421–74.

———. *Phaedrus.* Trans. R. Hackforth. *The Collected Dialogues of Plato.* Eds. Edith Hamilton and Huntington Cairns. New York: Bollingen Foundation-Pantheon, 1961. 475–525.

Scholem, Gershom. *Kabbalah.* Jerusalem: Keter, 1974.

———. *Major Trends in Jewish Mysticism.* New York: Schocken, 1941.

———. *On the Kabbalah and Its Symbolism.* Trans. Ralph Manheim. New York: Schocken, 1965.

———. *Origins of the Kabbalah.* Trans. Allan Arkush. Jewish Publication Society, 1987.

——— (Trans). *Zohar: The Book of Splendor. Basic Readings from the Kabbalah.* New York: Schocken, 1949.

14 Expressivism, Pleasure, and the Magical Medicine of Gorgias

T. R. Johnson
University of Louisville

Although Composition regularly claims the empowerment of students as a primary goal, no one has effectively theorized the internal experience of such empowerment—that is, no one has theorized increases in literacy as keen pleasure. All of us have chosen careers in the teaching of writing, I suspect, because we know that the process of writing, when it is going well and enlarging our powers, can yield an almost holy exuberance so delightful that we spend our professional lives, in various ways, trying to make that feeling available to students. In fact, the way many of us evaluate our own work as writers during the composing process is to ask ourselves, "How does this feel—good and right and strong, or not so much?" The issue of pleasure in writing then is crucial, and yet it remains untheorized.

In order to construct such a theory, Composition must begin by reconsidering Expressivism, a rhetoric that addresses the internal, emotional experience of the writer and that has sustained harsh, virtually dismissive criticism for roughly 15 years now. Allegedly, Expressivists mystify the composing process and disempower students by fostering the naive belief that texts materialize spontaneously and magically, like rabbits out of hats, instead of through the various institutional and disciplinary machineries and cultural conventions that shape the composing process. By those who dismissively equate Expressivism with "magical writing," literacy or empowerment is cast as increased fluency in discourse conventions.

However, if I am to define *literacy* as more than fluency in the academic discourses that are of such limited consequence in the lives of most of my students, I need to reimagine Expressivism, finding new precedents and fresh

119

warrants for this rhetoric, populating this tradition with new figures. Most specifically, I need to develop a theory of writing-as-magical that is more useful than the one so negatively associated with Expressivism today; one that will help me stimulate my students' appreciation of advances in literacy and that will help me to teach writing as the ecstatic process that I know it can be. Ultimately, I must key these revisions of Expressivism to reflect an awareness of the circulations of power through the social field, for the main charge against Expressivism and the magical orientation to writing is that they neglect the issue of social power.

Literacy or rhetorical sophistication, in addition to meaning fluency in discourse conventions, is also equated with critical consciousness, an ability to read, interpret, and judge that stands in binary opposition to magical consciousness—the naive belief that texts and meanings and events spontaneously appear, and that power merely circulates in ways no individual can influence. Rhetorician Covino, however, recently offered strong warrants for destabilizing this binary, for valuing rhetoric-as-magic. To wit: As rhetoricians, we all believe that words have the power to shape reality, and therefore we bear a striking resemblance to magicians and sorcerers who, historically, claim precisely the same power for their chants, spells, and incantations. Rhetoric, Covino suggested, can recover a rich history by examining its close intertwining with magic ("Magic and/as Rhetoric" 350). In particular, I recast literacy as the "magical" power to influence reality through language, and, still more particularly, I appropriate this "magical" theme in the history of rhetoric for Expressivism—because the feeling that one's writing has the power to alter, however slightly, socially constructed "reality" must be a feeling of exquisite pleasure, what Expressivists traditionally label "inspiration" and place at the center of their values.

Rather than theorize magic or inspiration and revise Expressivism in ways that might reduce this rich experiential domain to a generalized formulae, I suggest we research and teach rhetorical performances that foreground these themes. We could begin with any number of figures, from Protagoras to Cornelius Agrippa to William Blake to Helene Cixous, but I plan to restrict myself to Gorgias today because his work marks the earliest engagement of these themes in the rhetorical tradition and is probably most familiar to an audience of rhetoricians.

In his *Encomium of Helen*, Gorgias explicitly claimed for language the power to transform reality:

> Speech is a powerful lord, which by means of the finest and most invisible body, effects the divinest works . . .
>
> The power of incantation is wont to beguile the soul and persuade it and alter it by witchcraft.
>
> The effect of speech upon the condition of the soul is comparable to the effect of medicaments upon the condition of the body. (Bizzell and Herzberg 41)

Given these early, powerful claims for rhetoric-as-magic, Gorgias seems an appropriate figure through which to stage an expansion of Expressivist theory and an opening for discussions of writing as magic and pleasure.

Many in our field primarily know Gorgias from the Platonic dialogue named after him. Although a Sophist, a great orator and deeply revered teacher of oratory, Socrates got the better of Gorgias in the dialogue, persuading him that rhetoric is inferior to philosophy because rhetoric only produces belief or probability, not knowledge or truth. In the dialogue, Gorgias implicitly conceded that truth exists. Historically, however, the actual Gorgias de Leontini did not accept the possibility of any foundational, absolute truth or knowledge. In one of the fragments of Gorgias's writing that survived, he claimed, "There is no Truth, and even if there were, we could not know it, and, even if we could know it, we could not articulate it." Some have recently taken that remark as precedent for the radical localism, pragmatism, and pluralism favored by our own period in the aftermath of traditional philosophy's quest for foundational or transcendent truths. In other words, the philosophic program launched by Plato having come to an end, we might return to Gorgias, as Crowley and others have, as an important precedent for the poststructuralist era.

Gorgias' aversion to generalized truth also makes him a predecessor of contemporary Expressivists. Elbow, Macrorie, and other leading Expressivists produce terrifically popular, practical handbooks, something like "lore," for the successful day-to-day execution of writing tasks. They do not, however, publish generalized theory. As Rohman asserted in his early statement of Expressivist theory, "Prewriting," general principles held in advance of a particular writing situation can often impede rather than facilitate the composing process, presumably by deflecting attention away from the nuances that distinguish the context at hand from others. Although one may associate this theoretical position with a naive aversion to theory, with an anti-intellectualism, with a lowly absorption in the merely practical, one may also hear in it echoes of Gorgias and, for that matter, Derrida. Instead of neglecting the social contexts of writing, as so many charge Expressivism, we might recast Expressivism as practicing a degree of sensitivity to contexts that forbids generalized theory. This hypersensitivity to context may smack of mystification and allow a naive, asocial conception of the writer's "true self" to flourish, as many insist that among Expressivists it has; but to correct this, we must only examine very closely figures who engage these themes.

Gorgias's interest in the magical power of language centered, specifically, on the power of language to heal. Medical historian Pedro Entralgo wrote, "[Gorgias maintained that] verbal persuasion, the medicament of the persuasive word, not only dominates the will, but modifies the entire *physis*, body and soul, of the man upon whom it acts" (99). Although no one knows quite how Gorgian performances worked, he is known to have made such abundant use of rhythm, alliteration, repetition, assonance, and rhyme that some cast him as kind of incantatory jingle writer, whose performances literally spellbound the audience and aroused in them "intense sensual pleasure" (Bizzell and Herzberg 38). Arousing pleasure in an audience presumably arouses pleasure in the rhetor, too, especially because many classical rhetoricians maintained that in order to move an audience to experience a certain emotion, the rhetor first had to experience it in him- or herself. Gorgias's practice of rhetoric-as-magical medicine, then, puts us on the trail of a theory of writing and pleasure.

We might speculate that Gorgias practiced something like an ancient version of the Rogerian or Laingian psychotherapy so important to Expressivists in Composition during the ascendance of their rhetoric in the mid-1960s. These therapists supposed that the neurosis and misery that afflicted their patients stemmed from a division between the patient's self and his or her body. Thus, these therapists aimed to bring about a cathartic reintegration of the patient with his or her body, regrounding the alienated, defensive static ego in material, sensory experience; emphasizing the self as a process among the larger processes of the external world. The split between the ailing subject and his or her body sponsors in turn the split between language and the felt sense of meaning, and so these therapists sought ultimately to foster the experience of language and meaning as richly interconnected, very much as experienced in magical incantations and performative utterances. It must be emphasized that none of these psychotherapists explicitly aimed at fostering a naive belief in magic. Rather, they sought precisely the sort of social empowerment for their patients that felt like inspiration or magic, and that was the opposite of the madness that threatened them. Rogers, in particular, maintained that the sort of integration toward which he hoped to lead his patients came to these patients as a rich pleasure, a kind of euphoria of "self-actualization," a cathartic awakening or rebirth.

Can the therapeutic, spellbinding pleasure that Gorgias generated in audiences differ very deeply from what Rogers sought for his patients and what Expressivists seek for their students?

Gorgias's interest in magic led posthumously to his marginalization. Plato and the mainstream philosophic tradition that followed him lumped magic and rhetoric together and dismissed them as some combination of intellectual quackery and criminal dishonesty, the province of fools and charlatans. Magic and rhetoric produce only illusions, not truths. The entire discourse of rhetoric nearly disappeared in this general purge of magic, only surviving as an area of inquiry at all thanks to Isocrates's careful disentangling of it from the discourse of magic (see Deromilly). That Gorgias conflated the two, as demonstrated in the line about the "power of incantation . . . to beguile the soul . . . by witchcraft," perhaps explains in large part why this work has generated comparatively little interest among scholars. Magicians, in general, serve as the scapegoats against which intellectuals identify themselves, the Other against which they build and perpetuate a discourse community. Curiously, the word for magician (*pharmakeus*) also means scapegoat (Neel), suggesting that Gorgias was always already operating in the position of the Other, the outsider who wandered from town to town and made a home nowhere. As Diogenes Laertius is reputed to have said, "He astonished the Athenians with the *strangeness* of his diction."

Perhaps we can go so far as to suggest that Gorgias' interest in what we would today call *psychotherapy* stems from his own flirtation with "madness." In classical Greece, the mad, although outcast, spat on, and stoned, were also seen as carrying a special wisdom, a special intimacy with the gods (Dodds 64). Poets and divine seers sought to spread therapeutically through their audiences precisely the cathartic, frenzied fits of divine possession exemplified and feared in the "mad." Plato banished all poets from his ideal republic precisely for this practice. And, presumably, Gorgias, too, would have been banished, given the "intense sensual pleasure" he stirred in audiences.

Expressivists in Composition also may be seen as always already working from a position of exile. Even during the 1960s, their period of sharpest ascendance, they operated in a spirit of subversion and reform. A classic of the period, Macrorie's *Uptaught*, identified its purpose in the opening pages very closely with those of the student protestors who have generated enough campus unrest to warrant the intervention of the National Guard. Shortly after *Uptaught*, Elbow published *Writing Without Teachers*, the title of which speaks for itself. Twenty years later, Expressivism is more marginalized than ever, assumed to be a "meaningless concept" (Harris) and an all-but-dead tradition (McCarthy and Fishman), almost as if the institution has exacted a degree of vengeance on this prodigal strand of its discourse.

The Expressivist, accused of ignoring social contexts, might, on the other hand, be only too aware of them, consciously choosing to drift toward the margins, to the position of Other, where one risks the label of madness, but stands to gain the status of sorceress or magician. As Clement reminded, the Other is always flagged as either magical or mad, and for the Expressivist and for Gorgias, these are the proper stakes of writing, the proper stakes to live by.

If Gorgias and the Expressivists share an interest in writing as a therapeutic pleasure that inclines them toward magic (the last chapter of Elbow's *Writing With Power* is called "Writing and Magic"), and if both share an interest in radically contextual ways of knowing, and both are marginalized, how might we begin to synthesis these themes into coherent and manageable pedagogy?

The most ambitious sociology of magic recently produced—Daniel O'Keefe's *Stolen Lightning*—brings these ideas together and clarifies them very usefully. O'Keefe theorized that magic always occurs as a discourse in dissent from the community's mainstream religion, a symbolic mechanism by which individuals achieve a degree of difference or autonomy from the community. O'Keefe charted the development of magical phenomenon through a sequence of steps: first, during dramatic group experience, a group of people becomes conscious of itself as a community, with each person identifying this group feeling or *mana* feeling in each of the other persons. The group then symbolizes these feelings with *mana* objects, around which beliefs and rituals soon accumulate. Once these beliefs and rituals become systematized, we have a religion. Religion then is a kind of symbolic representation of a particular group's experience of itself. Magic occurs when tensions in the group produce a subgroup, people who wrench from the religion fragments of the *mana* objects, appropriating elements of the symbols, rituals and myths, recombining them into a new order to signify the subgroup's divergence from the dominant majority. Magic is always subversive, always used to signal and establish an "outside" position.

Poststructuralist critical theory has debated long and hard as to whether or not the subaltern can speak, whether or not an actual position of otherness can exist articulately. And O'Keefe's theory of magic as a mixing and matching, a scrambling of hegemonized codes, seems to provide precisely the sort of model for a rhetoric of the Other or underclass that critical theorists have sought in a variety of places (Butler in transvestites, Kristeva in avante-garde literature, and Deleuze and Guattari in schizophrenia, to name a few). To provide a voice for the subaltern in Composition—for example, the basic writer—O'Keefe's idea of magic seems a manageable synthesis of these.

This Magical Expressivist rhetoric is therapeutic and empowering because, according to O'Keefe, magic is the primary way that the institution of the individual self is maintained: Magic counteracts the power of the social institutions that might otherwise overwhelm and erase the subject's experience of self. The academy can pose such a threat, especially to the beginning student or minority student. Specifically, as much as we might resist this notion, some students' writing actually deteriorates through the course of English 101: The exposure to strict rules of correctness and absolutized discourse conventions provokes in them a distrust of their own linguistic intuitions, their ability to perceive error, and their physical felt sense of what sounds good (see McCutcheon et al). In these cases, the academic institution overwhelms the student's experience of him- or herself as a user of language, making the student feel that writing and speaking are nerve wracking, miserable, perhaps even impossible activities. The anxiety can begin to scramble his or her thoughts to the degree that the student feels he or she is slipping into madness. Such a student needs fresh experience of his or her own literate power, or magic, lest the student ultimately be driven out of the institution, if not driven mad by it. More humbly, these students need a reverse rhetoric if they are to learn anything about writing, especially if they are to learn to love writing. They need assignments that invite the sorts of language play through which they can discover the powers inherent in language.

As a colorful way to introduce students to the power of language, to the ultimate possibilities of literacy and rhetorical sophistication, this Magical Expressivism seems especially useful in the Basic Writing class, where students are most apt to see themselves as Other in relation to the writing situations and discourses in which they find themselves and therefore are poised to construct their relation to writing as either magical or mad, ecstatic or miserable.

By looking to the age-old overlap between magic and rhetoric, as it occurred with Gorgias and numerous others, our field begins to provide Expressivism with a much richer legacy than many in Composition have recently imagined for it. What is more, it opens up fresh ways to talk about writing as rich, empowering pleasure, which drastically increases the chances that our students will fall in love with it and continue to reflect on it and practice it long after they have left our classrooms.

WORKS CITED

Bizzell, Patricia and Bruce Herzberg. *The Rhetorical Tradition*. Boston: Bedford, 1990.

Butler, Judith. *Gender Trouble: Feminism and the Subversion of Identity*. New York: Routledge, 1990.

Clement, Catherine, and Helene Cixous. *The Newly Born Woman*. Trans. Betsy Wing. Minneapolis: U of Minnesota P, 1986.

Covino, William. "Alchemizing the History of Rhetoric: Introductions, Incantations, Spells." *Writing Histories of Rhetoric*. Ed. Victor Vitanza. Carbondale: Southern Illinois UP, 1994.

———. "Magic and/as Rhetoric." *Journal of Advanced Composition* 12, No. 1 (1992): 349–58.

———. "Magic, Literacy, and the National Enquirer." *Contending with Words: Composition and Rhetoric in a Postmodern Age*. Ed. Patricia Harkin and John Schilb. New York: MLA, 1991.

Crowley, Sharon. "Of Gorgias and Grammatology." *College Composition and Communication* 30 (1979): 278–85.

Deleuze, Gilles and Felix Guattari. *Anti-Oedipus: Capitalism and Schizophrenia*. Trans. Robert Hurley, Mark Seem, Helen Lane. Minneapolis: U of Minnesota P, 1983.

Deromilly, Jacqueline. *Magic and Rhetoric in Ancient Greece*. Cambridge: Harvard, 1975.

Dodds, E. R. *The Greeks and the Irrational*. Berkeley: U of California P, 1951.

Elbow, Peter. *Writing with Power: Techniques for Mastering the Writing Process*. London: Oxford UP, 1981.

Entralgo, Pedro Lain. *The Therapy of the Word in Classical Antiquity*. Trans. L.J. Rather and John Sharp. New Haven: Yale UP, 1970.

Harris, Jeanette. *Expressive Discourse*. Dallas: Southern Methodist UP, 1990.

Kristeva, Julia. *Revolution and Poetic Language*. Trans. Margaret Waller. New York: Columbia UP, 1982.

Macrorie, Ken. *Uptaught*. New York: Hayden, 1970.

McCutcheon, Glenda, et al. "Editing Strategies and Error Correction Basic Writers." *Written Communication* (1987): 139–54.

McCarthy, Lucille, and Stephen Fishman. "Is Expressivism Dead? Reconsidering Its Romantic Roots and Its Relation to Social Construction." *College English* (1992): 647–61.

Neel, Jasper. *Plato, Derrida, and Writing*. Carbondale: Southern Illinois UP, 1988.

O'Keefe, Daniel. *Stolen Lightning: The Social Theory of Magic*. New York: Continuum, 1982.

Rogers, Carl. *On Becoming a Person*. Boston: Houghton Mifflin, 1961.

Rohman, D. Gordon. "Pre-writing: The Stage of Discovery in the Writing Process." *College Composition and Communication* 16 (1965): 106–12.

Wagner, Julia. "Glamour and Spelling: Reclaiming Magical Thinking to the Composition Classroom." Unpublished CCCC presentation. Cincinnati, 1992.

15 Individualism or Personhood: A Battle of Locution or Rhetoric?

LuMing Mao
Miami University of Ohio

The word *individualism* and its concomitant conceptual implications often crop up in studies of other, non-Western rhetorics. This phenomenon is also true of studies of Chinese rhetoric. Namely, Chinese rhetorical practices have often been characterized as lacking individualism, as impeding or suppressing its expression or development. For example, Oliver suggested that Chinese classical rhetoric was based on an intricate system of prescribed ritual that calls for an unconditional acceptance of a hierarchical order and that suppresses, rather than encourages, individualism (91–93). In discussing Confucian rhetoric, which has served as a foundation for Chinese rhetorical practices, Oliver further suggested that Confucius's idea of lasting persuasiveness hinges on the authority of tradition rather than on a rhetor's individual ideas (137). He argued that ritual action represents a peculiarly Chinese type of rhetoric of behavior, whose basic tenet is that everyone should always adhere to expected patterns of behavior or behave in a predictable and traditional manner (143). In short, what is "missing" here is individualism or its conceptual implications.

Jumping ahead to the 1990s, one notices that Jolliffe has continued this tradition. While analyzing the social, cultural influences on Chinese rhetorical practices (267–72),[1] Jolliffe stated that "the ideal Chinese writer is a cooperative member of a collective, not a novel, independent, individual" (268), and "this subordination of the individual to the group, moreover, leads the ideal Chinese writer to employ a characteristic, recognizable mode of reasoning" (269). In associating individualism, or more precisely a lack thereof, with Chinese rhetorical practices, Jolliffe sided with, and in fact drew heavily on, Matalene's frequently cited essay—one that argues that the primary function of rhetoric for the contemporary Chinese is not so much in valuing individualism or originality as in preserving communal harmony and cohesion. Again, Chinese rhetorical practices and individualism become intertwined—only in a "negative," "deficient" way.

It is one thing for these and other similar studies (e.g., Becker 77; Erbaugh 15–16) to suggest that Chinese rhetorical practices do not favor or privilege the abstract, reified self or autonomous expression and development; that they cherish discursive practices of their community or their past tradition—suggestions that I totally agree with. It is entirely another, though, to associate the word *individualism*, negatively, with Chinese rhetorical practices, *without* unpacking the word's inherent linguistic and conceptual "baggage." Such "baggage," once unpacked, will in fact be nonapplicable to Chinese rhetorical practices—practices that are embedded in their own philosophical milieu.

So, what is this "baggage?" Three distinctive, but no less related, features come to mind. First, the word *individualism* invokes a belief in Western cultures that there is an inherent separateness of distinct persons and that its normative imperative is to become independent from others and to discover and express one's distinct attributes (Markus and Kitayama 226). Such a belief perceives an individual as a bounded, distinctive whole set both against other such wholes and against its own social and cultural background (Geertz 59). Second, the word *individualism* necessitates an exclusive dependence on one's own internal repertoire of thoughts, feelings, and action for achieving this kind of distinctiveness and independence. Although this self-dependence fits nicely, and further enhances the image of a "lone ranger," it does set itself apart from relying on any external resources such as systems of ritual action for guidance and counsel.[2] Third, the word *individualism* epitomizes a systemic, teleological model for self-actualization, a model that is "fundamentally progressive, entailing an efficient, a formal, a final cause," and "suggest[ing] a steady advance toward a *predetermined perfection*" (Ames, "The Focus-Field Self" 200–201; emphasis added). There is, in other words, a pragmatic closure in sight to this process of self-actualization.

What transpires, then, when Chinese rhetorical practices become negatively associated with individualism or with these three features? Or to put it more specifically, is it accurate or simply informative to claim that Chinese rhetorical practices lack individualism and impede its expression or development?

My answer to this question is, I am afraid, no. To develop my answer, it is necessary to review briefly *The Analects*, a collection (20 books) of Confucius's sayings put together by his disciples. *The Analects*, reflective of Confucius's rhetorical thinking, has frequently been invoked to buttress this "negative claim." Here I focus on three passages.

The claim that Chinese rhetorical practices lack individualism finds a sympathetic voice in the first paragraph of Book 7 where Confucius said: "I transmit but do not create. Being fond of the truth, I am an admirer of antiquity. I venture to be compared with our old Peng" (24).[3] This famous saying lends sufficient credence to the view that Chinese rhetorical practices value practices over innovation and privilege imitation over creation. In doing so, so goes the argument, they discourage, impede, and stifle individualism. It has also been suggested (e.g., Matalene; Jolliffe) that contemporary Chinese rhetorical practices are still very much "indebted" to this passage.

The lack-of-individualism claim is also being supported, at least at first glance, by Confucius's emphasis on following ritual action to achieve "humaneness" (rén).[4] When asked about "humaneness" in Book 12, the Master had this to say:

> To subdue oneself and return to ritual is to practice humaneness. If someone subdued himself and returned to ritual for a single day, then all under Heaven would ascribe humaneness to him. . . . Do not look at what is contrary to ritual, do not listen to what is contrary to ritual, do not speak what is contrary to ritual, and make no movement which is contrary to ritual. (44)

This kind of emphasis on an external system of codes (that is, ritual action) in one's effort to practice humaneness is at once central to Confucian rhetoric and antithetical to "individualism" (that is, to its yearning to look to one's own internal thoughts and feelings for self-actualization).

In the context of performing filial responsibility and maintaining the existing social hierarchy, Confucius said: "Avoid breaking the rules. . . . When you serve them [your parents] while they are alive do so in accordance with the rites; and after they are dead, when you bury them, do so in accordance with the rites and, when you sacrifice to them, do so in accordance with the rites" (6). Once again, what is being preached here seems to be no less than a total compliance with a prescribed set of rules and rites. If there is anything called *self-actualization*, it has already been consummated by these rules and rites. Apparently, this passage is not very keen, to say the least, on individualism.

These three passages (and other similar ones) in *The Analects* seem to have become a natural ally with the negative claim that Chinese rhetorical practices lack individualism. However, this "naturalness" is only an apparent one. That is, if there is any association between Chinese rhetorical practices and the word *individualism*, it is a nonassociation rather than a negative association. Such a nonassociation actually becomes inevitable if we examine the classical Chinese philosophy, and if we adopt a different locution that does not embody the same kind of illocutionary baggage as does the word *individualism*.

Undoubtedly, it is methodologically appealing when there appears to be some kind of direct opposition or polarity between Chinese rhetorical practices and what individualism stands for in Western cultures; this kind of opposition or polarity creates an apparent ease of exposition and subsequently lends plausibility and persuasiveness to such a *contrastive* study. Unfortunately, it is precisely this kind of easily attained opposition or polarity that tends to prevent us, so I would argue, from studying Chinese rhetorical practices in their own philosophical context, and from conceptualizing or categorizing them accordingly. Simply put, the negative application of individualism has a decontextualizing effect. Moreover, even studies of Chinese rhetorical practices sensitive to their philosophical context are still likely to be skewed or potentially contradicted by such an application. Namely, either such studies become a half-hearted exercise because the methodological appeal to direct opposition and to ease of exposition is too great to resist, or they imply problems or contradictions because, as I would suggest shortly, Chinese rhetorical practices seen in their own philosophical context cannot be adequately represented by a negative association with individualism. The representation of Chinese rhetorical practices simply calls for a shift of locution and a change of rhetoric.

It should be commonplace now to claim, I think, that there is an intricate relationship between Chinese rhetorical practices and their classical philosophy, that they have never been differentiated or codified from each other in the same way as has been the case in the West. Otherwise stated, Chinese rhetorical practices have been deeply influenced by, and indeed reflective of, their classical philosophy (Cheng 24–25; Jensen 219). What is at issue here, then, is how the classical Chinese philosophy, or more specifically Chinese ontology, provides a conceptual foundation for the relationship between the individual and his or her community in a Chinese setting.

According to Chinese ontology, form and substance cannot be separated; that is, "there cannot be pure forms without informing forms in matter, nor can there be pure matter without being informed by form" (Cheng 27). Ames also suggested that *polarism*, rather than *dualism*, constitutes a major principle of explanation in the initial formulation and evolution of classical Chinese metaphysics. He defined *polarism* as a kind of symbiosis, as "the unity of two organismic processes which require each other as a necessary condition for being what they are" ("The Meaning" 159). And each existent is, ontologically, a consequence of every other, and each existent is both self-determinate and determined by every other existent (159). It is this symbiotic unity in Chinese ontology that conceptually informs the relationship between the individual and his or her community and that underlies Chinese rhetorical practices.

What should be highlighted here is the fact that the existence of each individual requires another as an absolute condition for being what he or she is; although autogenerative and self-determinate for change and interaction, no individual absolutely determines his or her own being and relation. Cheng stated: "Each individual participates in the change and interaction of *all* individuals, not only fulfilling its individual potentiality but also advancing the totality of individual things to a more developed and more structured and newly developed and newly structured network of relations"(28).[5] Moreover, this process of self-cultivation and self-actualization through the participation of all others is always ongoing and ever expanding. Instead of embodying an internal closure or eyeing for a "predetermined perfection," it represents an individual's raison d'être without denying his or her own sense of uniqueness or identity (more about this "uniqueness" later).

This symbiotic conceptualization of the relationship between the individual and his or her community (or all other individuals) is central to Confucius's *The Analects* and to his ideas of the self (see also Tu 231–32). It should also serve as a necessary conceptual apparatus to study Chinese rhetorical practices with respect to an individual rhetor's relationship to his or her audience and community. Obviously, we are handicapped in trying to represent this symbiotic, "one part/whole" relationship by employing the word *individualism* and its above-mentioned features; they are simply nonapplicable. Hence, I suggest that it is not so much of a negative association as of a nonassociation that exists between Chinese rhetorical practices and individualism.[6]

A different locution is then needed if we want to initiate a different kind of categorization that will encode this symbiotic conceptualization and that will help generate a more accurate representation of Chinese rhetorical practices. I propose to use the word *personhood* for this purpose. More specifically, I suggest that the following threefold definition be developed.

First, the word *personhood* will emphasize that there is no inherent mutual exclusiveness between an individual and his or her community—an exclusiveness that seems to have been imposed on Chinese rhetorical practices by the word *individualism*. One of the features shaping individualism has to do with its belief that an individual is a bounded, distinct whole set both against other such wholes and against its own social and cultural background. It follows that there is a built-in antagonism between such an individual and his or her social and cultural background. On the contrary, personhood should seek to convey a symbiotic relationship between an individual and his or her community—a relationship that privileges coexistence and co-enrichment. In this sense, it is only reasonable not to claim that Chinese rhetorical practices lack individualism, but to suggest that they celebrate personhood.

Second, personhood will distinguish a unique being from an autonomous being. According to Ames, there is an unnoticed conceptual equivocation in the word *individual*; that is, *individual* can mean either one of a *kind*, or *one* of a kind ("The Focus-Field Self" 194). To quote Ames, "'individual' can refer to a single, separate and indivisible thing that, by virtue of some essential property or properties, qualifies as a member of a class. . . . Individual can alternatively also mean uniqueness: the character of a single and unsubstitutable particular" ("The Focus-Field Self" 194).

The word *individualism* seems to foster the former meaning: a single, autonomous, indivisible individual, generating notions such as "autonomy, equality, liberty, freedom, and individuated will" ("The Focus-Field Self" 194). In contrast, personhood is intended to legitimate the latter meaning: a single and unsubstitutable individual that echoes and validates Chinese ontology in that each individual is both self-determined and determined by others. After all, neither Confucius nor the classical Chinese philosophy denies the uniqueness or importance of a given individual. One ultimate objective for Confucian rhetoric is how to realize one's personhood as the heaven-endowed humaneness through the participation of all others in the community. As a result, the word individualism either misses the mark or commits the error of equivocation when it is applied negatively to Chinese rhetorical practices.

Third, personhood will stress an ongoing, lifelong process of self-cultivation and self-realization. In doing so, it separates itself from individualism which appeals to a teleological model and welcomes a pragmatic closure to the process of self-realization. Seen in this light, the Chinese rhetor's appeal to history and to the authority of the past as a mode of reasoning may not have anything to do with his or her lack of individualism, but may have everything to do with the view that one's appeal to history constitutes another way of invoking the participation of all others and of honoring the lifelong commitment to the process of self-cultivation and self-realization.[7]

Not only will this threefold definition so far developed for personhood enable us to transcend the conceptual boundary delimited by individualism, but it will also shed new light on the three previously-discussed passages from *The Analects* and on our understanding of Chinese rhetorical practices.

For example, the first "I transmit" passage does not have to be viewed now as a paradigmatic example of Confucius's direct opposition to individualism. In other words, Confucius's reverence for ancient ways does not have to be established at the expense of his readiness to discover the new. In fact, Confucius sees the ability to provide understanding of the new by keeping the old warm to be the main qualification for being a teacher (7). And there is enough textual evidence in *The Analects* itself to substantiate the suggestion that Confucius's love of antiquity may have become his means of interacting with others within the broad cultural continuity of his world. Just in Book 7, where this "I transmit" passage is taken, Confucius expresses both his love for antiquity and his desire to discover: "I am not one who knew about things at birth; I am one who through my admiration of antiquity is keen to discover things" (25).

This kind of interpretation very much echoes Chinese personhood. The individual's self-cultivation and self-actualization depend on his or her ability to discover and understand the new by interacting imaginatively with ancient ways and practices. It is part of the development of Chinese personhood. Similarly, the perceived tendency in Chinese rhetorical practices to "subordinate the self to the communal" may be nothing more than defining oneself in all others or performing the communal act of self-cultivation through the participation of all others. The reason that a number of scholars have suggested that Chinese rhetorical practices privilege a capitulation of the individual to the general will has to do with individualism, with its associated conceptualizations—as though the lens of individualism had clouded their view of Chinese personhood.

The second and third passages are equally supportive of this Chinese personhood. Undisputedly, these two passages placed a tremendous emphasis on adhering to ritual action in order to practice humaneness and filial piety. However, while shaping and regulating its participants, ritual action provides a necessary means for self-cultivation as it embodies a significant and often overlooked creative dimension (see also Tu 240, for a similar discussion of the father–son relationship). As Ames rightly observed:

> Ritual practices not only inform the participants of what is proper, they also are performed by them. They are formal structures which, to be efficacious, must be personalized and reformulated to accommodate the uniqueness and the quality of each participant. In this sense, ritual actions are a pliant body of actions for registering, developing, and displaying one's own sense of importance. ("Introduction" 153)

In the context of Chinese rhetorical practices, what has often been characterized as Chinese rhetors' apparent propensity to respect the established genres and to repeat the maxims, exempla, and analogies can now be seen as performing a set of ritual actions. Far from arresting personhood, this kind of action not only demonstrates Chinese rhetors' virtuosity with their past tradition, but provides them with a creative dimension as they reformulate and reinvent these formal structures in their process of self-cultivation and self-actualization. Once again, these characteristics in Chinese rhetorical practices, I believe, do not reveal a lack of individualism; instead, they exemplify personhood.

I phrased the title of this short essay in the form of a question: "*Individualism* or *Personhood*: A Battle of Locution or Rhetoric?" I hope that I provided my answer to this question. That is, the use of individualism over personhood or vice versa is not merely a battle of locution; it is, indeed, a battle of rhetoric. Because the word *individualism* carries with it a set of its linguistic and conceptual features unique only to Western cultures and their rhetorical practices, its negative application not only falls short of adequately describing Chinese rhetorical practices, but imposes on them a different way of thinking. On the other hand, the word *personhood* aims to convey a symbiotic relationship between an individual and his or her community. In doing so, it foregrounds the philosophical underpinning shaping Chinese rhetorical practices and restores them to their own art of persuasion, their own rhetoric indeed. Conceived as such, the word *personhood* may also have a serendipitous effect. It seems that its symbiotic characteristic parallels, to some extent, a postmodern Western perspective on self, on multiple subject positions. If so, such a parallelism will give new meaning to the dynamics of Chinese and Western rhetorical practices. In this sense, the battle of rhetoric initiated by the debate between *individualism* and *personhood* may after all be turned into a genuine quest to bring together the rhetorics of these two different cultures.

ENDNOTES

1. He dubbed such influences, in light of Kinneavy's original concept of "ethnologic," "ethnologic principles" or "ethnocomposition" (261–65).

2. It does not mean, on the other hand, that this kind of individualism excludes being responsive to the external, social environment. However, "[its] social responsiveness often, if not always, derives from the need to strategically determine the best way to express or assert the internal attributes of the self. Others, or the social situation in general, are important, but primarily as standards of reflected appraisal, or as sources that can verify and affirm the inner core of the self" (Markus and Kitayama 226).

3. It is not clear who old Peng was.

4. This word has a number of English translations, including "benevolence," "love," "goodness," and "human heartedness." I adopted Dawson's translation here largely because the word *humaneness* seems to be more inclusive.

5. Or as Kincaid suggested, "The part and the whole ultimately cannot be separated. One way to say this is that there is no part *and* whole but rather one part/whole. Each "one" defines the other, and indeed *is* the other" (332).

6. Not surprisingly, Chinese biographies are also not so much about exploring personality and individuality as about demonstrating this symbiotic relationship between the historical and the social (Wang 196).

7. My proposal here for adopting the word *personhood* in studies of Chinese rhetorical tradition, in some ways, echoes Lu and Frank's argument that the Chinese word *biàn* be used over the English word *rhetoric* to convey Chinese senses of persuasion and speech behavior in association with ancient Chinese rhetoric. For example, they suggest that although the Greek sense of rhetoric and its English translation conceptualize rhetoric as more of an end, Chinese *biàn* places emphasis on means and process (451–52).

WORKS CITED

Ames, Roger T. "Introduction to Part Three: On Body as Ritual Practice." *Self as Body in Asian Theory and Practice*. Ed. Thomas P. Kasulis, Roger T. Ames and Wimal Dissanayake. Albany: SUNY P, 1993. 149–56.

———. "The Meaning of Body in Classical Chinese Philosophy." *Self as Body in Asian Theory and Practice*. Ed. Thomas P. Kasulis, Roger T. Ames and Wimal Dissanayake. Albany: SUNY P, 1993. 157–77.

———. "The Focus-Field Self in Classical Confucianism." *Self as Person in Asian Theory and Practice*. Ed. Roger T. Ames, Wimal Dissanayake and Thomas P. Kasulis. Albany: SUNY P, 1994. 187–212.

Becker, Carl B. "Reasons for the Lack of Argumentation and Debate in the Far East." *International Journal of Intercultural Relations* 10 (1986): 75–92.

Cheng, Chung-Ying. "Chinese Philosophy and Contemporary Human Communication Theory." *Communication Theory: Eastern and Western Perspectives*. Ed. D. Lawrence Kincaid. San Diego: Academic, 1987. 23–43.

Confucius. *The Analects*. Trans. Raymond Dawson. Oxford, Oxford UP, 1993.

Erbaugh, Mary S. "Taking Advantage of China's Literary Practices in Teaching Chinese Students." *The Modern Language Journal* 74 (1990): 15–27.

Geertz, Clifford. "'From the Native's Point of View': On the Nature of Anthropological Understanding." *Local Knowledge: Further Essays in Interpretive Anthropology*. New York: Basic, 1983. 51–70.

Jensen, J. Vernon. "Rhetorical Emphasis of Taoism." *Rhetorica* 5 (1987): 219–29.

Jolliffe, David A. "Writers and Their Subjects: Ethnologic and Chinese Composition." *A Rhetoric of Doing: Essays on Written Discourse in Honor of James L. Kinneavy*. Ed. Stephen P. Witte,

Neil Nakadate and Roger D. Cherry. Carbondale: Southern Illinois UP, 1992. 261–75.

Kincaid, D. Lawrence. "Communication East and West: Points of Departure." *Communication Theory: Eastern and Western Perspectives*. Ed. D. Lawrence Kincaid. San Diego: Academic, 1987. 331–40.

Lu, Xing, and David A. Frank. "On the Study of Ancient Chinese Rhetoric/Bian." *Western Journal of Communication* 57 (1993): 445–63.

Markus, Hazel Rose, and Shinobu Kitayama. "Culture and the Self: Implications for Cognition, Emotion, and Motivation." *Psychological Review* 98 (1991): 224–53.

Matalene, Carolyn. "Contrastive Rhetoric: An American Writing Teacher in China." *College English* 47 (1985): 789–808.

Oliver, Robert T. *Communication and Culture in Ancient India and China*. Syracuse: Syracuse UP, 1971.

Tu, Wei-ming. "Selfhood and Otherness in Confucian Thought." *Culture and Self: Asian and Western Perspectives*. Ed. Anthony J. Marsella, George DeVos and Francis L.K. Hsu. New York: Tavistock, 1985. 231–51.

Wang, Gungwu. "The Rebel-Reformer and Modern Chinese Biography." *Self and Biography: Essays on the Individual and Society in Asia*. Ed. Gungwu Wang. Sydney: Sydney UP, 1975. 185–206.

16 Private Voices and Public Acts: Reform in the Teaching of Literacy

Hephzibah Roskelly
University of North Carolina–Greensboro

Susan Faludi's *Backlash* is more than a narrative of recent setbacks in the long struggle for gender equality. It is a story about how reactionary movements are fueled—by fear of damage to traditionally held values or traditional structures. The perceived success of women's rights issues unleashed a passionate counterattack that now pits community traditions against feminist values, values described as antifamily, or at least selfishly personal. In English studies, we suffer now from our own not-unrelated backlash, a reactionary movement that responds to the emergence of, and perceived success in using, the personal as a part of composing in writing and interpretation. Called by many names—*narrative* as a possible form for writing, *nurture* as a possible strategy for teaching, *subjective* as a possible method for interpretation—the personal is attacked as destructive to good academic prose, or as merely self-indulgent.

Ross Winterowd has no doubt about the problem in English studies. In "Where Is English: In the Garden or the Agora?" he wrote, "It can be argued (and I *do argue*) that the unholy combination of rationalism, associationism and romanticism . . . resulted in English department humanities, but whatever the cause, the consequences are obvious and undeniable: the exaltation of the imaginative and the degradation of the 'non-imaginative' . . . the exaltation of 'creative' writing and the degradation of composition . . . the high value placed on theory and the degradation of practice" (66). Winterowd blames the romantics—Socrates, Elbow, and many in between—for the ills that beset English classrooms, particularly the ill of poor, thoughtless writing.

In many ways, the attack from Winterowd seems overdone, just as the attack on feminists seems premature. It is not as though the personal and subjective have overturned traditional forms of writing or traditional methods of instruction. The typical first-year composition textbook is not notable for its insistence or encouragement of metaphorical thinking, fictionalized account, or personal reminiscence. Recent textbooks are notable for only one change in the last 20 years—the overt emphasis on envisioning writing as a process. A generally enlightening concept to student writers, a negative outcome of this emphasis has been that personal strategies, forms, or ideas are often explained as merely the beginnings of the process. Students are invited to practice, then dispose of, the personal. Not surprisingly, the typical first-year student is not anxious to employ the personal in writing or thinking. A typical batch of writing tasks from composition courses reveals far more objectified than subjective thinking, many more attempts at analysis than narrative, and an often extraordinary desire to hide rather than display voice.

Even as composition courses at all levels take account of the personal in composing—discuss strategies for fostering invention, encourage the keeping of journals as stimulants to writing, consider with serious attention words such as *voice* and *aim*, suggest the story as a possible form for writing, advocate the use of interviews as well as the library to document claims—even with this attention, the personal is displaced by the public eventually in the courses we teach. Narrative begins, not ends, composition courses. Nurturing teachers evaluate with rigor by semester's close. Subjectivity gives way to more highly prized objective assessment by student and teacher in the course of one assignment or one discussion.

It is not just our students' prose that is devoid of the personal and subjective. A look at many of our journals as well as many of the texts we ask our graduate students to read reveals the attempt, not unlike the first-year student's, to escape the personal in depersonalized prose. Limerick's essay "Dancing with Professors; The Trouble with Academic Prose" is a ringing indictment of the sterility of much of academic writing:

> When you write typical academic prose, it is nearly impossible to make a strong clear statement. The benefit here is that no one can attack your position, say you are wrong or even raise questions about the accuracy of what you have said, if they cannot *tell* what you have said. In those terms, awful indecipherable prose is its own form of armor, protecting the fragile sensitive thoughts of timid souls. (3)

The rigid dividing line we maintain between personal and public hurts our teaching and our writing as well as limits our ability to talk about the larger issues that rhetoric has historically been mindful of—social action and public responsibility. So how should we understand the personal, turn back the backlash? Toni Morrison indicated how we might:

> There is a conflict between public and private life, and it's a conflict that I think
> ought to remain a conflict. Not a problem, just a conflict. . . . It's a conflict that
> should be maintained now more than ever because of the social machinery of this
> country at this time that doesn't permit harmony in a life that has both aspects.
> (339).

Morrison promotes conflict—recognition of opposing claims—between personal and public. Hers is an argument for conversation, for relationship, in a time when the two seem to be mutually exclusive. Morrison, along with Cornel West and Patricia Williams, are writers who make their writing live out the conflict. Their work suggests strategies and models for rethinking the way we conceive and nurture the literate behavior of our own students, and for encouraging in ourselves a writing "life that has both aspects."

All of Morrison's fiction explores the personal/public conflict. I think of Stamp Paid's anguished whisper in *Beloved*: "Who are these people? You tell me Jesus. Who are they?" At once a personal statement of disbelief, grief, and loss, it is also a cry from a people and a narrator's reproach to readers who would gloss over the evils of humans who deny the humanity of others. But personal and public writing become more explicit in her essays and criticism. The following excerpt is from *Playing in the Dark*, a book about the American literary imagination that suggests that the presence of "blackness" provokes the white imagination and hovers at the edge of all the fiction. This aim is not simply literary; it is social and cultural, overtly rhetorical and deeply personal. Morrison traces in the first few pages of the book a growing awareness of an Africanist "other" presence in American fiction and the reason she reached such awareness. The excerpt reveals Morrison's method for making the personal and public converse:

> It is as if I had been looking at a fishbowl—the glide and the flick of the golden
> scales, the green tip, the bolt of white careening back from the gills; the castles at
> the bottom, surrounded by pebbles and tiny, intricate fronds of green; the barely
> disturbed water, the flecks of waste and food, the tranquil bubbles traveling to the
> surface—and suddenly I saw the bowl, the structure that transparently (and invisibly)
> permits the ordered life it contains to exist in the larger world. In other words, I
> began to rely on my knowledge of how books get written, how language arrives; my
> sense of how and why writers abandon or take on certain aspects of their project.
> (17)

The fishbowl metaphor illuminates a process of coming to awareness and suggests how we have been blind as readers and critics. Metaphor itself relies on public/personal dialogue, for metaphor expresses a writer's authority, a kind of confidence in both the idea and in the reader. In this piece, Morrison insists that a public, academic matter—a literary critique of American fiction—makes a personal difference. Her quietly controlled but nonetheless definite contention makes a statement about the ethics of literary criticism that she invites other critics to take personally: Matters of race in literary criticism and in literature itself have been skillfully deliberately evaded.

West—philosopher, religious studies professor, and lecturer—has written much about the public/personal connection in culture and philosophy. In interviews and speeches, West worries about the demise of "public conversation" and the loss of public life. He calls for a personal and community solution: "There can be no black freedom struggle, no radical democratic tradition without some universalism. It has much to do with love, the kind that asks your neighbor, 'What are you going through? Can I be of service?'" (14).

His most scholarly work is *The American Evasion of Philosophy*, analyzing the work of a number of American philosophers in an argument for pragmatic theory. Its academic intent makes the personal stance even more powerful:

> This book is principally motivated by my own disenchantment with intellectual life in America, and my own demoralization regarding the political and cultural state of the country. For example, I am disturbed by the transformation of highly intelligent liberal intellectuals into tendentious neoconservatives. . . . I am disappointed with the professional incorporation of former New Left activists who now often thrive on a selfserving careerism while espousing rhetorics of oppositional politics of little seriousness and integrity. I am depressed about the concrete nihilism in working-class and underclass American communities—the pervasive drug addiction, suicides, alcoholism, male violence against women, white violence against black, yellow and brown people, and the black criminality against others especially other black people. (7–8)

West's careful examination and reappraisal of Emerson, Peirce, James, Dewey, and Rorty and their pragmatic theories is motivated and informed by a personal need as well as a personal belief. "I have written this book," West said, "convinced that a thorough reexamination of American pragmatism, stripping it of its myths, caricatures, and stereotypes and viewing it as a component of a new and novel form of indigenous American oppositional thought and action, may be a first step toward fundamental change and transformation in America and in the world" (8). In pragmatic philosophy, there is no move from subjective vision to objective realization; the move is back and forth between other and self, I and thou. Pragmatism insists on the contingency, experiment, negotiation. It insists on belief.

For West, the doctrine he investigates is also one that he feels can make a difference in helping to cure the world's ills, ills that he admits depress and stymie him. The use of words that express his emotional and intellectual state as he begins to explore the theory—words such as *depressed, convinced, disenchanted*—suggest the power of belief to move readers. It is an unusual philosophy text indeed that provokes the kind of emotional assent that West's book calls forth. West makes ethics a personal responsibility and a public issue and demonstrates how putting the two in opposition—conversation—makes a difference in the world.

Williams is a law professor at New York University who wrote about her profession and its connection to her life in *The Alchemy of Race and Rights*. The first chapter is subtitled "Some Parables About Learning to Think like a Lawyer," and the book itself can be read as a kind of parable, a lesson on how the private interest and the public good must meet in legal practice, in teaching, and in life. It is an emotional book, a personal one, and a soundly researched and argued claim for a new kind of ethics in public life.

Williams used case studies and outcomes, a venerable technique from law books, to establish her position. She also used stories from her childhood, examples of her classroom dynamic, historical precedents, and her own ancestral slave narrative to push readers to new understanding about the dimensions of personal will and public act. The structures of legal discourse were manipulated and embedded in personal anecdotes and passionate argument.

Notions of private interest that seem disconnected from public responsibility are cited often in cases drawn from personal experience. The following is a rather long excerpt, but it serves to follow the course of Williams' argument through personal and public dimensions in such direct ways that I quote it at length:

> A little way down Broadway from the 14th St. subway station in Manhattan, there is a store called the Unique Boutique. Yards from the campus of NYU, it is a place where stylish coeds shop for the slightly frumpy, punky, slummy clothes that go well with bright red lipstick and ankle-high black bootlets. One winter day I saw a large, bright funcolored sign hanging in the window; "Sale! Two dollar overcoats. No bums, no booze." Offended, and not wanting to feel how offended I was, I turned my head away toward the street. There in the middle of the intersection of Broadway and Washington Place stood a black man dressed in the ancient remains of a Harris Tweed overcoat. His arms were spread-eagled as if to fly, though he was actually begging from cars in both directions. He was also drunk and crying and trying to keep his balance. . . .
>
> So the sign was disenfranchising the very people who most needed two dollar overcoats, the so-called bums. Moreover, it was selling the image of the disenfranchised themselves. . . . In discussing the tension between liberty and authority, John Stuart Mill observed that self-government means "not the government of each by himself but of each by all the rest. . . . But what Mill did not anticipate was that the persuasive power of the forum itself would subvert the polls, as well as the law, to the extent that there is today precious little 'public' left, just the tyranny of what we call the private." (42–43)

Williams began with a narrative, noted her emotional reaction to it, made an argument that proceeded from the implications of the narrative, suggested a generalization that reflected a position the chapter as a whole takes with regard to consumerism, and moved to a critique of a social theory that underlies much of the legal decision making in the past century. Williams's strategy integrated personal and communal in a logical, and lawyerly, framework. And her linguistic manipulation of the words *public* and *private*—in which both are at different times oppressor and oppressed—lets readers see how deeply intertwined the two concepts are.

The fact that these writers come from three separate disciplines indicates how much rhetoric and our discussions of literacy must remain embedded in cross-disciplinary approaches. Teachers and students must find their knowledge and their models from the law, philosophy, anthropology, and psychology as well as from literary criticism. That they are all African-American writers suggests how much voices that have been historically silenced long to speak in Winterowd's agora as persons. As Paula Giddings wrote in her account of black women feminists, "All of those things—and the hopes they inspired—were passed down to my great grandmother, who, in turn, kept them alive for succeeding genera-tions. But the story behind those eyes remains largely untold. That is why for a black woman to write about black women is at once a personal and an objective undertaking" (5).

Each writer uses the discipline and its forms to examine a position, make an argument, propound a theory. Each makes that public, social, professional position personal in similar ways. The voice in these excerpts is capable of great range and projection, and the syntax, diction, and tone let us hear the power of the sound. These writers make the public personal by asserting that the arguments they make have real consequences in their own lives and in the cultural life of our society. What they have discovered matters to a world larger than their own peers. Finally, each writer acknowledges that the conflict between individual and social, private and public, emotional and analytical informs their thinking and writing. As they wrestle with the forms of their disciplines, they transform them.

To rethink literacy by making personal and public conflict, we have to examine what we fear in the personal, because as Faludi shows, it is fear that fuels our negative reactions. "I don't want any stories of grandmother death," said the professor in declining to teach 101 for the 10th time in as many years. Grand-mother death is the new cliché for the personal/subjective/narrative/nurturing that is presumed to be the focus for the first semester writing course. Why don't we want stories of grandmother death? Limerick might say that the fear that prevents academics from talking in a real voice and keeps them talking in their own esoteric tongues also prevents academics from wanting to read those voices. Teachers themselves might say that they fear not doing the writing teacher job. If we encourage grandmother death—in writing—are we doing a service to public discourse?

But it seems that we believe in personal voice. Our belief is manifested in the joy with which we greet books by Williams, West, and Morrison, as well as by Elbow, Rose, and Bloom. What teachers fear from students, I believe, is not the personal voice, but the unexamined personal response. Wordsworth, after all, the great and much Winterowd-maligned romantic, is the one who insisted on spontaneous overflow of emotion *recollected in tranquility*. The reflection allows for connection, as Wordsworth knew, for the kind of negotiation that makes of intensely personal experience a communal participatory event. The teachers who would ban dying grandmothers from the classroom hardly wish to substitute the passive and passionless voice of the life insurance document in papers students produce.

No, what teachers want is negotiated response, a careful and real blend of public act and personal belief, a dialogue between private thought and social speech, and above all, a realization that an ethics of communication insists that public words hold within them personal responsibility, that personal writing carry with it a responsibility to communication. Blanche Clinchy calls this negotiation "connected knowing" (14). How might we teach this new kind of literacy in our classes?

We need to employ models in the classroom that encourage students to breathe the fresh air of personal style within, as well as without, the academic community of writers. One way to do that is to relearn stylistic analysis. It is easy to recognize in the writers discussed previously the use of qualifiers that diminishes the presumption of objectivity: the delight in personal anecdote, the hard-edged verbs that signal responsibility to ideas, metaphors that insist on readers' active engagement, logical argument that forces critical thinking. Students who examine texts in this way get help in finding their own strategies for connecting personal and public in their writing.

We must foster oral speech and oral communication in groups in our classrooms. West is right to insist on public conversation, on reasoned understanding as a premise for ethical behavior in society. It is also a premise for personal investment in writing public documents. The community is nurtured, as the pragmatists knew, in the exploration of the personal. And literacy is nurtured by helping students to recognize that what they bring with them to a course—their personal negotiation with the world of texts and people—is essential in making meaning within the classroom community.

West began his study with the romantic pragmatist Emerson, who recognized the tension between public and personal in 1837 in "The American Scholar" and came up with a pragmatic realization that Morrison, West, and Williams rediscovered for themselves:

> The poet in utter solitude remembering his spontaneous thoughts and recording them, is found to have recorded that which men in crowded cities find true for them also . . . the deeper he dives into his privatest, secretest presentiment, to his wonder he finds this is the most acceptable, most public and universally true. (49–50)

Graduate students concluded my course in gender and writing this spring by reading Williams and learned the truth of Emerson's statement firsthand. Over and over again, students wrote in journals that the chord Williams struck was their own as well: "I want to write like this," they said. "I've always known there was something missing about my own writing." "I know her anger. I've never been able to write mine." A new literacy insists on a new ethos of teaching and of writing, making it possible for students to enact writing that engages the personal and public, to act on the belief that guides Emerson. In diving deep within we can reach out to discover the commonality that binds us all.

WORKS CITED

Clinchy, Blanche. "On Critical Thinking and Connected Knowing." *Liberal Education* (Nov. 1989): 14–19.

Emerson, Ralph Waldo. "The American Scholar." *Selected Prose and Poetry*. New York: Holt Rinehart, 1969.

Giddings, Paula. *When and Where I Enter*. New York: Bantam, 1984.

Limerick, Patricia Nelson. "Dancing with Professors: The Trouble with Academic Prose." *New York Times Book Review*, October 31, 1993, 3.23.

Morrison, Toni. "Rootedness: The Ancestor as Foundation." *Black Women Authors: A Critical Evaluation*.

———. *Beloved*. New York: New American Library, 1988.

———. *Playing in the Dark: Whiteness and the Literary Imagination*. Cambridge: Harvard UP, 1992.

Poinsett, Alex. "Cornel West: Extending the Public Conversation." *Ebony* (Sept./Oct. 1993).

West, Cornel. *The American Evasion of Philosophy*. Madison: U of Wisconsin P, 1989.

Williams, Patricia. *The Alchemy of Race and Rights*. Cambridge: Harvard UP, 1991.

Winterowd, W. Ross. "Where is English—In the Garden or in the Agora?" *Focuses* 2 (1992): 65–86.

17 A Rhetoric of "Cultural Negotiation": Toward an Ethos of Empowerment for African-American Women Graduate Students

Juanita Comfort
Ohio State University

In her recent study of writing strategies among successful academic women, Gesa Kirsch wrote that "women are not only participating in but are also transforming the academy with their writing. . . . They are redefining what it means to be a writer and researcher in the academic context" (xix). This dynamic of enfranchisement suggested by Kirsch is, I believe, largely a rhetorical one. The perceived strength of one's scholarly writing plays a significant role in "composing" oneself as a member of an academic community. Judgments about the effectiveness of a scholar's work—and through those judgments, the according of collegial respect and the distribution of material rewards—are made by readers of her work who have the power to advance her or hold her back.

As African-American women, however, we often experience difficulty eliciting positive judgments about the quality of our work, especially if, in foregrounding perspectives on spirituality, community survival, and human development, we sometimes resist the traditional values of rationalism and materialism that privilege the secular over the spiritual, the political over the personal, and the individual over the community (James and Farmer 121). bell hooks points to several specific pitfalls for African-American women attempting to use academic prose. She observed:

> For Black women scholars and/or intellectuals, writing style may evoke questions of political allegiance. Using a style that may gain one academic acceptance and recognition may further estrange one from a wider Black reading audience. . . . Choosing to write in a traditional academic style may lead to isolation. And even if one writes along the lines of accepted academic style, there is no guarantee that one's work will be respected. (hooks and West 157)

145

In order to achieve our own intellectual, spiritual, and social/community goals (goals that are not necessarily shared by all academics), we may aim to employ scholarly discourse as a vehicle for putting on the academic agenda perspectives that we perceive to have been overlooked there. When we employ certain discursive options derived from our own particular life experiences—which we consider essential for the expression of those ideas—we tend to push the boundaries of academic convention.

Contemporary discourse theories claim that language, and the communities within which language is generated, actually shape knowledge and the knower. It would seem, then, that our fate as African-American women in the academy must inevitably be tied to the relative effectiveness of our discourse within the exigencies presented by the academic institution. Our enfranchisement as makers of knowledge in an academy that many believe to be plagued by racism and sexism may very well hinge on the daunting task of distinguishing ourselves to our largely White male (and White-male identified) audiences, specifically as African-American and female in our grounding assumptions, strategies of argument, and writing styles. Simultaneously, we must elicit from those very same audiences a favorable impression of our perceived characters. Like all rhetors, we must invent effective ways to answer our readers' fundamental question: "Who is this person and why should I believe what she says?"

Brooke's discussion of identity negotiation theories provides a useful framework for understanding how a sense of a writer's "self" develops in the act of writing. In these theories, according to Brooke, "individuals are seen as having to construct their particular sense of self from the competing social definitions of self which surround them" (4). Thus, it can be posited that the rhetorical exigencies of a given discourse, plus the writer's own personal history, beliefs, and values, define a range of possible roles she might assume in her text. The voice emanating from that text results from negotiation through a maze of social forces as she accepts some allowable roles and resists others. This image of *negotiation*—in the dual senses of making tradeoffs among valued but competing options, and winding one's way through complex cultural terrain—seems to aptly describe our experiences as writers developing self-representation strategies. Collins used a similar image, in fact, when she asserted that "Black women's lives are a series of negotiations that aim to reconcile the contradictions separating our own internally defined images of self as African-American women with our objectification as the Other" (94).

The impact of race, gender, and culture on identity formation and consequently on voice and ethos has been increasingly recognized in research across disciplines. Moreover, Afrocentric scholars such as Molefe Asante (Arthur Smith) and sociolinguists such as Geneva Smitherman have demonstrated that African-American culture indeed exhibits significant features of traditional African culture. They make particular note of a sense of unity between the sacred and the secular; a synthesis of dualities in order to achieve balance and harmony, both in the universe and in the community; and a balancing of long-standing group norms with individual improvisation. And as the work of Carol Gilligan and the Belenky team to reclaim women's voices emphasizes the impact of gender-related influences on identity, Collins, hooks, and other womanist theorists maintain that it is the complex *combination* of race, gender, and culture that shapes the African-American woman's experience of self.

These racial, gendered, and cultural elements of identity and voice are acquired through the discursive practices of our nonacademic communities and also include extensive formal schooling in academic discourse. The diverse ways in which discursive features come together in our texts result from conscious and unconscious decisions about how we position ourselves within (and/or outside of) the constraints imposed by both our academic rhetorical situations and our own backgrounds. As we struggle to generate a particular kind of ethos in our writing, we negotiate what we believe to be an appropriate speaking voice by means of specific, purposeful strategies. Roger Cherry observed that these "decisions about self-portrayal are not independent, but vary according to the way in which *writers characterize* their audience and other facets of the rhetorical situation" (252, my emphasis). For us, this characterization is conditioned by our awareness, as expressed by Collins, that "oppressed groups are frequently placed in the situation of being listened to only if we frame our ideas in the language that is familiar to and comfortable for a dominant group. This requirement often changes the meaning of our ideas and works to elevate the ideas of dominant groups" (xiii).

I am thus deeply concerned that African-American women face the very real danger of intellectual and even physical erasure from the landscape of academia (our documented numbers and status within the faculty ranks, for example, are both alarmingly low). In our desire to make ourselves known to the academy, we often work toward developing an ethos that sets us apart from the academy's dominant groups. However, in order to make ourselves more attractive to those same groups, we find ourselves obliged to suppress some of the very aspects of our identities that set us apart, so that we effectively render ourselves invisible.

This brings me to the threshold of my current research. Where do we learn how to assert a distinct—yet effective—scholarly presence in our academic writing? Certainly graduate programs function as important settings. It is within the rhetorical context of writing for instructors, examination and dissertation committees, and conference reviewers—all of whom represent the academy at large—that we begin to develop the kind of authorial presence that, theoretically at least, should empower us in the academic arena. For myself, and for many of my peers, the distance between our academic and nonacademic worlds is significant. For those of us who have come to predominantly White universities from historically African-American colleges or universities, the distance between academic worlds may also be great.

We have of course been educated in academic institutions whose rhetorical traditions are traceable to ancient Greece and Rome. We are also strongly conditioned by cultural forces whose roots are African in character, adding a sense of integration and synthesis to the typically Western approaches of compartmentalization and analysis that we draw on as rhetorical resources. As we engage our identity frameworks where potentially conflicting influences, experiences, and perspectives converge, our impulse as writers would be to bring them all into balance in an effort to achieve unity and harmony in our work.

When our rhetorical choices foreground these kinds of impulses over our training in the academy's conventions, however, our attempts at self-portrayal can be dangerous. If we are to write effectively for our graduate school audiences and for ourselves, we must learn how to bring academic and nonacademic resources into balance within our texts, regardless of whether the institution itself intends to teach us how to do this. I am learning that our rhetorical options may range from total compliance with the values and expectations of our readers to almost total resistance to them. From a position of total compliance, I speculate that we might imitate the dominant discursive models of our fields so closely that our writing would seem almost neutral in character. The more we make ourselves "visible"—that is, the more we signal to readers that we hold a different status from theirs, that we write as people who are different from them and who seek different goals—the more distinctly we may be identified as African-American women, with all the consequences (both positive and negative) attached to such an image. Given the often competing constraints between our academic rhetorical situations and our sociocultural backgrounds, we must continually negotiate—comply and resist—on our way to establishing effective scholarly voices that are also comfortable for us.

I have begun interviewing African-American women doctoral students from a range of disciplines who are planning academic careers and who write extensively in their programs. My research design consists primarily of in-depth interviews with these women and close readings of their texts. Because my methods assume that individuals "construct" the reality they experience, this project attempts to record the shape and direction—the "reality"—of my participants' academic experiences from their own points of view, as they consider the extent to which they are able to develop effective scholarly voices. I am discovering that although there are certain resonances among them given the similarity of their academic situations, their rhetorical practices, and the life experiences upon which those practices are based, make each woman unique. Their backgrounds are richly diverse in terms of their ages, educational paths, social classes, faith traditions, family makeup, and so forth. A few have served in the military and/or civil service, and several of them have had extensive nonacademic careers that included significant amounts of work-related writing.

These are women for whom issues of voice and identity in written discourse are issues of their very survival. Sadly, I have sensed very little empowerment in the conversations I have had with them so far. Some participants complain that their writings are often viciously criticized or else dismissed as lacking "rigor" or "complexity." An image comes to mind, for example, of one woman's seminar paper, returned by her professor heavily marked to point out everything from grammatical errors to the "suspect" quality of her evidence. Even her title had been crossed out. This writer spoke to me at length about the choices she had made in composing that paper and the particular effects she had hoped to achieve at the very points the professor disapproved of. Although many of my study participants can relate similar horror stories, some find that even when their work is judged to be well written, it elicits the kind of patronizing comments that imply that such "competence" is unexpected. From what I have been able to observe thus far, the discursive practices of many of these women simply do not seem to resonate with the expectations of the communities they are attempting to join.

One of my participants, whom I will call Maya, has been particularly articulate about the issues that have been raised by hooks and others. At 42, she is finishing a master's degree in education, while simultaneously taking course work toward her doctorate. I consider her graduate experience one of several success stories that I have found, but not necessarily because she has been validated by her academic readers. On the contrary, she has told me of numerous occasions when her writing has been devalued, dismissed, or misinterpreted. I consider her successful because, in the face of all the frustrations she has endured, she seems to be developing an ever stronger sense of identity and purpose in her writing, while keeping an eye squarely on the basic reason she committed herself to graduate school in the first place—to serve the youth of the African-American community as an educator. She observed:

> I've seen Black people who have set off to educate themselves, and when they're finished, they're so dysfunctional that they will not be accepted into a White community in positions commensurate with the level of their studies, and Black people will reject them because of their communication process: they've been taught to use empirical evidence only. I think that true thinking intellectuals use their thinking AND their feeling—they use their whole being.
>
> I often ask myself what I can do in my writing to establish credibility. It's very important for me to write to real audiences—not just an instructor, but an audience of people whom I can trust to be truly receptive to me both as a person and as a researcher. I believe there are many people who have been given credibility by virtue of the color of their skin, by virtue of the fact that someone says they have a degree. That's what a degree from a university says: When you show up you don't have to prove yourself; you've been certified, you've been licensed. It's a concept that carries equity, and that is attractive to me as a Black woman scholar. If there is something that I have to say, if there is something that I've been able to see in a unique way, that needs to be spoken to audiences who would benefit, then I have a responsibility to make my voice heard. And yet, many times within the university, messages are not designed to reach the most appropriate audience. The vehicle is short-circuited, changed so that the message intended for relevant readers would not be understood or even recognized by them.
>
> This sets up a tremendous dilemma for me—I have to continually ask myself

whether or not the white instructors that I'm writing for can in fact understand the scope and depth of what I'm talking about, because it seems they either don't understand my language or they don't understand the experience that I'm describing. They've only been able to see my message on a surface level. They may read it and file it away as folly, or they may read it and file it away as something to use against me later. So, I have to ask myself a question: How much of what I do in my writing can I allow someone else to control?

I have a real problem when a researcher's credibility is called into question. And I believe that generally happens with black scholars. When I say "this is my experience," it can always be negated because my eyes are not judged by my readers as being credibly perceptive. There are times when I feel I must write two separate papers: one for myself and my intended audience, and one containing those portions I intend for the professor.

Although my research project focused on African-American women, Maya's remarks send a message to those who teach, examine, and mentor all graduate students. Graduate faculty would do well to consider how they might be more sensitive to the dynamics of, and rationales behind, the rhetorical choices of their students, to consider how well their students' experience of writing in their programs empowers them to become effective academic rhetors capable of creating space for themselves and asserting power within the academy. Certainly, in an institution that increasingly desires to be recognized as a multicultural community, students should be able to develop as intellectuals without feeling the need to compromise their distinctive voices at the very start of their careers.

WORKS CITED

Asante, Molefi Kete. *The Afrocentric Idea*. Philadelphia: Temple UP, 1987.

Belenky, Mary Field, et al. *Women's Ways of Knowing: The Development of Self, Voice, and Mind*. New York: Basic, 1986.

Brooke, Robert. *Writing and Sense of Self: Identity Negotiation in Writing Workshops*. Urbana, IL: NCTE, 1991.

Cherry, Roger D. "Ethos Versus Persona: Self-Representation in Written Discourse." *Written Communication* 5 (July 1988): 251–76.

Collins, Patricia Hill. *Black Feminist Thought: Knowledge, Consciousness, and the Politics of Empowerment*. New York: Routledge, 1990.

Gilligan, Carol. *In a Different Voice: Psychological Theory and Women's Development*. Cambridge: Harvard UP, 1982.

hooks, bell, and Cornel West. *Breaking Bread: Insurgent Black Intellectual Life*. Boston: South End, 1991.

James, Joy, and Ruth Farmer, eds. *Spirit, Space & Survival: African-American Women in (White) Academe*. New York: Routledge, 1993.

Kirsch, Gesa. *Women Writing the Academy: Audience, Authority, and Transformation*. Carbondale: Southern Illinois UP, 1993.

Smith, Arthur L. "Markings of an Afrocentric Concept of Rhetoric." *Today's Speech* (Spring 1971): 13–18.

Smitherman, Geneva. *Talkin and Testifyin: The Language of Black America*. Detroit: Wayne State UP, 1977.

Part IV

Institutional Concerns

18 The Rhetoric of Writing Requirements

Rolf Norgaard
University of Colorado at Boulder

Open virtually any college catalog or registration packet, and you will find information about required course work in composition and rhetoric—that is, writing requirements. Those requirements are typically offered as neutral prescriptive statements about the study of rhetoric. A few institutions preface the statement with a lofty defense for writing well. More often, the statements amount to little more than a list of what courses to take when.

Writing requirements, however, lead an institutional life that is far more complex than catalogs would have us believe. Requirements may prescribe a course of study in rhetoric, yet they are themselves rhetorically inscribed. This chapter explores how institutional sponsorship of writing, through requirements, licenses a variety of competing behaviors, creating in effect a curricular underlife. This underlife develops because the rhetoric accompanying requirements can engender behaviors that undercut officially sanctioned positions. Whether those behaviors occur elsewhere in the institution or in writing programs themselves, they tend to marginalize what the requirements supposedly make central.

Writing requirements bear on some of our field's most engaging discussions. Historical studies about rhetoric in American colleges often use requirements as indicators of curricular and pedagogical trends (e.g., Berlin; Russell). Likewise, discussions about the politics of composition take as their point of departure the irony that an institution requires vast numbers of students to take a course that has little academic standing (e.g., Bullock and Trimbur; Miller). Small wonder, then, that we contest the nature and role of freshman composition in our professional journals and at conferences (e.g., Crowley; France; Larson). These studies

153

document what we know all too well from our daily professional lives. As rhetoricians, writing requirements shape the history we study and the new issues we debate. As writing program administrators, those requirements rule our lives. As teachers, those requirements shape our classrooms. As for our students, those requirements shape their perception of academic life.

My own focus is more modest than these studies, but perhaps more fundamental. Most presume the existence of requirements as they engage broader issues. I examine the rhetorical nature of those very requirements, with this question in mind: How can it be that requirements, often thought to express an institution's commitment to writing, can undercut their stated aims?

To understand the competing behaviors bred by requirements, we start by examining the rhetoric of those requirements and the special influence that they have in the field of rhetoric and composition. We then consider the sociological concept of "underlife" as a way to understand the tension between institutional sponsorship of writing and the tacit license given to competing behaviors. Those competing behaviors operate at two levels: throughout the institution, and within writing programs themselves. At both levels we find a curricular underlife that shadows, even satirizes officially sanctioned positions. In the tension between institutional sponsorship and licensed underlife behaviors we discover that requirements lead a strange double life.

A RHETORIC THAT SHOUTS

Few would question that requirements express institutional norms in a highly visible fashion. Actually, most requirements are far more ambitious. They do more than embody norms, they try to reshape norms to fit some high-minded educational ideal. In this light, requirements express an institution's fiction of itself.

We generate this fiction because institutions are fond of using requirements as a kind of performative speech act. Recall, if you will, Austin's prime example of a performative speech act: "I now pronounce you man and wife." Saying so means having accomplished the act. As a performative speech act, requirements pronounce a marriage of their own—a marriage between a particular course and desired student achievement of the broadest sort. Stating a requirement means fulfilling an overarching educational purpose. Yet the competing behaviors licensed by the requirement can all but guarantee a divorce.

Writing requirements are thus a form of institutional rhetoric that shouts. Requirements shout not merely so that the institution's commitment to writing will be heard, but so that the institution itself will believe in that commitment and, what is more, consider that belief fully realized. Yet the underlife behaviors elicited by the requirement can subvert the rhetorical education envisioned by providing a tacit instruction of their own. What students learn through underlife behaviors toward writing requirements in classes elsewhere on campus often contradicts what we teach in our own.

Habit easily inures us to the rhetorical dimension of requirements and the curricular underlife accompanying them. These concerns often become visible only when faculty discuss changing those requirements. Such was the case on my own campus, the University of Colorado at Boulder. The deliberations foundered on predictable issues: the nature and level of the requirement, what kind of problems the requirement should address, and matters of staffing and funding. What caught my attention was that those discussions also revealed behaviors that accompany requirements, but are rarely acknowledged as the specific formulation of the requirement is hammered out.

INSTITUTIONAL SPONSORSHIP

The rhetoric of requirements follows from the distinctive way that our institutions sponsor them. This sponsorship has a profound effect on our discipline and is divided in ways that often undermine writing instruction.

Although our own professional lives as rhetoricians may be governed by an institution's writing requirements, required courses of various kinds have a far more modest effect in other disciplines. Economics or physics, for example, have their own requirements for the major and contribute courses to a core curriculum that may be required of all students. Yet the work of these disciplines goes on largely unaffected by whatever requirements are in place.

Not so in rhetoric and composition. The matter of core requirements, incidental to most academic disciplines, goes to the heart of our field. Ours is one of the few disciplines in which requirements imposed by other academic units— economics or physics—actually define the courses offered and constrain our ability to propose new courses.

Those requirements also define the very character of composition programs and even determine the nature of our discipline. Requirements, along with entrance and enrollment policies, clearly have had a hand in how we conceive of such fields as basic writing and advanced composition, and how we approach disciplinary and professional writing, even critical thinking. In short, we become what others ask us to teach.

Moreover, institutional sponsorship is divided in ways that invite underlife behaviors. At one level, various schools and colleges, perhaps the entire institution, approve and thus sanction the requirement, usually by general faculty vote. Here, rhetoricians and physicists have an equal say in the matter. Actually, faculty outside of our field most relish the opportunity to make a statement. Yet at another level, the writing program must sponsor, exclusively or in large part, the specific courses that fulfill and thus embody the requirement.

This disjunction between two levels of sponsorship—by the institution and by the writing program—carries with it a corresponding gap between the idealized intention of the requirement and the actual embodiment of that requirement in section after section. Moreover, the divided sponsorship usually sets writing program courses apart from, even against, other courses on campus that may ask students to write.

UNDERLIFE BEHAVIORS

The troubled nature of institutional sponsorship licenses, in turn, a curricular underlife, a variety of competing behaviors that undercut officially sanctioned positions. To understand those behaviors, we can turn to the concept of "underlife," one that has acquired currency in sociology through the work of Goffman and has invited some interesting applications in rhetoric and composition—for example, by Brooke and by a group of students working with Miller (Anderson et al.).

Exploring the behaviors of students and teachers in a writing classroom, Brooke understands *underlife* to mean "the activities (or information games) individuals engage in to show that their identities are different from or more complex than the identities assigned them by organizational roles" (142). For Brooke, these underlife behaviors can help students accomplish a shift in identity from student to writer. Miller extended Brooke's work by taking a cross-curricular perspective and arrived at a far more vexing conclusion. Writing courses have at best a limited claim to helping students prepare for writing in college, for they usually fail to address the underlife of writing in the university— that is, the writing that students actually do in other classes (Anderson et al. 12).

These two perspectives on academic underlife flirt with but never directly address the role of writing requirements in establishing "official" institutional expectations and eliciting underlife behaviors. In the context of my argument, an institution's writing requirements imply certain roles and identities and thus form the stage for social interaction that develops through the information games we play. The rhetoric we teach and use in the context of required writing courses thus becomes a way of responding to, and not just representing, institutional norms.

Although Brooke sees classroom underlife as "contained," not "disruptive," and therefore a normal part of institutional life, I find that the underlife associated with writing requirements has a darker side. Indeed, the degree to which writing requirements elicit underlife behaviors may have much to do with what Miller described as the dysfunctional, carnivalesque status of composition in the academy.

REQUIREMENTS AS TACIT INSTRUCTION

If the idealized rhetorical education envisioned by requirements elicits underlife behaviors that subvert its aims, what, then, do those behaviors accompanying writing requirements really teach? Three sets of behaviors from faculty across campus offer an unsettling answer, for the behaviors marginalize what the requirements supposedly make central.

The first set of underlife behaviors has to do with the fact that requirements presume a clear correspondence between the broad intent of the requirement and the actual required course. This presumption elicits the following underlife behaviors:

- The sponsorship of a requirement licenses faculty to hold a specific course accountable for virtually utopian goals. That is, a requirement licenses faculty to snipe at a specific course by asking, in essence, "Didn't that course teach you to write?"

- It also encourages faculty and students alike to misunderstand the broad goal of academic literacy by identifying it with just one course, or, conversely, to misunderstand how that one course might contribute to some vague notion of academic literacy that they may have.

A second set of behaviors concerns the interplay of obligation and freedom. Required courses create zones of freedom elsewhere in the curriculum. These curricular zones of freedom, unencumbered by expectations about writing, can elicit the following underlife behaviors:

- Although faculty may have voted for a writing requirement that expresses the institution's commitment, its existence licenses their own neglect of writing in the courses they teach. One might expect that the writing-across-the-curriculum movement would mitigate this effect; it actually duplicates it. WAC programs can wither precisely because a few writing-intensive classes sanction a more general apathy.

- Even if faculty do address writing in their courses, the existence of a requirement often licenses them to take approaches to writing instruction that differ from or even contradict approaches used in the required writing courses. Diverse approaches to writing can be healthy, but given the rhetoric that accompanies requirements, students often view these behaviors as competing with, not complementing, stated institutional goals. Varying approaches to and expectations about student writing usually undermine the required course.

- Furthermore, the sponsorship of a writing requirement can often license grades on papers in other academic courses that undermine evaluations given in a required course. Students become confused when papers that would otherwise merit a C are given As or Bs because professors in other disciplines say they cannot be expected to look at the writing. Nothing erodes a writing requirement more profoundly than mixed signals about the quality of student writing, especially when the required course comes in with the low grade.

Although institutional sponsorship of writing may seek to express the importance of writing and encourage high standards, faculty usually see those same requirements as a way to remedy deficiencies in student work. A third set of underlife behaviors follows from this deficit model of writing instruction:

- Because institutional sponsorship of a writing requirement licenses faculty in other disciplines to focus on severe deficiencies, usually surface errors, they tend to elevate mediocre work to an acceptable, even praiseworthy status. A cleanly written paper, however ill conceived or poorly argued, will usually pass muster.

- Courses are required of our worst students, with the best given exemptions that only serve to dumb down the course. Thus, requirements do not encourage high performance, but actually conspire against it.

- This preoccupation with deficiency, in turn, licenses a perverse approach to staffing and funding these required courses. Requirements pay lip service to the importance of writing while sanctioning high classroom enrollments, as well as low wages and little if any job security for instructors. Actual teaching conditions conspire against courses ever fulfilling the intent of the requirement they supposedly meet.

In these three ways (and many more), the behaviors accompanying writing requirements offer an unsettling rhetorical education of their own. Students learn to play their own writing class off against both the institution's idealistic rhetoric and the actual use and evaluation of writing assignments in other courses. If they content themselves with mediocre work, they have learned all too well that the institution itself, whatever its official rhetoric, has set the mark embarrassingly low. Even as an institution shouts its commitment to writing, it licenses behaviors that undermine its own rhetoric.

PLAYING THE RENEGADE

But lest we point fingers at our colleagues across campus, we might examine our own behaviors. The presence of this curricular underlife can engender yet another dimension of sponsorship and license: that within composition programs themselves. Saddled with official sponsorship for administrating requirements that other faculty have approved, writing program faculty often seek to deal with this charge, and the student hostility that can accompany it, by inventing themselves in ways that counter or diffuse officially sanctioned positions. That is, institutional sponsorship of writing requirements licenses underlife behaviors even among those who actually teach the required courses.

Witness the opening classes of any term. Teachers invent for themselves a persona that is apart from or even satirizes expectations bred by the requirement. Syllabi for courses meant to fulfill the requirement go to great lengths to revise perceptions bred by the course catalog. And as we discuss and respond to student work throughout the term, we who teach the required courses are ever mindful to distance ourselves from the conventional identities fashioned for us by an institution's sponsorship of writing.

Thus, even those of us saddled with administering or teaching required writing courses succeed insofar as we play the renegade. A good teacher, to be sure, will often call on a bit of self-irony, or demonstrate a willingness to question institutional roles. Yet it is a measure of the carnivalesque status of composition, and the pervasive underlife behaviors accompanying requirements, that we end up satirizing our own received identities, impoverished as they are, to accomplish our goals.

THE PRESUMPTION OF REQUIREMENTS

Given the underlife behaviors that accompany writing requirements, it may be tempting to conclude that required courses have no redeeming virtues. That is not entirely the case. Required courses *can* help students—but for reasons that are largely incidental to the requirement, and usually in spite of hollow rhetoric. In short, requirements work when actual behaviors render the requirement superfluous.

But that is the rub. The worst fate for any requirement is that it be deemed superfluous. We have gotten it into our heads that a requirement should do something, that it should assert an institution's high-minded commitment, that it should refashion behaviors through a catalog text. And yet, with this overreaching rhetoric, the institution actually licenses a curricular underlife that can satirize our best intentions.

My cautionary tale about the rhetoric of writing requirements should give us pause when we engage broader issues in our field. Curricular histories, for example, would do well to consider catalog copy and institutional requirements with some skepticism, for underlife behaviors complicate their actual implementation enormously. Likewise, today's debate about the appropriate goals of freshman composition cannot lose sight of the required status of this course—a status that invites overblown official rhetoric even as it elicits competing underlife behaviors, no matter what the course's focus. Moreover, as we struggle to administer the requirements in place, and negotiate with those ever eager to propose new requirements, we would do well to temper official pronouncements by anticipating the underlife that is bound to accompany them.

Requirements, if we must endure them at all, should require of ourselves a seriousness of purpose, one demonstrated in our actual behaviors. But as soon as we use requirements to elevate our purpose, to shout our commitment, we license underlife behaviors that can expose our hypocrisy. Little wonder that today's requirements actually prompt us and our colleagues across campus to write ourselves out of the official catalog text, and write ourselves into its ironic gloss.

WORKS CITED

Anderson, Worth, Cynthia Best, Alycia Black, John Hurst, Brandt Miller, and Susan Miller. "Cross-Curricular Underlife: A Collaborative Report on Ways with Academic Words." *College Composition and Communication* 41, No. 1 (Feb. 1990): 11–36.

Austin, John L. *How to Do Things with Words*. Cambridge: Harvard UP, 1975.

Berlin, James A. *Rhetoric and Reality: Writing Instruction in American Colleges, 1900–1985*. Carbondale: Southern Illinois UP, 1987.

———. *Writing Instruction in Nineteenth-century American Colleges*. Carbondale: Southern Illinois UP, 1984.

Brooke, Robert. "Underlife and Writing Instruction." *College Composition and Communication* 38 (May 1987): 141–53.

Bullock, Richard, and John Trimbur, eds. *The Politics of Writing Instruction: Postsecondary*. Portsmouth, NH: Boynton/Cook, 1991.

Crowley, Sharon. "A Personal Essay on Freshman English." *Pre/Text* 12, Nos. 3–4 (1991): 156–76.

France, Alan W. "Assigning Places: The Function of Introductory Composition as a Cultural Discourse." *College English* 55, No. 6 (Oct. 1993): 593–609.

Goffman, Irving. *Asylums: Essays on the Social Situation of Mental Patients and Other Inmates*. New York: Anchor, 1961.

———. *Stigma: Notes on the Management of Spoiled Identity*. Englewood Cliffs, NJ: Prentice-Hall, 1963.

Larson, Richard. "Freshman Composition: Is It a Waste of Time?" *The Council Chronicle* 1 (April 1992): 9.

Miller, Susan. *Textual Carnivals: The Politics of Composition*. Carbondale: Southern Illinois UP, 1991.

Russell, David R. *Writing in the Academic Disciplines, 1870–1990: A Curricular History*. Carbondale: Southern Illinois UP, 1991.

19 Resisting and Revising Culture: From Modernist Theory to Postmodernist Pedagogy

Kristine L. Blair
Texas A&M University

From a modernist perspective, the term *text* encompasses the traditional canonical classics taught in literature classrooms or the public speeches of a great male orator. From a postmodernist perspective, however, the term *text* extends to most cultural and rhetorical artifacts: a Beatles' ballad, a Madonna video, a child's toy, a crucifix. Indeed, postmodernism is distinguishable from modernism in its refusal to privilege one textual form over another, its critique of the separation of textual production, distribution, and consumption from hegemonic forces, and its denial of the text as a source of univocal meaning created by an atomistic self (McGowan 25). But even for those of us who accept these broader, postmodern implications of *text*—particularly those of us engaged in the development of cultural studies approaches to composition—such examples mentioned here do not always make the transition to the composition classroom as topics of cultural and rhetorical study. Instead, both literature and composition teachers are often constrained by institutional obligations to uphold a more modernist definition of text in hopes that our students can somehow emulate what both university administrators and often students themselves consider to be the sacred texts of English studies: the academic essay and the literary artifact. As Paul Smith contends, such definitions become static and assume that culture is "containable in its most essential and fixed forms in anthologies and in the works of a few privileged writers" (33). Despite the theoretical acknowledgments of these competing definitions, my goal in this chapter is to call for more dialogue with students to address the conflicts over textuality and culture as well as conflicts over authority and subjectivity.

Of course, with these shifting definitions of *text* come overall shifts in the definition of culture. As Raymond Williams observes, the term *culture* initially took on a harvesting motif, at first denoting the tending of crops and animals and later connoting the tending of the human faculties (11). For Williams, the term later becomes associated with civilization, only to break away once more when philosophers from Rousseau through the Romantics insist on *culture* as individual, internal, the finest impulse of the "human spirit" and *civilization* as social, external, the required codes and luxuries of class consciousness (14). Such a distinction between culture and civilization, or culture and society, also becomes a distinction between production and consumption, for it is the highly spiritual, intuitive individual who will become the producer of works of art and literature, and the middle class who will later come to consume these works through such mass distribution sites as museums or the popular monthly serial.

Today, it appears that culture becomes as broad a term as the distribution processes used to disseminate its products, and it will be the influence of technology that helps to redefine different forms of culture—high culture as opposed to low culture—in a 20th-century clash between modernist epistemology and postmodernist technology. This clash comprises those—particularly such members of the Frankfort school as Theodor Adorno and Max Horkheimer—who see popular culture to be the new opiate of the duped masses and those—Jean Baudrillard, for example—who see issues of representation, meaning, and value to carry little weight in the face of fragmented textuality and fragmented subjectivity, both coming together to form only a surface knowledge about the world, the text, and the self.

Inevitably, the definitions, redefinitions, and value assigned to culture are significant not only for their broadened scope, but for their underlying epistemological assumptions, as well as the historical and material conditions that shaped these assumptions about culture. Traditional modernist definitions have maintained a distinction between high and low culture and have delivered a verdict of inferiority to mass culture that contemporary cultural critics are still struggling to overturn. Moreover, some postmodern assumptions include the concept of the individual as a cultural product to be multiplied and disseminated through various discursive practices. Admittedly, some theorists are more interested in that aspect of cultural study in which these discursive practices constitute the subject than in that aspect in which subjects both conform to and resist the culture industry. In my own resistance of these assumptions of both modernism and postmodernism, I hope to show that culture must be redefined as something lived and experienced by human agents capable of action, reaction, and resistance, an empowered subject position that neither modernist conceptions of preferred texts and their univocal meanings and postmodernist conceptions of text and information overload can fully foresee. Finally, because of the pressing need to challenge the backlash against cultural work as "politically correct," I argue that rather than talk only to ourselves in our major theoretical journals and anthologies, we must also actively engage our students in the question of culture so that such under-standing and attempts for change can take place outside the halls of academe.

The distinctions between theories of culture include the traditional Arnoldian paradigm of the best that is thought and said throughout Western civilization, the denigration of mass culture by certain members of the Frankfort school, and more recent discussions of the effects of technology on the production, distribution, and consumption of culture. Despite these distinctions, it becomes clear that the term *culture* evolves from a totalizing, cohesive emphasis on art, literature, and general ideas of the aesthetic to a concept that is at once fragmented and technologically mediated. Yet our definition of culture must also focus on the politically localized experience of marginalized and mainstream groups who both acquiesce to and struggle against the hegemonic forces that shape and are shaped by this broader sense of mass-mediated culture that has come to typify the postmodern era. Such a reconfiguration of our theory of culture has in turn reconfigured the nature of our pedagogy, necessitating a shift in writing and literature pedagogy that calls for both the critical strategies for understanding, critiquing, and resisting the technological and ideological production of mass cultural forms as well as the synthesis of mass culture into the classroom along with the traditional texts of composition and literature to acknowledge the power of all texts, literary or popular, to shape perceptions about self and other. Ultimately, such strategies are necessary so that such perceptions can be revised to acknowledge a politics of difference, yet foster a politics of equality, in resisting and revising gender, race, and class representations within popular cultural forms.

In defining *postmodernism*, Aronowitz and Giroux claim that:

> Postmodern criticism call[s] attention to the shifting boundaries related to the increasing influence of the electronic mass media and information technology, the changing nature of class and social formations in postindustrialized capitalist societies, and the growing transgression of boundaries between life and art, high and popular culture, and image and reality. (59)

Although Aronowitz and Giroux contend the challenge of postmodernism is important to educators in general because it raises crucial questions regarding certain hegemonic aspects of modernism, some versions of postmodern discourse, as such postcolonial theorists as Gayatri Spivak have asserted, want to theoreti-cally value the "other" without considering what social conditions need to exist before such groups can actually exercise self- and social empowerment. Meanwhile, the more negative tendency of postmodernism is to privilege theoretical discussions in which space, textuality, and signs overpower all tangible forms of historicity. Consequently, Aronowitz and Giroux call for the breakdown of the binary between modern and postmodern theory in an attempt to link the modernist reliance on agency and reason to the construction of a democratic public sphere (59). And however much we may want to distance ourselves from modernist theory that posits a rational, objective subject position, in doing so we must not loiter at the other extreme, opting for what Ebert and others have termed a *Ludic* and ultimately *postpolitical* postmodernism, one in which the free-floating nature of signifiers supposedly limits the power of the subject to resist existing representations and to create new ones (Ebert 887). As a result, modernism needs to be defended within the existing conditions of the postmodern sphere, with critical pedagogy drawing from the best aspects of *both* modernism and postmodernism.

But whether subscribing to a more unified notion of culture as in a modernist perspective or a more fragmented notion of culture as in a postmodernist perspective, it is clear that with the current influences of both mass media and multicultural hegemonies that no systematic theory of culture can exist. It is also equally clear that there are many factions who propose that such a dominant culture needs to exist, the rationale falling into the traditional Arnoldian paradigm of offering society a sense of the best it has to give. Consider, for example, the recent battle at the University of Texas at Austin in which the proposed course "Writing About Difference" came under such attack for supposedly imposing political correctness at the expense of more traditional paradigms. In analyzing the situation, James Berlin and Michael Vivion argued that:

> One of the ironies of these unmistakably political disputes is that one group of contestants—those representing the right—offer their transparently ideological judgment in the name of a transcendent value-free commitment to the best that has been thought and said. That this "best" is nothing other than an ideological designation . . . remains unacknowledged. (vii)

Although there exist more conservative factions within both theoretical and pedagogical camps that attempt to label any multicultural theory as indoctrination into the politically correct, Blitz and Hurlbert, in discussing pedagogy, finally question, "What set of pedagogies have we packaged . . . in an attempt to transmit a view of culture which looks less and less like us—or like anybody" (21).

Furthermore, in arguing for a cultural criticism that acknowledges hegemonic structures within social, political, as well as educational institutions, we must question the role of the academic as cultural and social critic. One important discussion of this issue comes from Frank Lentricchia's *Criticism and Social Change*. Lentricchia's book is about culture, intellectuals, their authority and power, and how, in their work, they involve themselves inescapably in the political work of social change (6). Discussing the intellectual, Lentricchia focused on the literary intellectual, one who works mainly on texts and produces texts, such as poets, novelists, critics, and so forth. This is in direct contrast to the radical intellectuals, those who are actively involved with the working class, as well as traditional intellectuals, those who eschew the supposedly outer political world in favor of those more universal beauties and truths. Although many may argue about the role of the literary intellectual, Lentricchia asserted that the most powerful political work of the university humanist is to be carried on in what the intellectual does or is trained to do within the institution (7). Believing that criticism, as the task of literary intellectuals, "is the production of knowledge to the ends of power, and, maybe, of social change" (11), Lentricchia's goal is to have a situation in which intellectuals work without the regret that not everyone can hear them.

Although his academic audience may find his conclusions comforting, Lentricchia does not seem to envision situations that would allow for dialogue among intellectuals or even, more importantly, pedagogical dialogue between those who teach and those who learn, so that students, once outside the halls of academe, can continue to launch similar questions in a search for increased citizenship, an issue of central concern to many of us working in cultural studies. Yet the role of students, be they graduate or undergraduate, remains unaddressed by Lentricchia's mix of modern and postmodern theory. Without student empowerment, the notion of criticism as a vehicle of social change is too compact: Only certain people will fit behind the wheel and be allowed to drive. Thus, it is possible that Lentricchia and his compact community of intellectuals may be talking to themselves and not "changing" anything. Indeed, the limits of theory and criticism have been noted in various approaches, including feminism; for example, as Kolodny concluded, "any consciously ideologically premised criticism . . . is vitiated by confining those ideas to the study . . . or the pages of our books" (163).

In addition, intellectual politics must do more than critique racism, sexism, or militarism without incorporating the popular; rather, it must acknowledge the tradeoff between the popular appeal to bodily pleasures as opposed to a political rationality that calls for the denigration of that appeal. Indeed, Andrew Ross asserted that the history of popular culture involves intellectuals because of their role in culture as "experts, whose traditional business is to define what is popular and what is legitimate" (5). Education is culture's way of earning respect, but because the study of popular culture has been marginalized if not absent from most educational systems from kindergarten to college, it lacks the legitimacy of the great books approach to education (6). Yet, as in any cultural studies project, it is important to consider the dialectical relationship between intellectuals and popular culture to analyze what has become a mutual disrespect of the intellectual for popular culture and the masses for the highly educated. Although the educated cringe at those cultural genres that disseminate racist, sexist, and classist messages, because of their academic shield from much of these genres, they do not understand that cultural forms, "steeped in chauvinism and other bad attitudes," draw their popular appeal from expressions of disrespect for the lessons of educated taste and are thus a form of resistance (231). Ross concluded that part of the intellectual's dismissal of popular culture stems from the knowledge that the popular is an arena in which the expert knowledge and power granted to the intellectual no longer applies.

For these reasons, culture must not be solely a theoretical issue, but a pedagogical practice to be implemented both inside and outside the classroom. It is safe to say that as cultural critics concerned with revealing the hegemonic practices and textual representations that empower some and exclude others, we do not delude ourselves that our ideological premises have become "mainstream" and widely accepted by both the academic and surrounding communities. Often, those most resistant to our theory are those we most want to reach: our students. Despite the recognition of marginalized groups within our society, the voices of the margin are well subordinated into all too brief news images of inner-city poor or young gay men dying of AIDS, images that many of our students feel comfortable leaving in the margin. Depending on the philosophy of the thousands of university newspapers, we are bound to find editorials such as "Sexual Harassment is Not a Problem" or "Indulge in a Conservative's Diet," editorials that further reflect the marginalization of the Other. And whereas conservative writers such as Dinesh D'Souza may hope to take credit for fostering the ideological backlash against "political correctness," the likely influences are those more directly tied to mass consumption, for example, the radio and television shows of talk-show pundit Rush Limbaugh, who has often termed his liberal bashing *entertainment*.

As we quickly approach the year 2000, the legacy of the 1980s conservatism has left its traces on those who now sit in our college classrooms. Lest we forget the impact of this conservatism, Stuart Hall reminded us that:

> If the global postmodern represents an ambiguous opening to difference and to the margins and makes certain a kind of decentering of the Western narrative a likely possibility, it is matched . . . by the backlash: the aggressive resistance to difference; the attempt to restore the canon of Western civilization . . . the return to grand narratives of history, language, and great literature; the defense of ethnic absolutism, of a cultural racism that has marked the Thatcher and the Reagan eras. (25)

Given the political conflicts over the content of college-level courses, from composition to literature and to history as well, Hall's observation that a grand narrative of culture lives on is an astute one. But because of the influence of media technology and media representation, culture has become more fragmented, and although some view this fragmentation negatively, we must consider the ways in which such fragmentation can first be critiqued, perhaps focusing on the ways in which mass media can offer only partial representations of women, ethnic, and other cultural minorities. Part of this critique necessitates that our students question the distinction between the discursive representation of these groups and the social, historical, and local frameworks in which such individuals experience cultures. We must also consider the way in which this fragmentation, both cultural and technological, can be used as a tool of resistance and change by providing more opportunity for the student production of discursive alternatives, be they verbal, visual, or aural.

Because it is clear that despite the efforts of Marxist and feminist theory, dominant hegemonic practices continue to place women, ethnic minorities, lesbians, and gays in the category of "other," we must look for more public avenues for the critique and resistance of these practices. As the University of Texas incident indicates, scholars certainly need to dialogue with each other about the question of culture and the role of mass media in producing and distributing images of that culture, yet without dialogue between teachers and students, change seems less likely. Thus the place for such discussion is the classroom, and the question of culture must move from theory to pedagogy, blending our revised theories of culture with pedagogies that acknowledge the value of studying the discursive practices of student culture, from toys to music to shopping malls, within the academy.

Although we do not wish to merely reindoctrinate our students with a counterhegemony, what we hope to do is to call into question those hegemonic forces that uphold a univocal version of culture, a version in which there is a standard of "the best that has been thought and said," a version in which popular culture remains inferior to other cultural texts, a version in which issues of concern to women and other minorities are of little concern to anyone else. Because of the increasing importance of this endeavor, we must look at both the history of our supposed cultural and media studies' pedagogies as well as our most current cultural approaches to reveal strengths and weaknesses and to argue for those practices that offer a critique of culture, media, technology, and society, as well to offer strategies for resistance and revision so that those seen as "other" need not remain underrepresented in our media and marginalized in their own communities.

WORKS CITED

Aronowitz, Stanley, and Henry Giroux. *Postmodern Education: Politics, Culture, and Social Criticism*. Minneapolis: U of Minneapolis P, 1991.

Berlin, James, and Michael Vivion, eds. *Cultural Studies and the English Classroom*. Portsmouth, NH: Boynton/Cook, 1993.

Blitz, Michael, and C. Mark Hurlbert. "Cults of Culture." *Cultural Studies and the English Classroom*. Eds. James Berlin and Michael Vivion. Portsmouth, NH: Boynton/Cook, 1993. 5–23

Ebert, Teresa L. "The 'Difference' of Postmodern Feminism." *College English* 53 (1991): 886–904.

Hall, Stuart. "What is This 'Black' Popular Culture?" *Black Popular Culture*. Ed. Gina Dent. Seattle: Bay Press, 1992. 21–36.

Kolodny, Annette. "Dancing Through the Minefield: Some Observations of the Theory, Practice, and Politics of a Feminist Literary Criticism." *The New Feminist Criticism*. Ed. Elaine Showalter. New York: Pantheon, 1985.

Lentricchia, Frank. *Criticism and Social Change*. Chicago: U of Chicago P, 1985.

McGowan, John. *Postmodernism and its Critics*. New York: Cornell UP, 1991.

Ross, Andrew. *No Respect: Intellectuals and Popular Culture*. London: Routledge, 1989.

Smith, Paul. "Pedagogy and the Popular Culture Commodity Text." *Popular Culture, Schooling and Everyday Life*. Eds. Henry Giroux and Roger Simon. New York: Bergin and Garvey, 1989. 31–46.

Williams, Raymond. *Marxism and Literature*. London: Oxford UP, 1977.

20 Literacy Among Undergraduates: How We Represent Students as Writers and What It Means When We Don't

Joyce Neff Magnotto
Old Dominion University

For many years I was active in the writing across the curriculum (WAC) movement, leading workshops at schools and universities, directing a WAC program, and serving on the Board of Consultants of the National WAC Network (see Magnotto et al.; Stout and Magnotto). That work put me face to face with professors from all disciplines who wanted to know why those of us in the English department were not doing our jobs, and why students who had passed our composition classes were, according to these professors, still "illiterate."

The frequency with which my colleagues voiced their concerns pushed me to reexamine my own assumptions about college writing classes and their impact on academic literacy. Literacy, as we well know, is a slippery term. It is not always synonymous with writing, and it is no longer limited to functional literacy. As Ellsworth, Hedley, and Baratta reminded us in their recent book, there are multiple literacies—everything from electronic literacy to cultural literacy to environmental literacy, even family literacy.

Nevertheless, I, like many others who teach rhetoric and composition, expect my work to improve my students' levels of academic literacy. I assume that guided instruction in composition enables students to become critical readers and writers of academic texts. But my colleagues from other disciplines were persistent, so I decided to address their concerns by researching some of my own: Just what is academic literacy for an undergraduate? And how do college writing courses contribute to academic literacy, if they do?

I investigated the construct of *literacy* as it manifests itself in the writing that undergraduates do for their professors across disciplines. In other words, I looked at how various people involved in a particular writing program (students, professors, and writing center tutors) represent college writing as a social practice (see Brodkey). The most surprising finding of my study is that students were rarely, if ever, constructed as writers in either college writing classes or in classes in other disciplines where writing assignments were part of the pedagogy. My study shows that pseudocomposition (a term coined by Robert Scholes) continues to thrive, and that academic institutions continue to define undergraduate literacy in very narrow terms.

In the following pages I explain my methodology briefly and then discuss the implications of these findings.

THE STUDY

During the 1989–90 academic year, I conducted a naturalistic study of a cross-disciplinary, faculty-staffed writing center located at a large (36,000), metropolitan community college (Magnotto). My purpose was not so much to study the writing center itself, but to use that site to analyze college writing as a social practice. I selected the writing center rather than a classroom setting because this center is somewhat unique. The tutors are faculty who agree to tutor in place of teaching one course out of their teaching load. They represent different disciplines: English, biology, mathematics, computer science, foreign languages, and philosophy; and they work with students who bring assignments from different courses. Furthermore, the faculty selected to serve as tutors are versed in writing across the curriculum, and they engage in biweekly training sessions that often involve conversations with other faculty who are not tutors. Thus, the setting allowed me to collect different kinds of talk about college writing: (a) tutor–student talk from tutoring sessions; (b) interview talk with tutors and students; and (c) training-session talk between tutors and other faculty. I also collected the written texts brought to the center.

Using methods from grounded theory (open, axial, and selective coding and memoing), I focused on how students, tutors, and other faculty represent college writing in their talk, in their assignment directions, and in the writing produced in response to those assignments (see Strauss for further explanation of grounded theory). After coding hundreds of pages of transcripts and other texts, I classified statements about college writing into five dimensions: audience, purpose, product, process, and student-as-writer.

The names of the first four dimensions are, of course, from composition theory and were familiar to all of the 10 tutors in my study. None of these dimensions needed to be explained to students visiting the writing center, but in almost all instances, tutors rather than students first used the terms during the writing center conferences. The fifth dimension, "student-as-writer," names the most intriguing dimension to emerge from the data.

DATA ANALYSIS

Table 20.1 shows the five dimensions listed along the left side of the chart. Across the top of the table are the core categories that emerged when I further analyzed the data using additional coding methods (memo sequencing and integrative diagrams). The core categories are: student representations, tutor representations, faculty representations, and writing center constructs. Each box in the matrix summarizes the predominant assumptions that individuals in a particular group (students, faculty, tutors) hold about one of the dimensions. These assumptions were embedded in the talk of the people I studied, and as often as feasible I used their language to construct the chart. In the case of the last column, the assumptions emerged from the whole data collection, including field notes and the recordings of writing center sessions and meetings.

"AHA" MOMENTS

As I further analyzed the transcripts, another interesting feature to emerge was the discursive interruption (Silverman and Torode) or what I call the "aha" moment. During "aha" moments, one person realizes that the other holds different assumptions about writing and therefore represents writing differently. "Aha" moments signify tensions within and across representations of writing. I define *representation* as a discursive expression of a belief or notion that is used (consciously or unconsciously) as the basis for practice. The following are two examples of "aha" moments followed by a discussion of the presence and absence of tensions in representations of college writing.

One type of "aha" moment occurred in several conferences. The student came to the conference assuming that her classroom teacher/examiner was her only audience. In the writing center session, the student met an additional audience discursively represented by the tutor—the audience of an "interested, nonexpert reader." The "aha" moment unfolded as the student realized that there were ways for her paper to be read other than by a teacher/examiner.

In another example of an "aha" moment, the tutor assumed revision was a meaning-making process for the student until the tutor could no longer ignore the student's discursive representation of revision as "making it right":

"You're going to tell me how to make it right, right?"

"I'm thinking of criticism on what I'm doing wrong, so I can do it right."

"Aha" moments typically occur well into the conference after much circling and repetition. They are signaled linguistically by responses such as the following:

1. "Oh! I can do the rest of [the essay answers] the same way!"

2. "Okay! When I say 'why' that's the cause!"

3. "That makes sense. That feels much better. At least I have a guideline I can go by, and you said I can just go right into it. I thought I had to work around [it]."

4. "Okay! That sounds workable. It's removed the fear anyway."

TENSIONS

To return to Table 20.1: Tensions become evident when we look across the chart and notice conflicts between different assumptions about college writing. Both the presence and absence of tensions are unsettling.

The first box under the column labeled "tutor representations" shows assumptions tutors make about audience: audience as teacher/examiner, and audience as interested, nonexpert reader. These representations suggest that tutors balance different notions about audience, but may not realize any conflict or tension between these notions except in "aha" moments (and in later reflection about "aha" moments, such as in workshops I gave to cross check my analysis).

There is also tension among the different purposes for college writing that tutors name. For example, displaying knowledge (to an expert) versus communicating one's exploratory ideas on a subject. I read this tension as a reflection of the traditional distinction between student writing and professional writing. The former is a "test" of what a novice knows about a subject that is already known by the audience. The latter purpose is generally reserved for writers constructed as having the authority to explore a subject in a nonhierarchical context.

We can see tension across representations when we look at tutor representations of products versus student representations of products. Students assume a separation of content and form (style) in products. Tutors assume an interrelationship of content and form—mutual support of one for the other.

STUDENT-AS-WRITER

One of the most revealing lines in Table 20.1 is the bottom one: student-as-writer. When students come to the writing center, they do not discursively represent themselves as writers. Neither do the faculty who send them. The following statements illustrate students' views of themselves as *non*writers:

"I can't write."

"I'm not a writer."

"I'm not good at writing."

Table 20.1: Representations of College Writing

	Student representations	Tutor representations	Faculty representations	Writing Center Constructs
Audience	Teacher as examiner	(1) Teacher as examiner (2) Interested, non-expert readers	Teacher as examiner	(1) Teacher as examiner (2) Tutor as interested reader (3) Writer as reader
Purpose	To earn a grade by satisfying a professor.	(1) To display knowledge (2) To learn content (3) To learn to write (4) To communicate one's ideas	(1) To test learning (2) To teach content (3) To assist student learning	(1) To satisfy the professor/ institution (2) To meet writer & reader needs
Products	Content and form are separable. Writing is right or wrong.	Content + Form. Professors want deductive, thesis-driven essays, relatively free of error.	Formal products "count." Writing-to-learn products "uncountable." Ideal texts vs student texts.	Institutional constraints determine form & content.
Process	Linear, mysterious, painful, constrained by slippery rules, solitary. Revision = polishing.	Recursive, messy. HOCS & LOCS. Revision = meaning-making	A means to the product rather than a means of developing the writer.	Collaborative, social. Strategies can be taught & learned by moving between the particular and general.
Student as writer	Students are students, not writers.	Students can also be writers.	Unexamined dimension	Students can be constructed as writers.

173

"The whole class was on writing. We wrote the whole entire class, and I did good! I mean I made a B in the class, and I mean I don't even know how to write."

DISCUSSION

The tensions that emerge because of differing representations of what it means to write in college are striking: Students who do *not* see themselves as writers find themselves in writing center conferences talking to writing tutors who do see them as writers; professors give assignments that ask students to role play as "experts" and then evaluate the responses for formal features of correctness; collaborative writing and learning are encouraged in the writing center but prohibited in many classrooms.

Most writing center advocates accept the premise that writing center work influences the tutor as much as it does the student, and different theorists suggest how that influence works. As Roswell showed, in the case of peer tutors, the influence may work to reproduce the academy as much as to change it. However, when the tutors are faculty, as they are in the writing center I studied, the influence of writing center work can be quite the opposite. In follow-up interviews with the faculty tutors in my study, they told me writing-center work had pushed them to reconsider their assignments, their grading, their class policies, their deadlines, and their understanding of students. I would claim that their reconsidered pedagogies resulted in part because tutoring situates them differently. When tutoring, they experience the dilemmas of school writing from the students' perspectives—writing as linear, mysterious, painful, constrained by arbitrary rules, solitary. Tutors also see college writing as it is constructed by their colleagues who design and evaluate the assignments that students bring to the writing center (see the column labeled "faculty representations").

The good news is that writing-center talk between a faculty–tutor and a student allows some representations to be reconstructed and opens up others for reconsideration. Reconstruction of beliefs is a possibility in the writing center because differing assumptions are allowed to surface. I found instances in which students' notions of audience and purpose were expanded, and in which assumptions about writing-as-process became more sophisticated. However, I found only a few instances in which notions of "product" were reconstructed. Ideally, writing-center culture allows a tutor and student to relate as one writer/reader talking to another writer/reader during the conference. But it is not that simple. The tutor also represents the institution and fellow teachers. Thus, the tutor, him- or herself, is in a position of tension and balances many issues: Who does and who does not belong in college? Where in school do writers find places to write about their own ideas and tell their own stories? How writer-like or unwriter-like do schools make students feel?

Susan Miller traced the history of college writing classes as gatekeeping mechanisms that became necessary in the mid-19th century when colleges opened their doors a bit wider to admit a few more men than had been previously selected. My study provides evidence that institutional practices regarding writing have not moved much beyond gatekeeping. Even WAC programs and writing centers that have helped individual teachers and groups of teachers reexamine their pedagogies have not significantly altered the institution's representation of undergraduate literacy. Thesis and support essays, relatively free of error, remain the products that count in the academy.

When we design writing programs, we usually deal with goals and outcomes and with what will be a core course and what will be an elective. My study suggests that we must go deeper than that. We must evaluate how we construct undergraduate students as writers, what counts as academic literacy, and who is credentialed as literate. We must think about the combination of cultural literacy and critical thinking we are aiming for. We must ask how our often unexamined assumptions about who is and who is not a writer impact on our success (or lack thereof) in producing literate graduates. Finally, we must consider where the resistance to constructing students as writers lies, and what we want to do about it (if anything)? What tensions will emerge if and when we *do* treat students as writers?

WORKS CITED

Brodkey, Linda. *Academic Writing as Social Practice*. Philadelphia: Temple UP, 1987.

Ellsworth, Nancy, Carolyn N. Hedley, and Anthony N. Baratta. *Literacy: A Redefinition*. Hillsdale, NJ: Erlbaum, 1994.

Magnotto, Joyce. "The Construction of College Writing in a Cross-disciplinary, Community College Writing Center: Student, Tutor, and Faculty Representations." Diss. U of Pennsylvania, 1991.

——— et al. "Prince George's Community College." *Programs that Work: Models and Methods for Writing Across the Curriculum*. Ed. Toby Fulwiler and Art Young. Portsmouth, NH: Boynton/ Cook, 1990. 65–81.

Miller, Susan. *Textual Carnivals: The Politics of Composition*. Carbondale: Southern Illinois UP, 1991.

Roswell, Barbara. "The Tutor's Audience Is Always a Fiction: The Construction of Authority in Writing Center Conferences." Diss. U of Pennsylvania, 1992.

Scholes, Robert. *Textual Power: Literary Theory and the Teaching of English*. New Haven: Yale UP, 1985.

Silverman, David, and Brian Torode. *The Material Word: Some Theories of Language and Its Limits*. London: Routledge & Kegan Paul, 1980.

Stout, Barbara, and Joyce Magnotto. "Writing Across the Curriculum at Community Colleges." *Strengthening Programs for Writing Across the Curriculum*. Ed. Susan H. McLeod. San Francisco, Jossey-Bass, 1988. 21–30.

Strauss, Anselm. *Qualitative Analysis for Social Scientists*. Cambridge UP, 1987.

21 Scholarship, Promotion, and Tenure in Composition Studies

Richard C. Gebhardt
Bowling Green State University

In my final Editor's Column in *College Composition and Communication*, I sketched a number of issues confronting rhetoric at a time when many of its scholars are within a few years of important personnel evaluations, and I urged "a widening consideration," by individual scholars and professional organizations, "of the way scholarship in composition studies is viewed, of how it should be evaluated, and of ways scholars in our field can more effectively present themselves for tenure and promotion" ("Scholarship" 442). That goal stands behind this chapter addressed to women and men who—as individuals and as members of Rhetoric Society of America and other organizations—are affected by the issues involved in scholarship, promotion, and tenure in composition studies.

These issues are numerous, complicated, and entangled with one another in a way that has made writing this chapter a frustrating experience for me. In an effort to reduce your frustration, I begin with an overview, in the form of four generalizations:

1. The breadth of composition studies—the range of its research approaches and of its scholarly products—makes it difficult to define the standards of scholarship that should apply to the field and to explain them to people working in more focused scholarly paradigms.

2. The important place of pedagogy in composition studies poses special problems as we define and explain our field, for many individuals—within rhetoric and throughout American higher education—consider teaching and

177

students lesser objects of research and publishing than arcane and theoretical topics.

3. Composition studies has established itself as an academic field through research and scholarship, a development that has put into sharp relief the field's dual (or some would say, conflicting) interests in research and in undergraduate teaching.

4. The field of composition studies is part of a system of American higher education that is reappraising the roles publication and teaching play in the work and the evaluation of faculty members.

The diversity of research approaches, evident in the pages of the journals and the programs of professional meetings of composition studies, is a source of strength and vitality for our field, as well as a source of difficulty for scholars. This dual aspect of our diversity shows in Andrea Lunsford's "The Nature of Composition Studies." She wrote that composition studies tends "to look well beyond its own borders and to challenge divisions between disciplines. . . . Thus a scholar may draw on anthropology, psychology, philosophy, literary theory, neurobiology, or other disciplines in studying the creation and dissemination of written texts" (9). Then, in the next sentence, she noted that "the blurring of disciplinary boundaries raises a number of difficulties for graduate students and scholars in the field" (9). Similarly, Gesa Kirsch wrote that the "diversity of research questions raised by scholars, the broad territory encompassed by rhetoric and composition, and the multidisciplinary backgrounds of researchers all invite the use of multiple research methods" (255). But this "methodological pluralism," she immediately notes, "is not unproblematic. Researchers steeped in different research traditions often speak different languages and describe their observations with different sets of vocabulary" (255–56). And Janice Lauer described composition studies as a "multimodal discipline" that works "through the use of at least three modes of inquiry—rhetorical, historical, and empirical" (44). But she also wrote candidly about the "costs" of multimodality: for instance, the way the difficulty of studying several "forms of inquiry" can lead people "to ignore or marginalize a mode or two" (50), and the fact that, in promotion and tenure review, composition scholars "often face a double task—to produce first-rate scholarship and to explain its nature and value" (51).

It is no small matter for composition studies (or for individual scholars worried about their tenure or promotion) if a defining quality of the field interferes with understanding among scholars; promotes the privileging of some research approaches by those who "ignore or marginalize" other approaches; requires extraordinary efforts of those who try to do multimodal research; and burdens scholars with the need not just to do good research, but also to "explain its nature and value." To begin with, it takes a lot of time just to "keep up," generally, with research approaches. And, as Cheryl Geisler's essay about her own research suggests, the costs are far higher for those who try to use multiple approaches in their scholarship:

> When I'm done [with a multimodal text analysis], I'm fairly sure of my conclusions and I can explain and defend them, both to people who want numbers and those who want exegesis. But people who want numbers don't care about exegesis and those who want exegesis don't understand the numbers. Sure, I can talk to both, but it takes twice as long to get something to say.
>   The second highest cost comes in terms of comprehensibility. In building an argument across multiple methods and traditions, some parts of the logic are simply incomprehensible to some of the people to whom I think the argument should be important. (47)

In this extract Geisler emphasized audience concerns (whether readers want numbers or exegesis, for instance) and the comprehensibility of research to others *within* the community of composition researchers. But tenure and promotion reviews bring broader contexts for explanation. Records of scholarship presented by composition specialists may be viewed skeptically by faculty—outside English departments or within—who see our field still struggling to find its research methods and scholarly standards. This potential difficulty during personnel reviews is complicated further by a second defining quality of our field, its concern for pedagogy. As I phrased the second issue at the beginning of this chapter, the important place of pedagogy in composition studies poses special problems as we define and explain our field, because many individuals consider teaching and students less worthy objects of scholarship than arcane and theoretical topics.

Within higher education at large, Maryellen Weimer wrote that pedagogical journals often "are viewed as weak siblings of the favored and prestigious research journals," and many faculty report that "writing about pedagogy isn't regarded as legitimate scholarship" (44). And Lacey noted, in an article about the evaluation of faculty scholarship, that "writing about teaching and a number of other activities that keep teachers intellectually alive and effective in the classroom . . . are excluded by definition" in many tenure and promotion reviews (95). I offer these quotations not to describe the situation inside composition studies, but to illustrate the special problems composition scholars may face at tenure or promotion time.

A survey I made of teachers and administrators in composition studies (see Gebhardt, "Issues" 12–13) suggests that scholarship in our field is evaluated against such standards as these:

Object of Research: A rough hierarchy ranging from complex and theoretical topics and issues (at the high end) to practical and pedagogical matters.

Manner of Research: A rough hierarchy ranging from rigorous "original" research (at the top) through rigorous secondary or summarizing research, to work with a more personal or anecdotal slant.

Genre of Publication: "Major" scholarly articles and university press books are more important here than articles and books for nonspecialists, and textbooks and other overtly pedagogical publications bring up the rear.

Validity of Publication: Refereeing and the reputation of journals and publishers are important here, as are citation by others and comments by external reviewers during tenure and promotion reviews.

A scholar in our field can do rigorous original scholarship (the *manner* of research) and publish it in scholarly books and refereed journals of high profile (the *genre* and the *validity* of publication) and still find his or her scholarship undervalued by a personnel committee because of its focus on teaching (the *object* of research).

It does not always work that way, of course. But most of us know of situations in which faculty have been disadvantaged in personnel reviews by presenting research and publications that focused on the teaching of writing. And it seems pretty clear that sensitivity to the second-tier status teaching holds for many academics has been one influence on composition's evolution as a scholarly field. Richard Miller's words in a recent *CCC* article made this point:

> English studies [has long] taken for granted that meaningful work occurs in the realm of literary studies and menial labor takes place in the composition classroom.
>
> In the past decade, compositionists have openly begun to combat this all-too-familiar relegation to the economic and intellectual lower classes by attempting to organize and professionalize the field in a number of well-publicized initiatives. Among these has been the steady growth of graduate programs allowing concentration in composition, rhetoric, and/or literacy studies; the proliferation of monographs and book-length publications on the theory and practice of composition; and the elaboration of workers' rights initiatives like the Wyoming Resolution. (165)

This quotation—with what strikes me as an odd linking of graduate program growth and workers' rights statements—is a useful bridge to the third issue I sketched earlier: that composition's development as an academic field through scholarly means throws into sharp relief our field's dual interests in research and undergraduate teaching.

Over the past couple of decades, composition studies has evolved as a scholarly discipline with at least six dozen Ph.D. programs (Brown et al. 240). These programs graduate many women and men to faculty positions that provide the incentive to protect time for research and publication, and a fair number of these Ph.D.s have been absorbed into the graduate teaching required as the number of Ph.D. programs has doubled over the past decade. At the same time, America's colleges and universities have undergraduates to teach, virtually all of whom take at least one first-year writing class. Many of them take classes taught by part-time or temporary teachers with too many students, too many sections, low pay, and few benefits. But very few of these students are in classes taught by graduates of America's growing number of rhetoric Ph.D. programs. There are many reasons for this situation, of course, and as John Schilb put it in a commentary following *Rhetoric Review*'s recent survey of doctoral programs:

> When it comes to rhetoric and composition, universities are highly capable of schizophrenic behavior. On the one hand, they create doctoral programs in the subject; on the other, they continue to treat introductory writing as a mere "service" enterprise not worthy of "real" faculty. (403)

The growth of graduate programs in rhetoric and composition has not taken place in isolation. It has been accompanied by significant increases in the numbers of rhetoric and composition journals, specialized book series serving the field, and university presses and other publishers interested in books in composition studies and its developing subfields. As Jane Peterson said in her 1990 CCCC Chair's Address, "We have become a healthy and dynamic profession through devoting . . . years to establishing our identity as an emerging discipline, to becoming respectable through scholarship and research" (26). But we have developed scholarly identity within an academic system that has, as Peterson put it, long "institutionalized a hierarchy that places teaching far below research and scholarship" (26) so that, today, there is "evidence that a hierarchy exists within [our] profession, evidence that we consider teaching far less important than research or scholarship" (27).

Developing as a scholarly field, then, may be causing some separation of composition studies (as it is pursued through research and publication by specialists in faculty positions) from composition teaching (as it is organized and staffed at most colleges and universities). At least that is the way some people view the situation—for instance, two-year college teacher Howard Tinberg, writing in *CCC*:

> The rush toward theory in the field might just as well be described as a rush to get out of the classroom. The irony of such a development is palpable. Composition, which has been for so long committed to the importance of the classroom as the scene of learning and teaching, is determined to cut itself from its root. (37)

If composition studies (a field "devoted to the multimodal study of written discourse and its *facilitation*" [Lauer 44, emphasis added]) were to distance itself from composition teaching, it would be a critical loss of disciplinary identity. It also would mean the loss, for the field, of an opportunity to provide leadership at a time when (and this is the fourth issue I sketched earlier) American higher education is reappraising the roles publication and teaching play in the work and the evaluation of faculty members.

Many faculty members and professional organizations now are questioning the priority given to publication and are seeking better ways to evaluate and reward faculty. *Scholarship Reconsidered*, for instance, made it clear that a "strong undercurrent of dissatisfaction exists" with an emphasis on scholarship over teaching: "More than 60 percent of today's faculty feel that teaching effectiveness, not publication, should be the *primary* criterion for promotion" (Boyer 29, 31). More recently, the Director of the AAHE Forum on Faculty Roles and Rewards wrote that "[a]t every type of institution, faculty express a longing for an older and spiritually richer academic culture, one that placed greater value on the education of students and on the public responsibilities of scholars" (Lovett 3). Within English studies, the ADE recently indicated that "publication need not be the only or even the most important measure of a faculty member's accomplishments. In evaluations of scholarship, different kinds of activities and products should be given credit" ("ADE" 44). And the MLA Commission on Professional Service is trying to develop a new way to think about and evaluate the work of faculty by replacing the Teaching/Research/Service categories in personnel review with an evaluation matrix in which each of these activities is described in terms of its intellectual work and its professional citizenship (Phelps et al.).

Within this climate of review and reform, composition studies—its scholars and teachers and professional associations such as the Rhetoric Society of America— can and should play a significant leadership role. Surely, composition studies is *not* one of the fields the director of FIPSE's Institutional Priorities and Faculty Rewards Project had in mind when he wrote that:

> The process of expanding the scope of what is considered scholarly or professional work is far more difficult for some disciplines than for others.
>
> For many scholars, the effort to re-emphasize the importance of teaching, applied research, and community-related activities has created concern about how their disciplines will be perceived by others. (Diamond B2)

Teaching has long occupied an important place in rhetoric and composition. Most research published in the field's refereed journals and scholarly books, like most dissertations written in the field's doctoral programs, has some connection to teaching or students. We know that research can lead to pedagogical expressions such as textbooks, new programs, teaching materials, and workshops for college and high school teachers. And we do not have to worry about how others will perceive our treating pedagogical and applied research as "scholarship"; from past experience, we already know.

As long as composition studies maintains its historical connection to composition teaching, then, our field is in a very strong position to provide the leadership American higher education needs to refine the relationship between scholarship and teaching and to reform the way faculty members are evaluated. I'll end this chapter by suggesting a few ways we might work, as individuals and members of professional groups, to exercise such leadership.

An initial goal we might pursue is to help English departments take the "first step" *Scholarship Reconsidered* recommended to make "the reward system more flexible and more vital." This is to have "faculty assessment take into account a broader range of writing," including textbooks and articles about teaching— writing that "if done well can reveal a professor's knowledge of the field, illuminate essential integrative themes, and powerfully contribute to excellence in teaching" (Boyer 35).

Pursuing this goal would also involve broadening the current criteria for evaluating scholarship (e.g., the Object of Research, Manner of Research, and Genre of Publication) and developing additional criteria—perhaps evaluating publications in light of their relationships to the teaching assignment of the faculty member, the mission of the institution or department, and the needs and expectations of society (see Gebhardt, "Avoiding" xxx).

Such review and rethinking could be undertaken by individuals, writing program staffs, and departments, as well as by committees and task forces of scholarly and professional associations. These organizations could foster and coordinate local efforts by scheduling sessions at their conferences, featuring the subject in their journals and newsletters, and setting up clearinghouses or computer bulletin boards.

And RSA, CCCC, and other professional groups in composition studies can increase the impact of their leadership by working together to explore the way scholarship should be evaluated and by sharing ideas and approaches with other disciplinary and administrative groups that are grappling with the same issues.

These are but a few of the things individuals and professional organizations in composition studies *could* do to provide leadership in the reappraisal of scholarship now underway in American higher education. They also are some of the things individuals and organizations within composition studies *should* do. After all, we have considerable experience to share about scholarship focused on teaching and students. And it is in our vested interest to help other specialties— outside English studies and within—to understand such scholarship and to practice it.

WORKS CITED

"ADE Statement of Good Practice: Teaching, Evaluation, and Scholarship." *ADE Bulletin* 105 (Fall 1993): 43–45.

Boyer, Ernest. *Scholarship Reconsidered: Priorities of the Professorate.* Princeton: Carnegie Foundation, 1990.

Brown, Stewart C., Paul R. Meyer, and Theresa Enos. "Doctoral Programs in Rhetoric and Composition: A Catalog of the Profession." *Rhetoric Review* 12 (Spring 1994): 240–51.

Diamond, Robert M. "The Tough Task of Reforming the Faculty-Rewards System." *Chronicle of Higher Education,* 11 (May 1994): B1–B3.

Gebhardt, Richard C. "Avoiding the Research vs. Teaching Trap: Expanding the Criteria for Evaluating Scholarship." *The Politics and Processes of Scholarly Publishing*. Ed. Joseph Moxley. Forthcoming.

———. "Issues of Promotion and Tenure for Rhetoric and Technical Writing Faculty." *Studies in Technical Communication*. Ed. Brenda R. Sims. Denton: CCCC Committee on Technical Communications, 1993. 9–15.

———. "Scholarship, Promotion, and Tenure in Composition Studies." *College Composition and Communication* 44 (Dec. 1993): 439–42.

Geisler, Cheryl. "Exploring Academic Literacy: An Experiment in Composing." *College Composition and Communication* 43 (Feb. 1992): 39–54.

Kirsch, Gesa. "Methodological Pluralism." *Methods and Methodologies in Composition Research*. Ed. Gesa Kirsch and Patricia A. Sullivan. Carbondale: Southern Illinois UP, 1992. 247–69.

Lacey, Paul A. "Encouraging and Evaluating Scholarship for the College Teacher." *Excellent Teaching in a Changing Academy*. Ed. Feroza Jussawalla. New Directions in Teaching and Learning No. 44. San Francisco: Jossey-Bass, 1990. 91–100.

Lauer, M. Janice. "Rhetoric and Composition Studies: A Multimodal Discipline." *Defining the New Rhetorics*. Ed. Theresa Enos and Stuart C. Brown. Sage Series in Written Communication 7. Newbury Park: Sage, 1993. 44–54.

Lovett, Clara M. "Listening to the Faculty Grapevine." *AAHE Bulletin* 46, No. 3 (Nov. 1993): 3–5.

Lunsford, Andrea A. "The Nature of Composition Studies." *An Introduction to Composition Studies*. Ed. Erika Lindemann and Gary Tate. New York: Oxford UP, 1991. 3–14.

Miller, Richard E. "Composing English Studies: Towards a Social History of the Discipline." *College Composition and Communication* 45 (May 1994): 164–79.

Peterson, Jane. "Valuing Teaching: Assumptions, Problems, and Possibilities." *College Composition and Communication* 42 (Feb. 1991): 25–35.

Phelps, Louise Wetherbee, James Slevin, and Robert Denham. "Rethinking Intellectual Work and Faculty Reward: The MLA Commission on Professional Service." Conference on College Composition and Communication. Nashville, March 16, 1994.

Schilb, John. "Getting Disciplined?" *Rhetoric Review* 12 (Spring 1994): 398–405.

Tinberg, Howard B. "An Enlargement of Composition: More on Theory Building in the Composition Classroom." *College Composition and Communication* 42 (Feb. 1991): 36–44.

Weimer, Maryellen. "The Disciplinary Journals on Pedagogy." *Change* (Nov./Dec. 1993): 44–51.\

About the Contributors

Kristine L. Blair is an assistant professor of English at Texas A&M University in Corpus Christi, Texas, where she teaches computer-assisted writing courses. She received her Ph.D. in English from Purdue University, where she served as an assistant director of technical writing, and president of the English graduate student association. She previously taught at Sacramento City College and California State University at Sacramento. Her interests include rhetorical theory, feminist cultural theory, and technical and professional communication.

Dottie Broaddus is an assistant professor of American studies at Arizona State University West in Phoenix, where she teaches composition and professional writing courses in an American studies program. She received her Ph.D. in rhetoric and composition from the University of Louisville. Currently she is working on a book about 19th-century rhetoric and culture in Boston. She has previously taught at St. Meinrad College in Indiana.

Juanita R. Comfort, on leave from Old Dominion University in Norfolk, Virginia, where her work is supported by a presidential minority fellowship, is a graduate administrative associate and doctoral candidate in English at The Ohio State University. Her current interests include classroom enthnography and issues affecting African-American women academics. She has worked as a professional journalist and has taught a wide range of first-year writing courses, as well as advanced courses in American literature and literature by minorities.

Glenda Conway is a doctoral candidate in rhetoric and composition at the University of Louisville, where her dissertation examined issues of voice and ideology in U.S. Supreme Court decisions. In addition to her work at Louisville, she has taught at the University of Kentucky, Lexington Community College, and

Kentucky State University, and has been a writing consultant to General Electric, 3M Corporation, the Kentucky National Guard, and the Kentucky State Police Academy.

Sharon Crowley (Ph.D., University of Northern Colorado) is Professor of Rhetoric at the University of Iowa. Previously she was Professor of English at Northern Arizona University. From 1989 to 1992, she chaired the National Committee on Professional Standards in Postsecondary Writing Instruction. She is the author of *A Teacher's Introduction to Deconstruction* (NCTE, 1989), *Ancient Rhetorics for Contemporary Students* (Macmillan, 1994), and *The Methodical Memory: Invention in Current-Traditional Rhetoric* (Southern Illinois UP), which received the W. Ross Winterowd Award for the Outstanding Book in Composition Theory in 1990.

Richard C. Gebhardt (Ph.D., Michigan State University) is Professor and Chair of the Department of English at Bowling Green State University. Earlier he was chair of the humanities division and associate academic dean at Findlay College. From 1987 until 1993 he served as editor of *College Composition and Communication*. His "Avoiding the Research vs. Teaching Trap: Expanding the Criteria for Evaluating Scholarship" is forthcoming in *The Politics and Processes of Scholarly Publishing* (Greenwood Press).

Cheryl Glenn is an associate professor of English at Oregon State University, where she teaches courses in rhetoric, composition, and literature. She received her Ph.D. in English from Ohio State University, where she specialized in rhetorical theory and history, composition theory and practice, and medieval and Renaissance literature. She is, with Robert Connors, the author of the *St. Martin's Guide to Teaching Writing*, as well as numerous articles, reviews, and chapters in books. She currently serves as the Rhetoric Society's director of membership.

Mary Grabar began her doctoral work in English in the fall of 1994 at Georgia State University in Atlanta, where she serves as a graduate teaching assistant in the first-year composition program. In addition to her work here on Gadamer, she has presented research from her master's thesis on symbolism and intersubjectivity in *Paradise Lost* at medieval/Renaissance literature conferences.

T. R. Johnson is a doctoral candidate in rhetoric and composition at the University of Louisville, where he is a university fellow. He has taught courses in world literature, first-year composition, and writing across the curriculum at Louisville and at Bellarmine College. He has presented papers on Elvis at the Popular Culture Association, the human genome project at the Society for the Study of Literature and Science, and magic and the body at the Conference on College Composition and Communication. His article "Stamping Out Elvis" is forthcoming in the book *Elvisology*.

Steven B. Katz is an associate professor of English at North Carolina State University, where he has taught since 1986. He received his Ph.D. in communication and rhetoric from Rensselaer Polytechnic Institute, where he specialized in the rhetoric of science and technology. His *College English* article "The Ethic of Expediency: Classical Rhetoric, Technology, and the Holocaust" received a 1993 NCTE Best Article award, and his book *The Epistemic Music of Rhetoric: Toward the Temporal Dimension of Reader Response and Writing* is forthcoming from Southern Illinois UP.

John Kimsey is a doctoral candidate in English at the University of Illinois at Chicago, where he teaches courses in composition, literature, and reasoning. His research interests include modernism, the history of rhetoric, and cultural studies, and his dissertation "Spilt Religion: Ezra Pound and the Rhetoric of Heresy" is in progress. A professional musician, he has previously taught at the School of the Art Institute of Chicago.

Joyce Neff Magnotto is an assistant professor of English at Old Dominion University. Previously she was chair of the writing division at Prince George's Community College in Maryland. She received her Ph.D. in writing from the University of Pennsylvania, where her dissertation was a finalist for the Conference on College Composition and Communication's outstanding dissertation award. Her publications have focused on writing centers, WAC programs, and professional communication. She is currently a consultant to the General Accounting Office, for whom she teaches both onsite and by interactive television.

LuMing Mao (Ph.D., University of Minnesota) is an assistant professor of English at Miami University of Ohio, where he teaches undergraduate and graduate courses in rhetoric, composition, and linguistics. His research interests include pragmatics, discourse analysis, and cross-cultural communication, and his work has been published in the *Rhetoric Society Quarterly*, the *Journal of Pragmatics*, and *Rhetoric Review*, which honored his "I Conclude Not: Toward a Pragmatic Account of Metadiscourse" with an Outstanding Essay award in 1993.

Robert L. McDonald (Ph.D., Texas Christian University) is an assistant professor of English at the Virginia Military Institute, where he teaches rhetoric, writing, and literature courses, and coordinates the annual Spilman Symposium on the Teaching of Writing. His research interests include rhetoric, composition, popular culture, and American studies. He is the author, with Christina Russell, of *Teaching Composition in the 1990s: Sites of Contention* (Harper Collins, 1994), and his book on the letters of Erskine Caldwell is forthcoming.

Rolf Norgaard is a senior instructor in the university writing program at the University of Colorado at Boulder, where he coordinates advanced composition and writing across the curriculum programs. He received his Ph.D. in comparative literature from Stanford University and was previously a senior writer for the National Center for Higher Education Management. His research interests include rhetorical theory and criticism, argumentative writing, and curricular design. He is the author of *Ideas in Action: A Guide to Critical Thinking and Writing* (Harper Collins, 1994).

Donovan J. Ochs is Professor of Communication Studies and Rhetoric at the University of Iowa, where he received his Ph.D. and has taught courses in rhetoric, public address, and classics for nearly 30 years. He has received numerous grants, editorships, honors, and awards (including the 1993 Iowa Collegiate Teaching Award), and is the author of nine books, including *Consolatory Rhetoric: Grief, Symbol, and Ritual in the Greco-Roman Era* (U of South Carolina Press, 1993) and *The Rhetoric of Agitation and Control*, now in its second edition and currently published by Waveland Press.

John Frederick Reynolds (Ph.D., University of Oklahoma) is a professor of English at the City College of the City University of New York (CUNY), where he teaches courses in writing and rhetoric. Earlier he taught at Old Dominion University. He is the author of *Writing and Reading Mental Health Records: Issues and Analysis* (Sage, 1993); also *Rhetorical Memory and Delivery: Classical Concepts for Contemporary Composition and Communication* (1994) and *Professional Writing in Context: Lessons from Teaching and Consulting in Worlds of Work* (in press), both published by Lawrence Erlbaum Associates.

Hephzibah Roskelly (Ph.D., University of Louisville) is an associate professor of English at the University of North Carolina at Greensboro, where she directs the composition program, supervises student teachers, and teaches courses in rhetoric, writing, reading, literacy, and gender. She is the author, with Eleanor Kutz, of *An Unquiet Pedagogy: Transforming Practice in the English Classroom* (Heinemann, 1991), and is currently at work on *Reason to Believe: Romantics and Pragmatics in the Teaching of English*.

William T. Ross is Professor of English and chair of the department at the University of South Florida, where he teaches stylistics and 20th-century British literature courses. He received his Ph.D. in English from the University of Virginia. His work on Morris Peckham has been published in the *Rhetoric Society Quarterly*; his book on Weldon Keyes was published by Twayne; currently he is working on a book on Bertrand Russell's popular prose, an excerpt from which is forthcoming in *Centennial Review*.

Christina G. Russell is an assistant professor of English and the director of composition at James Madison University, where she teaches rhetoric, composition, and writing pedagogy courses. She received her Ph.D. in English from Texas Christian University, where she served as associate director of composition. She is the author, with Robert McDonald, of *Teaching Composition in the 1990s: Sites of Contention* (Harper Collins, 1994), and is a contributing bibliographer for the Conference on College Composition and Communication's *Bibliography on Rhetoric and Composition*.

Edward Schiappa (Ph.D., Northwestern University) is an associate professor and the director of graduate studies in communication at Purdue University. His work on classical and contemporary rhetoric has appeared in the *Quarterly Journal of Speech*, *Philosophy and Rhetoric*, *Rhetoric Society Quarterly*, the

Journal of Advanced Composition, Rhetoric Review, Pre/Text, and *Communication Monographs*. He is the author of *Protagoras and Logos: A Study in Greek Philosophy and Rhetoric* (University of South Carolina Press, 1991), and editor of *Warranting Assent: Case Studies in Argument Evaluation* (State University of New York Press, 1995) and *Landmark Essays on Classical Greek Rhetoric* (Hermagoras, 1994).

David W. Smit is an associate professor of English and the director of expository writing at Kansas State University, where he teaches courses in composition, rhetorical theory and history, and Henry James, among others. He received his Ph.D. from the University of Iowa, and taught for several years at Tarsus American School in Turkey, where he was chairman of the faculty. His work has appeared in the *Journal of Advanced Composition*, the *Writing Program Administration, Rhetoric Review*, and *Style*, and he is the author of the book *The Language of a Master: Theories of Style and the Later Style of Henry James*.

Rex L. Veeder (Ph.D., University of Arizona) is an assistant professor of English at St. Cloud State University in Minnesota, where he teaches a wide range of writing courses. At Arizona, he was assistant editor of *Rhetoric Review*; at St. Cloud he is managing editor of the *Rhetoric Society Quarterly*. He has taught high school English and speech, community college composition, and has been a professional writer for the Arizona Arts Commission. He is currently at work on *The History of Romantic Rhetoric from Plato to Burke*.

Author Index

Page numbers in *italics* denote complete bibliographic information

Subject Index